Alaska's Rural Development

Westview Replica Editions

This book is a Westview Replica Edition. The concept of Replica Editions is a response to the crisis in academic and informational publishing. Library budgets for books have been severely curtailed; economic pressures on the university presses and the few private publishing companies primarily interested in scholarly manuscripts have severely limited the capacity of the industry to properly serve the academic and research communities. Many manuscripts dealing with important subjects, often representing the highest level of scholarship, are today not economically viable publishing projects. Or, if they are accepted for publication, they are often subject to lead times ranging from one to three years. Scholars are understandably frustrated when they realize that their first-class research cannot be published within a reasonable time frame, if at all.

Westview Replica Editions are our practical solution to the problem. The concept is simple. We accept a manuscript in camera-ready form and move it immediately into the production process. The responsibility for textual and copy editing lies with the author or sponsoring organization. If necessary we will advise the author on proper preparation of footnotes and bibliography. We prefer that the manuscript be typed according to our specifications, though it may be acceptable as typed for a dissertation or prepared in some other clearly organized and readable way. The end result is a book produced by lithography and bound in hard covers. Initial edition sizes range from 400 to 800 copies, and a number of recent Replicas are already in second printings. We include among Westview Replica Editions only works of outstanding scholarly quality or of great informational value, and we will continue to exercise our usual editorial standards and quality control.

About the Book and Editors

Alaska's Rural Development

edited by Peter G. Cornwall and Gerald McBeath

This book examines the social, economic, political, and cultural concerns surrounding the development of rural Alaska. The authors explore the controversy over rural development from a variety of perspectives — some supporting economic development and its implications for rural communities, others arguing for alternative approaches. They raise the issues of external control over local development and the effects of the boom-and-bust cycle often associated with rural change.

Part 1 surveys the economic development of Alaska's resources, providing an historical overview of its fur, timber, and fishing industries and examining the current importance of oil, gas, minerals, and agricultural products. The section concludes with a discussion of the unique patterns of trade between Alaska and Asia. The second part turns to the organizations that have been, and are presently, the major vehicles for development — the village and regional corporations that grew out of the Alaska Native Claims Settlement Act of 1971 and the non-profit organizations responsible for social services and education. The authors also discuss the increasingly important role of governmental institutions.

The final section considers the conflict between the goal of economic development and traditional Native values of subsistence and cultural preservation. The authors ask whether the development of Alaska's rural regions must take place at the expense of the traditional lifestyle and cultural distinctiveness of Native society.

Peter G. Cornwall is associate professor and head of the Department of History at the University of Alaska, Fairbanks. **Gerald McBeath** is associate professor and head of the Department of Political Science, also at the University of Alaska.

Alaska's Rural Development

edited by Peter G. Cornwall
and Gerald McBeath

Westview Press / Boulder, Colorado

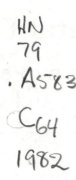

Copyright © 1982 by Westview Press, Inc.

Published in 1982 in the United States of America by
 Westview Press, Inc.
 5500 Central Avenue
 Boulder, Colorado 80301
 Frederick A. Praeger, Publisher

Library of Congress Cataloging in Publication Data
Main entry under title:
Alaska's Rural Development.
 (A Westview replica edition)
 Papers presented at a statewide conference held in Alaska in July 1978.
 Includes index.
 1. Rural development—Alaska—Congresses. I. Cornwall, Peter G.   II. McBeath, Gerald A.
HN79.A583C64   307.7'2'09798   81-21815
ISBN 0-86531-294-X   AACR2

Printed and bound in the United States of America

Contents

Tables, Figures and Maps

TABLES

FIGURES

MAPS

Tables, Figures and Maps

Foreword

Alaska is still the land of opportunity. Rich in renewable and non-renewable resources, virtually undeveloped, and with a tradition of freedom—we do have a chance to set our own course and to determine our own future. We will not repeat mistakes made in the south 48. We can guide our own economy and through it our growth, our commerce, our jobs. We can encourage the industries we want, and have a maximum impact on decisions affecting our land use, our environment, our population—our standard of living and our quality of life.

Portions of Alaska, though made, will inevitably be remade, and that remaking is our responsibility and our challenge. Decisions made by this generation of Alaskans will determine the options and range of opportunities open to those who follow. If we choose wisely and well, future generations will have the security and stability of a diversified economy. They will inherit both the freedom and opportunity offered by our vast wilderness and our rich natural resources.

This idyllic vision is within our reach. We must, however, exercise the restraint and the foresight needed to develop the foundation for that diversified, stable economy which will anchor Alaska's future.

Domestic and foreign markets are obviously an integral part of this foundation. Immediately, markets in the south 48 and foreign nations, especially Japan, need basic resources—including fish, timber, agricultural commodities, and petrochemicals—which we are able to supply at reasonable rates.

As we move toward development of Alaska, we must exercise caution and create an integrated approach based on our long-term interests. We cannot operate unilaterally. Our development programs must strike a mutually satisfying balance that:

- serves the needs of the people of Alaska;

- fulfills state socio-economic goals;

- serves the interests of the nation as a whole; and

- responds to the needs of our trading partners.

Equity and reciprocity are critical factors. We have strengths, but the south 48 and our foreign trading partners have strengths as well. Alaska is energy-intensive;

America, technology-intensive; foreign nations, labor-intensive. Our future development plans should fuse the three, so that we can develop from "strength to strength."

These papers focus on the potential of rural Alaska. They address some critical questions:

- what resources offer the greatest potential for rural development?

- what role can organizations—private and public—play in the balanced development of rural areas of the state?

- what are the critical values that should guide development efforts?

These questions and more must be asked and answered. The fundamental question, of course, is "What is best for Alaska?" The corollary question to this is "What type of economy do we want—do we need—to support and sustain the lifestyle and standard of living that we cherish?"

The obvious answer is that we want to establish a diversified economy that is not wholly dependent on our non-renewable resources. We want a stable economy which is not over-reliant on any one of our non-renewable resources. We want a technologically sophisticated economy which will not pollute our environment but will provide jobs for our resident population, their children and grandchildren. We want an independent economy which means investment and profit stay in the state and our exports do not depend on boom or bust cycles in foreign nations.

This means that we must embark upon a more diversified course in developing and marketing our products. Right now, we are mostly exporting unprocessed, raw materials to the south 48 and East Asia. The range of these exports is generally confined to petroleum, forest products, fish, and shellfish. Dependence on the export of limited resources to limited markets places us at the mercy of fluctuations in the economies of other regions and nations. We are the victims—the uneasy riders—of their boom and bust cycles.

An immediate solution is to expand the range of our markets and basic export commodities. Specifically, we should stress basic commodities—and here I am referring to renewable resources. The agricultural potential of the Yukon Flats and Tanana Valley has yet to be fully tapped. Rural Alaska provides the opportunity to diversify and expand our exports of essential commodities. Food is the one essential commodity that does not depend upon world economic fluctuations.

We have to expand our capability to export processed materials. Alaska must develop value added industries which capitalize on the proximity of natural resources to compensate for our distance from major markets. As an energy-intensive state, we can reduce production costs. As a technologically advanced society, we can compensate for our limited labor supply.

Alaska today has the opportunity to diversify its economy. It does not have to depend on the export of non-renewable resources to survive in today's world economy. We hold all of the cards; the key is to play them correctly.

This involves a well-reasoned and comprehensive strategy. By developing the various renewable resources of the rural areas of the state, we can become a stable and diversified economy not dependent on the ups and downs of one or even a couple of the raw resource purchases. We must and can do the thinking and planning necessary for such a stable and diversified economy. The thought and time put into the papers found in this book represent that kind of effort.

Senator Ted Stevens

Acknowledgments

We are grateful to those who helped us organize and present the statewide conference "Developing Rural Alaska" in July 1978, which was the foundation for this volume of essays—Lee Gorsuch and Thomas Morehouse, of the Institute of Social and Economic Research, Anchorage, William Phillips of the School of Management, University of Alaska, Fairbanks, and Claus Naske of the History Department, University of Alaska, Fairbanks. The Alaska Humanities Forum and the National Endowment for the Humanities sponsored the conference and have supported the publication of this volume, for which we are very grateful. We thank particularly Gary Holthaus, executive director of the Humanities Forum, for his advice and assistance.

We owe a debt of gratitude to the authors for permission to include their works in this volume and for allowing us the discretion to standardize the format and language of their articles to achieve some consistency in the final work. Lynne Rienner and Miriam Gilbert of Westview Press were helpful in advising us on matters of style and organization of the manuscript.

Finally, we owe Sheri Layral special and profound thanks. She typed the entire manuscript quickly and with nearly faultless accuracy. Her knowledge of language and style made our tasks as editors simple indeed. Throughout, she maintained her characteristic good humor, which made an otherwise arduous task pleasant for us.

Peter G. Cornwall
Gerald McBeath

Alaska's Rural Development

Introduction

Peter G. Cornwall

Alaska occupies an unusual position within the United States. Largest in overall size, it is the least populous state, with a concentrated, and somewhat diversified population. Its arctic and sub-arctic climate adds materially to the costs of production, and the state lacks a developed, articulated economic structure. Alaska, in fact, can in many ways be regarded as a developing region, and as such is unlike the other forty-nine states. Yet Alaska is rich in natural resources, both renewable and non-renewable; and at this stage of the state's development, there is a need to consider alternate patterns for the future, especially for the rural areas of the state.

Rural Alaska, sometimes referred to as the "bush," encompasses those regions of the state outside the major urban centers of Anchorage, Fairbanks, and Juneau. It is not an homogeneous region, ranging from the Arctic North Slope through the sub-arctic interior, to the island chain of the Aleutians and the heavily timbered Southeastern Alaska. Its population is sparse, less than one-third of the state's total population of some 400,000, and is predominantly Native (who comprise some two-thirds of the rural population). Native, in this context, refers to the Eskimo, Indian, and Aleut peoples. Its economic base is likewise varied, from subsistence hunting to gathering to timber and fish harvesting and processing, with prospects for future development in oil and gas, hard minerals including coal, and tourism.

This future development, however, is a source of controversy. Development can be an emotion-laden term, connoting for many the rapid exploitation of the state's resources, with no thought for anything beyond immediate profit. This point of view tends to create its opposite, represented by the so-called "conservationists," who would protect the environment even at the cost of halting resource utilization altogether. While simplistic, this dichotomy is everywhere evident throughout the state. To further compound the situation, the issue of subsistence hunting and gathering has been raised. Advocates of this centuries-old lifestyle see themselves threatened by both development and conservation, the one with its threat to the natural habitat of game species, and the other which seek to restrict the taking of endangered species, such as the bowhead whale, or to close great areas of the state to hunting and trapping.

An added dimension to the issue of development and utilization is to be seen in the problem of marketing Alaska's resources. For reasons which will be presented in the following chapters, Alaska, except in the area of oil and gas production, is not in a position to compete with other states in the domestic American market. The state can, however, find a ready market in Asia for a wide range of natural products. In recent

1

years, Japan has been Alaska's most important foreign trading partner, accounting for the major portion of the state's overseas trade. Moreover, Japan has influenced growth in Alaska through direct investment and joint venture arrangements, particularly in the timber and fishing industries. To a considerable degree, the two regions are complementary—industrialized but resource-poor Japan finding in Alaska a stable, relatively close source of necessary raw materials and food products. Other nations in Asia—China, India, Korea, and Taiwan among them—are becoming increasingly important as markets for Alaska's products. If the economic position of these countries strengthens, as it is expected to do, they will become even more important in the future.

Alaska, then, is one of the few American states oriented toward East Asia, and to examine this relationship a conference was held at the University of Alaska, Fairbanks, in July of 1978. The title of the conference was "Developing Rural Alaska: A Role for China and Japan?" But, as the meeting progressed, it became apparent that, for many participants, expanding Alaska-East Asia trade was not the only issue to be considered when talking of developing rural Alaska. The question of development versus non-development, or at least of the extent and nature of development was raised, but not answered. The related issue of the essentially Native subsistence culture and its future in the face of economic growth and change in rural Alaska also did not find a solution.

Development, however defined, involves a great number of groups representing government at all levels, profit-oriented associations, and non-profit groups concerned with social service delivery. These have to be considered in any study of rural development. The present volume is an attempt to address these and related questions. Some of the papers presented here were originally read at the conference; others illustrate the expanded scope of our study. Naturally, as discrete papers they do not necessarily present a plan for development, nor do they always agree, but all relate to the overall theme of rural development in Alaska.

Development, as already indicated, connotes many things. For some it is synonymous with economic growth and, in the case of Alaska, means the exploitation of natural resources. Opponents of this point of view argue that this pattern, so evident in the past, would mean the repetition of boom and bust cycles, and would perpetuate the dependent nature of the Alaskan economy. For others, development is seen as progress, expressed in an improved standard of living in the material sense. This is often associated with urban growth, and thus raises the question of urban-rural relations. In rural Alaska, the need for improvement in the standard of living is particularly evident, and therefore there are those who believe that some form of decentralization might be the answer, placing greater authority in decision making with rural residents themselves. In preference to a resource based economic growth pattern, they see a human resources approach, involving human values as a major determinant in policy planning.

Although Alaska does not have a discernable development program, many agencies are involved in the development process. The federal government has long been active in the rural areas of the state, through such agencies as the Bureau of Indian Affairs and the Bureau of Land Management. More recently, and with possibly greater impact, the passage of the Alaska Native Claims Settlement Act of 1971 placed land and capital in the hands of Alaska Natives, to be administered through village and regional corporations. The state government, using some of its oil income, contributed to this settlement. The state also provides assistance with many essential services, such as transportation and communications, and is deeply involved in the regulation and funding of large scale agricultural projects.

Until recently, the state provided educational services to rural areas through a State Operated School System but, in 1976, in a move toward decentralization, Rural Education Attendance Areas were created. These have resulted in greater local participation in educational policy making. Formal local government is not very much in evidence in the sparsely-settled areas of rural Alaska. Much of this area is unincorporated, although a significant exception to this general rule can be found on the oil-producing North Slope, where an essentially Native borough has made important contributions to that region's development.

For most of rural Alaska, the Native corporations stemming from the Alaska Native Claims Settlement Act play important semi-governmental roles at the village and regional levels. The profit-making corporations created by the act, endowed with land and some disposable wealth, stand in the forefront of what economic development is taking place. Some observers see the village corporations as holding the key to rural development, at least for village residents, while others believe that the larger, wealthier regional corporations are better suited to development along more conventional lines. Rural development does not rest exclusively in the hands of the profit-oriented corporations, however. Their non-profit counterparts, which grew out of the earlier land claims settlement movement, are deeply committed to providing social services in their areas, especially health care.

This volume presents the issues of development in rural Alaska under three general headings: resources, organizations, and values. We begin, appropriately, with an examination of the historical background of resource development, emphasizing its sporadic nature, and its reliance upon specific resources; furs, fish, and timber. Potential for future development is considered, in the areas of agriculture, particularly in the production of barley and rapeseed, and in the hard rock minerals, especially coal. Possible markets for these products exist in East Asia, and in particular in Japan; and we proceed to a consideration of the general patterns of Alaska-Japan trade both from the Japanese point of view and from the perspective of overall Japan-United States trade relations.

The second section examines the roles that are being and can be played by some of the more important organizations involved in the process of rural development. Again, we begin with a background study, in this case of conditions in contemporary rural Alaska, before considering the village and regional corporations and their experience in the first ten years after the passage of the settlement act. The prospects for rural Alaska-East Asia trade are approached through a survey of the actions and attitudes of Native corporations, at both levels, while the important social issues of resources and subsistence, alcoholism, energy conservation, and child care are examined through a study of the work on the non-profit Rural Alaska Community Action Program. Finally, the example of the North Slope Borough, while not typical nor necessarily a model for others, shows what a local government has been able to accomplish.

The third section considers the ways in which development and traditional values interact, and offers suggestions for alternate approaches to the general concept of development. A case study of the Northwest Arctic Native Association's human resources approach can be contrasted to the experience and results achieved by other regional corporations, while the opportunities these corporations have to follow different paths can be considered as an expression of the self-determination thrust in American political though and practice. A study of subsistence indicates that this issue is more complex than is often realized, and that it will require careful attention if traditional lifestyles are to be made compatible with other demands upon resources.

The section concludes with assessments of the difficulties being encountered in rural development in Alaska, and with tentative suggestions for the future.

The development of rural Alaska is a complex issue and one which presents, in the eyes of many Alaskans, unique problems. The geographic location of the state, its climate and terrain, and the needs of its indigeneous people, among other considerations, seem to suggest that special solutions must be found. This is not necessarily true, for many of the problems encountered in rural Alaska are common to sparsely populated regions, and comparative studies of rural development might suggest that the range of options available to Alaskans is wider than heretofore considered. The chapters which follow, to some degree, introduce the issue of comparison, and offer a series of perspectives that shows both the particular and general nature of rural development in Alaska.

Part One:
Development and Resources
in Rural Alaska

1
The Nature of Rural Economic Development in Alaska

George Rogers

My topic is the nature of Alaska's rural economic development, but I will expand the topic in two directions. I plan to include political as well as economic development, because if we exclude politics, we exclude the reason Alaska was acquired from the Russians in the first place. We avoid entirely the impact on rural Alaska of the defense development that took place in the 1940s and 1950s, and the impact of statehood and the Native Claims Settlement Act. I will also include exploitation as well as development, because when we deal in an historical sense with Alaska's economic or historical evolution, we are generally discussing exploitation rather than development.

In the beginning all of Alaska was rural. At the time of the first contacts with western civilization in the mid-eighteenth century, the ethno-historians have suggested that there were about 62,000 people in residence in Alaska. Approximately ninety two percent of these lived along the coastal regions of Alaska from Dixon Entrance to Barter Island. Only about eight percent lived in the interior of Alaska, north of the Alaska Range or south of the Brooks Range. These people lived along the river systems where they also participated in some of the same harvesting processes that were undertaken along the coast.

What I will discuss are three major economic or political frontiers that intruded upon this rural Alaska, sketching briefly the nature of the intrusions, their impact upon rural Alaska, and the residual left after they receded. I discuss "frontiers" because we are describing developments that came from outside Alaska.

Before contact with western civilization, a sort of balanced state had been reached between the residents of Alaska and the economic base. The people lived along the coastal areas mostly because these were the areas that were richest in harvestable resources. These were subsistence economies, for the scale of the society was contingent upon the availability of resources. Even in the most densely populated sector, the southeastern part of Alaska, the concentration of population very rarely exceeded about 500 people at one place, because the resource base and the technology used would not support denser human habitation.

A paper presented at a conference on "Developing Rural Alaska," held at the University of Alaska, Fairbanks July 20-21, 1978.

This was in sharp contrast to the developments occurring afterward. The new frontiers had several things in common. All of them were frontiers in the sense that the origin of the movement was outside the geographic boundaries of Alaska. The benefits that were derived from the activities taking place were primarily for interests outside of Alaska. The frontiers were transitory in nature. They came and went as conditions changed. The frontiers were specialized in the sense that they concerned one resource, generally, in many cases producing only one product. They were also specialized in the manner in which this was done. There was no concern about side effects; things were done in the most economical manner possible. They had a lasting impact upon rural Alaska, which changed the patterns of living of the people. Each frontier in varying degrees had some effect on the aboriginal self-sufficiency of the people, in that each required specialization of labor and division of labor; but the people who were subjected to this division of labor did not fully participate in the system that required the division of labor. The resource base that had supported the aboriginal systems was generally eroded in some sense. The cultural systems were eroded by the contact. Finally, in each case the frontiers also brought in some new technology which had an impact both upon the resources of rural Alaska and upon the people. In many cases the people adopted that technology, which made their subsistence activities more efficient in that they could harvest more resources, but which had a damaging effect upon the sustained yield of the resource.

The first major frontier was a marine frontier and in this case the first movement was from the west to the east, contrary to the movements with which we are familiar. The Russian fur trade followed the last exploratory probes into the Alaska area. The fur trade developed very rapidly from the middle of the eighteenth century until the turn of the century, and then declined by the middle of the nineteenth century. At its peak, no more than 500 people were involved in the fur trade. These were Russians (Siberians) that came as hunters, as traders, as administrators; they traded from Kodiak down to Fort Ross in northern California. In terms of population, they had little impact on rural Alaska. The impact they did have was initially on the Aleut people, a people who were destroyed in the real sense of the word as Margaret Lantis established in her ethno-history of southwestern Alaska.[1] The Aleuts were destroyed in the sense that their culture was destroyed, and they were removed from their homeland forcibly. Only their language and their memory culture (what they remembered from the old culture) survived.

The fur trade was primarily in sea otter and to a lesser degree fur seal. When the sea otter and fur seal resources were near depletion, there was no longer an economic reason for fur traders to remain in Alaska. This, combined with competition from the Hudson Bay Company and the threat of loss of Russian possessions in North America in any case, led to the purchase of Alaska by the United States in 1867. Resulting from the fur trade was a certain reorganization of the people—principally, the Aleuts—whose population had been scattered. The one unit that survived was the Pribilof Island operation, surviving to the present date essentially as it was organized in the Russian period. The Aleuts were located there for a single purpose, to herd, to kill, to skin, to flense, to salt fur seal hides. There was no other economic reason for their existing in the Pribilofs than this, and they were treated as though this was their only reason for existing.

During the Russian period, the Aleuts were provided with the means of survival. They were given barrels of salt to use in salting down the carcasses of the seals, so they would have some meat to eat during the period when they were not hunting. They were given a few other commodities such as flour, sugar, and tea. When the population declined, a few more women were brought in to keep the population stable. The Aleuts were managed very much as the animal resources were managed. With some modifications, this system was continued under American rule. There was somewhat more concern for the human and social aspects; but basically even today the only enterprise in the Pribilofs is a variation of the original Russian operation. The fur trade, of course, had a profound impact upon that part of rural Alaska out of keeping with the usual impacts. The only other features of this period which survived were the intermingling of the Russian and Native peoples, and the existence of the Russian Orthodox church which was a very powerful supportive force in the people's survival and which continues to this day as an important element of their lives.

Included in the period of the marine frontier were activities of the New England whalers, from the early part of the nineteenth century until the middle of the nineteenth century, and then later the steamwheelers which moved up into the Arctic Ocean proper. Again, there were impacts on the resource, sea mammals (the whale and walrus in particular), the extermination or the erosion of which influenced the people's survival. Diseases and alcohol were introduced which contributed very tragically to the decline of the population in that area. An additional impact was the intermingling of New England whalers and Native people. The technology the whalers carried with them was adopted by some of the Eskimo whalers to good effect. However, on the North Slope, the musk ox herds were wiped out by the whalers when they overwintered and had to have food to survive.

Overshadowing all these developments during this period was the salmon frontier. This began around 1878 when two canneries were established in Southeast Alaska. Shortly thereafter, several more canneries were set up along the coast. By 1884 the frontier aspect of this movement had come to a halt in Bristol Bay with the establishment of the canning industry there. Salmon fishing was a highly exploitive operation. The fish were not harvested, they were in effect mined. The canneries were fairly portable, and were moved around from place to place. The salmon catch rose from an average 32 million fish per year in the first decade of the present century to 99 million fish per year in the 1935-39 period, just before World War II. But the resource could not sustain itself, and after 1939 there was a dramatic decline in availability of the species. The nature of this period of development warrants a closer look.

The first thing that is interesting to note is that initially almost the entire labor force was imported, whether we discuss fishermen or shore workers. The reason for this was that in California there was a cheap supply of labor, namely Chinese who had been brought over for the building of the railroads. They were redundant to the needs of California, and they represented a cheap, exploitable labor force. This was Alaska's first China connection, via California. The workforce was brought into the Bristol Bay coastal area on sailing ships, along with the cans and cannery equipment; and at the end of the season, the workforce and canned salmon were returned to San Francisco. The process itself was a highly industrialized one, much in advance of those typical of the processes at the end of the nineteenth century. Eventually there developed almost totally automated cannery lines, including the "iron chink" that cut and skinned the salmon, preparing them for ultimate canning.

The harvesting of the resource was also highly industrialized. During most of the period up to 1939, half or more of the take was by salmon traps. The use of traps fluctuated by area and by year, but traps were a highly efficient and rational means of taking salmon. One simply put the trap in an area where the salmon had schooled and were moving into their home streams they were most vulnerable there and could be led into a trap, and then bailed out afterwards. It required little manpower. This practice became a subject of political agitation up until the time of statehood.

The salmon frontier developed in rural Alaska, but initially it had virtually no impact on the people outside of the Southeast. The Tlingit Indians of Southeast Alaska had been engaged in salmon fishing. They had an available labor force, and they were able to compete with imported labor. But in the Bristol Bay area, the resident population was scattered, and engaged in sheer survival. Subsistence fishing occupied all their time during the season. They were not interested, they were not hired, they were not trained; it was much more ecnomical to import Chinese and then later Filipino laborers from California. In 1939, a study of the breakdown of the labor force from fisherman through shoremen indicated that in Southeast Alaska forty percent of the labor force was non-resident. In central Alaska, which includes Prince William Sound, Cook Inlet, Kodiak, the Aleutian Islands and the Alaska Peninsula, fifty three percent of the labor force was imported from outside Alaska. In westward Alaska, which is primarily Bristol Bay, seventy nine percent of the labor force was imported from outside Alaska. This was in 1939, close to the eve of Alaska's involvement in World War II. The salmon frontier utilized a resource upon which the survival of the indigenous resident people was dependent; the resource was over exploited and used to benefit external forces more than residents.

During World War II, there were two new developments. Manpower was limited, and there were restrictions on transportation; and therefore, for the first time, the Bristol Bay fishery was manned quite heavily by resident Alaskans. After World War II, through the formation of associations and unions, this trend toward employment of residents was not reversed, so at the present time there is a higher participation of residents in the fisheries and in the processing. Unfortunately, this occurred when the resource was very nearly depleted. If one examines the fish catch after World War II, for example the period 1955-59, the number of salmon caught per year had dropped to 34 million fish. In the period 1959-75, it dropped to 30 million, and it is continuing to decline to a level about a third or less of the peak five-year period in the past.

Thus, Alaskans are involved in development of a resource when it is long past its prime. Of the several noteworthy changes in this time, I have already mentioned the manpower situation in World War II. A second important change was the development in the 1950s of a conservative fisheries management policy. Until that time management had been more or less a matter of form. One went through the motions of conducting investigations, and holding public hearings, and then finished by doing whatever the industry wanted done.

Another change was the abolition of the fish trap with the granting of statehood in 1959, resulting in a reallocation of the catch among gear which employed more local manpower. Then, in 1973, the limited entry program was enacted. This limited the number of people engaged in the harvesting of fish, as a conservation measure; it was also an economic measure designed to make fishing a viable industry, producing a regular income for those engaged in it.

Simultaneous with the limited entry program, a high sea fisheries began to develop. This was primarily a foreign fishery which had very little if any impact (except a negative impact) upon rural Alaska. The domestic crab fishery was primarily a Puget Sound, Kodiak-based fishery. The harvesting of halibut and other bottom fish has had very little impact upon rural Alaska.

Another frontier was developing concurrently, which could be called the lands frontier—although it included chiefly gold, copper, and timber in the last phases. The year 1878 was an important one since that is when the first gold mining camp was set up in Alaska, from that time until 1906 Alaska had a series of gold rushes. Prospecting activity by 1906 had identified almost all of the major gold finds, and a number of them were already well into the stages of commercial exploitation. The discovery of gold was one of the beginnings of urbanization in Alaska. In the 1900 census, for example, the only places of any size that were registered were the Juneau-Douglas area with 3,609 people, Skagway with 3,117 people, and Nome City with 12,488 people. (This census was taken a little bit past the boom.) At that time, mining in Juneau-Douglas had passed the prospecting stage, and entered the development and production stages. Skagway had reached the tail end of the Klondike rush, having developed the transportation for it; and mining in Nome was still in the phase of preliminary development. In the census of 1909 the population at Nome had dropped to 2,600, the population required to maintain the dredge operations that were then underway. The gold mining period was a time of an influx of people with headquarters at transportation points, who then fanned out to prospect; once the finds were identified, evaluated, and money invested, the population declined, because the actual operations of the mines did not require much labor.

A copper bonanza occurred between 1911 and 1938 (when the last ounce of copper was removed from the Kennecott-McCarthy mines). This also was a process of prospecting, discovery, development of access, construction of a railroad, construction of a port, and then the extraction of copper. When we talk about mining, we discuss an enterprise that is very uncertain. First, one has to discover, but that is only part of the problem. Second, one has to wait until the price is right, which may be a long time; and the price is right only for a short time in many cases. So one has to be able to move investments quickly. One cannot depend on local sources, because the amount of investment is very large and has to be made available instantaneously. One has to have a work force that can arrive, do a job quickly, and then leave. As a result, the impact upon rural Alaska was to create the beginnings of urban Alaska, and that was all. Some local people were involved in some of the operations once they developed, but this involvement was marginal.

Timber, the last part of the land frontier, was an intermittent economic enterprise. It was dependent upon local markets until the mid-1950s when the first pulp mill was constructed in southeast Alaska at Ketchikan, followed by a second mill at Sitka. By this time, the harvest of timber had increased from a few million board feet to almost half a billion board feet. Most of the timber development was a colonial exploitation. Initially, the market was divided between Japan and the U.S., but now it is totally Japanese, and at least half of the investment is Japanese. Again, the work-force was imported, because the local people fished, and a fisherman cannot be converted into a logger overnight. Urban centers grew around the mills, but they did not incorporate the rural population. The 1950 census was taken before, and the 1960 census after, this development. In my study of the effect of timber development on Native employment and Native population, I found a negative relationship. The Native people tended to move away from the centers in which the employment opportunities developed in mill operations and logging, because they were still part of the fishing culture and they were not ready to make that change.

The final frontier is one of the present, that I would call the defense and energy frontier. I have linked them together not because the products are alike, but because the patterns are very similar. Defense has always been part of Alaska's scene: it was the reason that Seward bought Alaska in the first place; strategic rather than economic considerations caused the negotiations to proceed. However, few military forces were stationed in Alaska. In the 1900 census, for example, only two defense sites were identified. One was Fort Seward in southeast Alaska, housing 255 infantrymen and officers, who were there to defend our borders against the Canadians. We brag that our border has not been fortified, but it was then, for there was a dispute about where the boundary should be drawn. Actually, the final boundary settlement was somewhat more to our benefit than Fort Seward would indicate. This infantry post was maintained intact until the Japanese invasion of the Aleutian Islands when it was suddenly realized that the war was taking place somewhere else and it was decommissioned. The second post was at Fort Davis near Nome, which housed 180 infantrymen and officers who had been sent up to establish order during the gold rush. A great deal of claim jumping took place, accompanied by other violence, and the soldiers joined in the fray very happily. In the 1939 census taken just before the onset of World War II, there were 524 military in Alaska. Half of them were still at Fort Seward waiting for the Canadians to come across the border. The rest were scattered around Alaska, operating the Alaska Communications System. This was almost as efficient as the system in effect now, and it cost less, taking about 200 men to operate. World War II and the Japanese invasion changed this picture, and by 1942 there were 152,000 troops stationed in Alaska.

The present military system was designed for World War II. Initially, the main point of the system was at Anchorage. This was a good strategic point, with access by sea, road, and by rail. A secondary point was at Adak, another at Kodiak, and a fourth at Fairbanks. There had been a point at Nome, but that was phased out. Most of the changes in the system were a function of technological change—the distance bombers and fighters could fly and shifts to jet and missile operations. Currently, the military presence in Fairbanks is based on an obsolescent technology, but we hedge our bets because we do not know what is going to happen. The military impact created urban Alaska, cities such as Fairbanks and Anchorage. Now these are the centers where growth is taking place. In rural Alaska, that is the balance of Alaska, the population either remained roughly the same or declined slightly. The distribution of population has not shifted very much, which means people continue to do what they always did.

The energy frontier began in 1957 with the oil discoveries on Kenai and the Cook Inlet, followed, of course, by the major discoveries at Prudhoe Bay in 1968 and construction of the pipeline. If we ignore the details and focus on the larger process, we see a pattern resembling that in defense. There was a large labor influx during the period of construction, when the defense system was set up. Great numbers of workers constructed defense facilities, but the completed garrison state was manned by far fewer personnel. The same pattern has been followed in the energy frontier. Also, the geographic relationships are the same which is seen in the population figures. In the 1970s, particularly in the two years 1974 and 1975, there has been an increase in population in the northern part of the state—the North Slope Borough area, the upper Yukon, and the Fairbanks area—resulting from pipeline construction, which parallels the experience in the 1950s in the construction of the defense establishment. There were comparable rates of increase in the population of Anchorage, but Anchorage continued to grow when people left the northern part of the state after the construction of the pipeline. The reason for this is that the energy operation has been manned from Anchorage. Workers are rotated to Anchorage, and the headquarters is there. Fairbanks operates as a supplemental support base, but the base of all operations is in Anchorage as it was for the defense establishment. Looking at the balance of the state over this period, the population from year to year has changed at a very nominal rate, generally one percent or less; and in one year it actually declined. This is the part of Alaska that is still "rural". Thus, both the defense and energy frontiers created a system or geographic entity of their own. Although they were superimposed upon rural Alaska, they did not interact very much with rural Alaska.

As to the present and future, I have mentioned the movement of support bases to Anchorage. There has also been a shift from Seattle and outside points to Anchorage which has augmented this change, so that Alaska is beginning to develop an urban center of its own, replacing the external bases of support of earlier frontier pathways into Alaska. This is the point at which things start, and this is the point to which things retreat in a number of cases.

In rural Alaska, there has been a decline in the resource base. The fisheries resource in salmon, as I have indicated, has declined precipitously. There is a bonanza now in crab, but it is fading. There is hope about bottom fish, but it is largely hope, with very little to support its development. Other resources, for example timber, are being cut back; that is levels of harvesting are declining. This is largely because of market conditions, but more importantly, the future for potential expansion has been threatened by the creation of wilderness areas within the forest areas and other parts of Alaska. The outlook for development in rural Alaska from exploitation of traditional resources—fish and timber—is rather dim. Prospects may improve, and they may not.

This leaves us only with minerals and energy resources which I think we can discount as being part of rural Alaska. The mineral situation is very hard to predict. We do know that we have some very interesting deposits that could be developed. However, we have to wait until the price is right, and we have to be ready to pounce when this happens.

NOTES

1. Lantis, Margaret et al., Ethnohistory in Southwestern Alaska and the Southern Yukon. Lexington: University of Kentucky Press, 1970.

2
The Coincidence of Rural Development and Major Resource Development

Lee Huskey

INTRODUCTION

By most indicators, Western and Arctic Alaska have recently experienced economic growth. Per capita income in the region increased by over 125 percent between 1970 and 1978, while employment increased by 237 percent during the same time period. The major determinants of this growth were increased public expenditures and natural resource production. This article addresses the effect of major resource production on the economic development of these rural regions.

The development of natural resources for export has long been considered an important source of regional growth. Encouragement of natural resource production for growth also has a long history as an important policy tool. Recently, the benefits of natural resource development as a growth-initiating factor have been challenged. Concern over the external effects of rapid energy development in the Western United States,[1] and of the long-run development consequences in the Third World has raised questions concerning the usefulness of this approach. The next section summarizes the current debate about economic development and draws implications for economic development in rural Alaska. In the third section, we examine the effect of Prudhoe Bay petroleum development on the economy of the North Slope region of Alaska and develop a model of this interaction. Finally, we examine some potential future resource developments in rural Alaska and their possible consequences for economic development.

ECONOMIC DEVELOPMENT AND DEPENDENCY

There has been much recent discussion in both the practical and theoretical literature about the definition of economic development. Much of the discussion originated in the Third World as a consequence of its experience with recent economic growth. A primary reason for the discussion is that past development programs, which were successful in terms of most economic indicators, have been less than successful in human terms. Agreement on the definition of economic development is needed, because the definition of the problem has much to do with the suggested solutions.

Originally presented at the American Association for the Advancement of Science— Alaska Section 1980 Conference, Anchorage, Alaska, September 17-19, 1980.

Henriot has suggested three alternative definitions of the problem of economic development;[2] each suggests alternative strategies and goals. In the first view, the problem of development is simply to increase the per capita output of the country. Output is increased through capital accumulation, resource production, and the application of new technology. This view assumes each underdeveloped region will follow a growth path similar to that of the developed regions of the world.

The second view of the problem emphasizes not only the increase in gross national product (GNP) but also the distribution of this output. It results from the experience of the Third World in the 1960s. During this period, the Third World experienced truly remarkable growth, but the benefits of growth were not shared by all of the population. The benefits of growth cannot be assumed to trickle down to the poor; an important development problem is how to spread the gains of growth in terms of jobs, distribution of income, and basic needs.

The final view of the problem of economic development is that of the dependency school which perceives not just a lack of development, but an active process of underdevelopment resulting from the interaction of the developed and Third World countries. Dependency defines economic development not just in terms of growth but in the quality of the process of growth.

The key question about growth is who controls it. The dependency school has observed that for the Third World most economic decisions are made outside the region, so that the economy of one region is determined by the expansion of another economy by which it is controlled. The control is through the economic relations and not through colonial or other political means. The process of underdevelopment is an active result of these relations.

Understanding the process of underdevelopment is helpful in describing the relation between rural development and natural resource production, since most Third World countries entered the world economy as producers of primary products to be exported. Initially, investment is made in primary products by expanding traditional crops in plantation agriculture or development of mineral deposits. In both of these cases, there is little change to the economies beyond the development of enclave sectors and links with developed countries. These links are not only paths by which production is exported from the less developed countries but also paths for the importation of goods and technologies. These links influence the tastes of the upper income elite, and they import not only the goods of the developed world but also the technology for producing these goods. These technologies may be inappropriate for the country, often being capital intensive in countries where labor is relatively cheap. This process leads to underdevelopment when traditional patterns of economic activity are destroyed but not replaced by new activity; increased production occurs in enclaves and is not integrated with the remainder of the economy; and the economy becomes geared to the demands of the world market.

What can we learn from the experience of the developing world? The lessons involve both definitions of development and results of primary production as a source of growth. The basic lessons for rural Alaska are:

- Economic development is distinct from growth. Economic growth is simply an increase in regional income which could result from a one-time exploitation of natural resource deposits. Economic development must in the limit be sustained growth; regional growth must continue after the resource is depleted. The ability to sustain growth requires structural change which allows the economy to replace declining sectors with new growing sectors. Economic development must also affect qualitative changes—jobs, income distribution, and basic needs must be considered. Finally, economic development must also assure a degree of control over the region's economic affairs.

- In most developing countries, although there are some obvious counter-examples, concentration on primary production has reduced the control of the region over its economy.

- Natural resource production may lead to growth but no development. This is a result of increased output in enclaves with only limited linkages to the rest of the economy.

- Finally, ties with the outside world may lead to the importation of tastes and technologies which are inappropriate to the region's culture, environment, resource availability, and level of development. This may actually hinder development through the fragmentation of the regional economy.

PRUDHOE BAY AND THE NORTH SLOPE REGION

The history of Alaskan economic growth has been importantly determined by the exploitation of natural resources. The exploitation of furs, fish, gold, and strategic location all resulted in major expansions of the economy. Prudhoe Bay petroleum development is the most recent example of this pattern. Beyond its effects on the state economy, the development of Prudhoe Bay can also be seen as a model of the economic consequences of major resource development on rural regions of the state. Prudhoe Bay is located on Alaska's Arctic coast within the lightly inhabited North Slope region of Alaska. This rural region provides a regional economy primarily because of the formation of the North Slope Borough government in 1972.[3] By examining the relation between Prudhoe Bay development and the economy of the North Slope region, we hope to learn lessons for the future of rural economic development.

We will examine the relation between Prudhoe Bay and the North Slope in terms of the staple theory of growth. Building our discussion around this model will allow us to isolate the important effects of growth. Staple theory is not a general theory of growth, but one that applies to frontier economies with a high level of resources per capita.[4] In such economies, staple exports (natural resources) are the leading sector of growth, and most capital and labor resources must be imported. Economic development is the process of diversification around the staple base.

The spread of development from the staple base is determined primarily by the characteristic of the exported staple. The production function, which describes the way the staple is produced, determines the extent of the economic development effects. Once the production function is determined, the demand for factors, the intermediate inputs used, and the distribution of income are all determined. The inducement to invest in the economy as a result of staple production can be broken into three linkage effects:

- Backward linkages—the inducement to invest in local production of inputs.

- Forward linkages—inducement to invest in local industries using the output as an input.

- Demand linkages—the inducement to invest in the local production of consumer goods and services.

The strength of these linkages determines the economic development inducement from the resource development. We can examine the economic development effects by looking at the strength of these linkages.

The prevailing conditions in Arctic climates—remoteness, lack of infrastructure, and separation—dictate the production attributes of successful Arctic commercial enterprises. Such enterprises must be large, have access to large amounts of capital, import technologies, affiliate with outside markets, and export the product in easily transportable form.[5] The high costs of production in frontier regions also dictate that only bonanza resource deposits are developed. The petroleum development at Prudhoe Bay fits this description; it is highly capital intensive, uses the most up-to-date technology , and produces crude for export.

The Arctic conditions and small markets in these regions constrain both forward and backward linkages of this development. Oil field services developed by both the Northwest Arctic Native Association (NANA) and Arctic Slope regional corporations are examples of backward linkages. The construction of the gas liquification plant at Prudhoe would be a type of forward linkage. More important than these links may be the pecuniary externalities resulting from construction of transportation and other infrastructure at Prudhoe, the existence of these facilities may make profitable future resource development in the American Beaufort Sea, the National Petroleum Reserve—Alaska (NPRA), and smaller fields near Prudhoe.

The final demand linkage is the most important for the economic development of the North Slope, as it will be in most of rural Alaska. The strength of this linkage is primarily a function of the effects of production on employment and income distribution. The capital intensity and technological advancement of the production process indicate a high level of skill required of employees. Of the jobs in the oil and gas industry, only slightly over 18 percent could be considered unskilled or entry level. The pattern of employment is also important: the development phase requires peak employment; and employment is reduced when production begins.

These characteristics have important implications for the distribution of income between regional residents and others. The high skill requirements and need for rapid expansion of the workforce for the development phase limit the proportion of jobs obtained by rural residents. When the high proportion of outside residents is combined with the location characteristics of production, this weakens even further the final demand linkage. The location of petroleum development is fixed by the location of the resource; this, combined with a lack of infrastructure and separation of communities, results in the development of enclaves. Enclaves are separate from existing communities, and their major links are with communities out of the region. Both material and labor inputs are imported from outside. With arrangements in work schedules, workers can live in outside communities so that the final demand-miltiplier effects occur outside the regions.

The strength of the final demand linkage depends on the number of local residents employed on the project and the number of employees who become residents. We would expect that, given adequate work schedules, the second effect is minimal. The first effect may also be small. A recent survey on the North Slope found that only 14 percent of North Slope Natives worked for oil or pipeline companies.[6]   Although this was a period of high employment in the region, as a result of North Slope Borough expenditures, it is an indication of the possible limited direct employment links. Evidence of Native employment on the Trans-Alaska Pipeline System (TAPS) is another limited indication of the weakness of this link. The weakness of this link results from both demand factors such as lack of appropriate training and supply factors such as unwillingness to leave the home region.

The large capital requirement of production and the development by national firms mean that a large portion of the income earned flows outside as remittance to capital. The formation of the North Slope Borough and its ability to tax the producers limit the flow of resources outside of the region and strengthen the final demand linkage. The tax revenues are substantial relative to the size of the Borough. The Borough spends the revenues on operating expenditures and a massive capital improvement program. Both of these programs create jobs, increase income, and strengthen the final demand linkage.[7] The importance of these programs for employment can be seen by contrasting the 14 percent of Borough residents who have worked for the Borough.[8]

There are also characteristics of the economy which place supply side constraints on the strength of the final demand linkage. The size of the market may be most important since this limits the type of goods and services which can be produced. The total population of the Borough may be a relatively large market in Alaskan terms, but the enclave nature of much of the population and the separation limit the effective size of the market. Technological change most probably weakens the demand link by improving transportation and the access to outside markets. Another supply constraint may be a limit of entrepreneurs. The small size of the population and the nonmarket opportunities to apply entrepreneurial skills may limit the number of local residents willing to take advantage of opportunities. The small size and relative riskiness of investment may limit the importation of entrepreneurs and the capital they require.

This brief discussion of the relation between Prudhoe Bay development and the North Slope economy provides a model for rural Alaskan attempts to maximize the economic development effects of resource development. The major characteristics of the approach is the use of the Borough's taxing power to increase the final demand linkage. This experience provides the following important lessons for future economic development:

- Even though Borough taxation secures a bigger share of Prudhoe Bay income for Borough residents, growth is still tied to the export of natural resources from Prudhoe. The ability of the North Slope Borough to create jobs depends on the existence of Prudhoe Bay (or its replacement by other natural resource producers).

- High wages which reflect resource industry employment may not reflect local labor market conditions. If these are exogenously imposed on the economy, they may limit the expansion of other sections. Some activities which may be possible at true market wages will not take place.

- To the extent that the Borough sets wages at nonmarket rates and has access to capital not available to local producers, a fragmented market may result.

- Success in securing a large portion of the natural resource surplus may develop an export mentality. Economic policy may concentrate on developing exports and ignore the vital role the supporting sector plays in economic development.

- Finally, both tastes and technologies which are inappropriate to the Arctic may be imported, as in the Third World. This may reduce the local production of goods and service by reducing the demand for these products. Inappropriate technology may also increase costs; for example, construction of non-Arctic type houses increases the cost of heating.

FUTURE RESOURCE DEVELOPMENT AND ITS LINKS TO ECONOMIC DEVELOPMENT

Future economic growth in rural Alaska will result from resource development. The development of Outer Continental Shelf (OCS) petroleum resources and of the bottomfish industry will be two major initiators of growth. This section will briefly examine the potential for economic development in terms of the linkages of these activities.

There are currently seven OCS sales scheduled off the coast of Arctic and Western Alaska. Marketable petroleum will not be found in all of these areas, but it is likely that peak mining employment associated with OCS development will be between 5,000 and 10,000. The OCS industry will result in a large increase in employment and income, but the spread effects will be weaker than in the Prudhoe Bay case.

In addition to the characteristics described for production at Prudhoe Bay, specific characteristics of OCS production limit the final demand linkages. The lease sale areas are geographically spread out—from the St. George Basin to the Beaufort Sea—which limits the effect of the large numbers. Most of the activity takes place in the ocean; this enforces the enclave nature of production. This also limits the taxable capital facilities and the government linkage. One positive aspect may arise from the necessity of obtaining good harbors for OCS activity. To the extent that past population concentrations have been at these harbors, onshore activities may have less of an enclave nature.

The bottomfish industry may be another important source of income and employment growth with the potential for stronger development linkages. Employment in the bottomfish industry has been projected to reach 18,000 by the year 2000 if all the foreign fleets within the 200-mile limit are replaced. Although there is some disagreement over the extent of this development, growth to even half these levels would provide significant effects.[9] Both fishing and manufacturing connected with fisheries have, in the past, been highly nonresident, resulting in a weak final demand link. The major production characteristic determining this nonresident nature is the seasonality of production. The bottomfish industry operates all year, which may increase the residency share of employment and the strength of the final demand linkages. The size of this activity (whether it is reached in 2000 or after) provides a scale which also increases the opportunities available within the region, particularly since the majority of activity will occur within one region, the Aleutians. This mass of activity may also provide opportunities for backward linkages such as boat repair and servicing.

The difference in production characteristics of the industries determines the economic development effects. The bottomfish industry seems to offer a greater chance for rural development than the petroleum industry; these effects, however, will be concentrated within one region.

CONCLUSIONS

The connection between resource development and economic development may not be as direct as a policy based on resource development assumes. The lessons from primary product production in the less developed countries and from the North Slope experience may allow rural Alaska to deal more effectively with future resource development and maximize its spread effects.

Two lessons are important. First, the residency of employment will determine the strength of the final demand linkage. The potential rural resource development may allow a separation of residence and workplace and weaken the spread of development. This separation may also provide a possible source of growth and development if the rural villages of Alaska become labor exporters. Rural workers may also take advantage of the chance to commute long distances to work. Maximizing this potential requires job training, providing transportation links, and union arrangements.

The second lesson for rural Alaska is the ease with which underdeveloped economies lose control through the export of natural resource products. One way this happens is through the import of a wage structure which does not reflect local conditions and limits the expansion of local economic activity. Another way in which control is lost is through the importation of tastes and technologies which are inappropriate to the region. These technologies and tastes may be extremely expensive in the long run. Policy must limit the extent of this effect by reducing those instances in which wages are determined exogenously, such as local government employment. Policies must also be devised which search for import substitutes which apply technologies appropriate to rural, small-scale regions and make use of local resources.

NOTES

1. S. Murdock and L. Leistritz. Energy Development in the Western United States: Impact on Rural Areas. New York: Praeger, 1980, pp. 1-3.

2. P. Henriot, "Development Alternatives: Problems, Strategies, Values." In The Political Economy of Development and Underdevelopment. Ed. C. Wilber. New York: Random House, 1979, pp. 6-13.

3. T. Morehouse and L. Leask, "Alaska's North Slope Borough: Oil, Money, and Eskimo Self-Government." Polar Record, Vol 20, No. 124, 1980. pp. 19-21.

4. M. Watkins, "A Staple Theory of Economic Growth." In Readings in Economic Development. Ed. Johnson and D. Kamerschen. Cincinnati: South-Western Publ. Co., 1972, pp. 461-470.

5. K. Rea, The Political Economy of Northern Development. Ottawa, Science Council of Canada, 1976, pp. 31-39.

6. J. Kruse, R. Travis, and J. Kleinfeld, Energy Development and the North Slope Inupiat: Quantitative Analysis of Social and Economic Change. Man in the Arctic Program. Monograph No. 1. Institute of Social and Economic Research, University of Alaska, 1980, Table 4-3, p. 36.

7. Morehouse and Leask, "Alaska's North Slope Borough," pp. 25-27.

8. Kruse, Travis, and Kleinfeld, Energy Development and the North Slope Inupiat, Table 4-3, p. 36.

9. M. Scott, "Prospects for a Bottomfish Industry in Alaska." Alaska Review of Social and Economic Conditions. Vol. 17, No. 1, 1980, pp. 19-23.

3

The Role of Agriculture in Alaska's Rural Development

Wayne Thomas

A BRIEF HISTORY OF AGRICULTURE IN ALASKA

Agriculture has been attempted in Alaska for 100 years, but until recently with indifferent success. The development of agriculture has generally followed the pace of more important economic activities.

The Russians grew food in the vicinity of their fur trading posts,[1] and these limited agricultural activities continued under the United States' ownership of Alaska. In the 1890s reindeer husbandry was introduced on the Seward Peninsula, initially to provide a more reliable protein source to the Natives of the region. However, the greatest growth in husbandry occurred after gold was discovered at Nome in 1898, an event which brought thousands to the Seward Peninsula.[2]

The Klondike gold discovery of 1896 was the event that stimulated governmental interest in Alaska agriculture.[3] Gold was discovered near Alaska's boundary with Canada, and the vast majority of miners were Americans. These facts, along with the expectation that more gold would be discovered in Alaska, led the United States government to establish several Alaska agriculture experiment stations, including one in Fairbanks in 1907. When gold was discovered near Fairbanks, the experiment station provided support to farmers producing products for local markets. A flour mill and a brewery were developed then too.[4] The pace of agricultural development matched that of gold mining, declining as mining declined.

Construction of the Alaska Railroad from Seward to Fairbanks, completed in 1923, created enough new economic activity to slow the downward slide of the regional economy. However, the 1930s depression seemed to adversely affect the prospects for agriculture in Alaska,[5] until the federal government sponsored the Matanuska Colony in the mid 1930s. This federal experiment provided funds for needy midwesterners with farming backgrounds to move to Alaska and establish farms to expand local food production and increase the population of the region.[6] Farm land improvements were provided at low costs, and the Alaska Railroad linked the colony to the growing city of Anchorage, forty miles away. By the early 1940s, this farming project had moved from the stage of subsistence agriculture to commercial agriculture, based on dairy farming and vegetable production.[7]

The dynamics of Matanuska Valley agriculture in the 1960s were much the same as those in many other parts of the United States: urban growth expanded into

23

surrounding farm areas. The population of Anchorage grew, and residents looked for land outside the city to purchase for home construction. The Matanuska Valley was near by, and it included large areas of patented, fee simple land which, unlike most land in Alaska could be sold easily. The number of farms declined, and agricultural land was sold for home sites, commercial uses, and development of light industries. The agriculture that remained in the valley took the form of dairy farms and truck gardening.

What happened to agriculture in other areas? The reindeer industry declined in the early 1930s, and the 30,000 head herded today are only 5 percent of the herds of the 1920s.[8] Commercial farming in the Fairbanks area had virtually ended by the early 1970s.

In one area, Delta-Clearwater, this trend was slowly being reversed. During the 1950s, some crop and livestock production associated with homesteading developed. After statehood in 1959, the state selected lands in the Delta area and conducted a few agricultural land sales, which transferred these lands to private citizens at public auction. By 1975, about 10,000 acres of patented farm land were in private hands, but only approximately 4,000 acres had been recently cultivated.

Several factors retarded the growth of agriculture in Alaska. Most food could be brought in from outside the state more cheaply than it could be produced in Alaska because, among other reasons, Alaska farms were small in size, and could not take advantage of economics of scale associated with highly productive agriculture in the lower 48, because of land limitations.[9] Also, the economic infrastructure, particularly the transportation network, did not facilitate marketing of products or supplying farms.

The Delta Agricultural Project

Government and oil were the prime ingredients in Alaska's agricultural expansion of the late 1970s. At the completion of the trans-Alaska oil pipeline in 1977, the economic condition of the private sector of the state's economy worsened, but the public sector improved. The state now taxed oil flowing through the pipeline and gained royalty oil. These two developments, softening of the private economy and the filling of the state treasury with oil revenues, were foreseen prior to 1977. Policy makers sought other economic activities to migitate the economic downturn, and considered agriculture seriously. The Federal-State Land Use Planning Commission for Alaska sponsored a study exploring agricultural development and in-state and export marketing opportunities.[10] The researcher proposed that barley be grown in the Delta-Clearwater area, 100 miles southeast of Fairbanks. A comparison study suggested that there be a 50,000 acre experiment in large scale agriculture in Alaska.[11] Simultaneously, in 1974 a local citizens-state government land use planning committee was studying the Delta area, and one outcome of this investigation was the designation of a 60,000 acre block of state land for agricultural use.[12]

The stage was set but a catalyst was lacking until the coordinator of the Governor's special projects office became interested in the prospect of agricultural development in Delta. He was influenced by state bureaucrats and private citizens who supported agriculture and by the two federal-state land use planning studies on agriculture.

In mid 1976, an ad hoc agricultural committee proposed that there be an agricultural development project in Delta. The Delta-Clearwater area was selected for three principal reasons: a major highway transversed the area; the regional population center was surrounded by an embryonic agriculture; and a 60,000 acre block of state land was available for agricultural development.

A feasibility study undertaken by the committee recommended the production of barley, for there was good marketing potential in Alaska and abroad for this crop. Barley had been grown in the Tanana Valley previously; and, not the least important, there was an adequate agricultural research base for large scale cultivation. The study recommended that farms be large, around 3,000 acres, to take advantage of economies of scale. Also, the study emphasized the importance of infrastructure, particularly a country elevator, to the success of project development. This proposed project differed from all previous agricultural development in that an export market (East Asia) was identified for all surplus products. Overall, the study indicated a reasonable chance for success of a "Delta" agricultural project.[13] On this basis, the committee recommended to the Governor that the state develop the Delta project.

At the Governor's request, the Division of Policy Development and Planning reviewed the feasibility study and found that the "plan" was based on possibly "optimistic" data, particularly concerning barley yields.[14] Simultaneously, a coalition of pro-agriculture legislators initiated legislation to create a development authority to undertake the Delta project, which passed both houses of the legislature. However, the Governor vetoed the legislation, for he opposed the creation of a new bureaucracy which would be empowered to dispose of state lands (a function of the Department of Natural Resources).[15]

At this time, new information became available on rapeseed, a crop that is compatible with barley, in that the crops can be rotated.[16] Rapeseed is an oilseed crop that has been grown successfully in northern areas of Canada; and it seemed likely to be adaptable to interior Alaska. A project benefit/cost ratio calculated at varying interest rates showed that, in most cases, there would be economic advantages to growing rapeseed and barley in rotation. This information made the idea of agricultural development in Delta more viable.[17]

In December 1977, the Governor agreed to support the Delta Agricultural Project, implementing it in existing state agencies. The 1978 state legislature provided funds for land clearing, loans for the country elevator, loan funds, land surveys, and project road construction. The project area was divided into tracts ranging in size from 1,900 to 3,700 acres; and these agricultural rights were sold in a lottery.[18] To be qualified to participate in the lottery, applicants were required to have Alaska residency and U.S. citizenship; a minimum of $35,000 in equity capital available for investment in the farming enterprise; and sufficient evidence of management capability.[19] Twenty-two applicants were chosen from the 103 who qualified for the lottery. The price of land averaged $51 per acre. Further, the state used the Agricultural Revolving Loan Fund for all loans except for land clearing. These loans were all made at subsidized interest rates.

The new farmers of the Delta project were required to clear their lands by 1982 and were encouraged to begin production immediately, so that they would use the grain elevators and other elements of the infrastructure, repaying construction loans on them. Farmers were not required to produce barley, but this crop has been relatively easy to grow, especially on new cleared lands. With approximately one fourth of the 60,000 acres under cultivation in 1981, barley is the major crop, and the development has truly become a Delta "barley" project.

MAJOR ISSUES IN ALASKA'S AGRICULTURAL DEVELOPMENT

Agricultural development is facilitated by low land prices, low interest rate loans, and government construction and financial support of transportation. These three key features characterize agricultural development in many countries of the world, including the United States. The American West was settled in part because of low land prices. Federal government support for agricultural loan programs has resulted in low interest loans for American farmers. Finally, there are numerous examples of highways and railroads built or subsidized by government, because the improvement of domestic transportation is a prime function of government. What has been used elsewhere to stimulate agriculture seems equally likely to aid its development in Alaska. Modern governments often work through the market system and create incentives to stimulate or accelerate regional growth. The Alaska state government has followed this approach in spurring agricultural development.

The Interface with State Government

The Delta agricultural project is unusual in the United States in that its chief sponsor is a state and not the federal government. The state of Alaska controls the agricultural project through its land disposal program and provision of financing for farms and infrastructure. The leading state agency has been the special projects office, within the office of the governor. Line agencies such as the Departments of Natural Resources (through its Divisions of Agriculture and Lands), Commerce and Economic Development, Transportation and Public Facilities, and Fish and Game have been involved to a lesser extent. There has been some confusion regarding agency roles and relationships, and questions concerning the responsibility (and accountability) of the Special Projects Office. These concerns over the direction and administration of the Delta project led the legislature to create in 1979 the Alaska Agricultural Action Council. Its responsibility is to coordinate and direct Alaskan agricultural development. The Council's five members include the special projects coordinator, two state cabinet members (the commissioners of Natural Resources, and Commerce and Economic Development), and two individuals appointed by the governor from the private sector. The Council now directs the Delta project, and it also suggests new agricultural projects annually to the state legislature and governor. Inter-agency disagreements continue, but the Council has exercised authority in overcoming administrative obstacles.

Periodically, there are calls for a more explicit governmental commitment to agriculture. The most frequently mentioned suggestion is that there be a state Department of Agriculture. This would consolidate in one agency the staff of several agencies now working on agricultural issues, and hopefully streamline the whole process. Of greater significance, a Department of Agriculture would symbolize the state commitment to agriculture. The merits of this proposal aside, Alaskan agriculture does not yet have the political power to gain its own department.

Capital Requirements

Two long term loan programs for land purchase and land clearing are the hallmarks of the Delta project. The new owners of the twenty-two tracts were required to make a 5 percent down-payment and then received long-term financing at low interest from the state of Alaska for the remainder of the land price, with payment to begin in 1980. A second loan, for land clearing, provided each tract owner with $165 per acre, a figure arrived at through negotiation with project farmers, in an attempt to cover all costs if efficient clearing techniques were employed. Repayment of principal and interest for this long-term low interest loan is not to begin until November 1982.

Capital requirements extend to more than just land clearing. Three major types of farm loans generally are needed to carry out crop production. Each year a short-term loan can be used to purchase seed and fertilizer in the spring, to be repaid when the crop is harvested. For the Delta project the amount of loan requirement would be approximately $3,000,000. The primary source of short term loans through the 1981 crop season is the Alaska Agricultural Revolving Loan Fund, a state loan program with a legislatively mandated limit on loan interest rates at 6 percent. Farmers go here first because of obvious economic advantages.

The second type of loan is for farm equipment. The loan period generally is more than one year and less than 15 years. The need for tractors in land clearing and farming and associated tillage equipment has been the major investment requirement of project farmers. To achieve full scale production for the Delta project, equipment requirements may total as much as $11,000,000. Most of this money, minus equity requirements, will likely be requested from the Agricultural Revolving Loan Fund.

The final major category of farm capital requirements is for land and farm improvements. Originally, project land loans were made to farmers by the Alaska Division of Lands. Project farmers who purchased more land for farm production or individuals who did not win in the lottery but who purchased Delta project farm tracts cannot use this source. Once again the cheapest money is available from the Agricultural Revolving Loan Fund. The other aspect of long-term capital requirements is farm improvements, buildings, and farm dwellings. In the beginning of the Delta project, these improvements were de-emphasized in favor of land clearing. In 1981, three years after the Delta project land lottery, property improvements are more evident on the farm tracts. As an example, a major investment in swine production has been made in one tract, with a total capital requirement for buildings, livestock, and equipment exceeding $1,000,000. Again, the chief source of loanable funds was the Agricultural Revolving Loan Fund.

Of course, there are other loan sources for short, intermediate, and long-term loans. They are not presently being used as widely as the Agricultural Revolving Loan Fund because of its lower interest rate. The apparent strategy that most project and non-project farmers are using is to attempt to obtain as much as possible of their capital requirements from the Loan Fund. When the Loan Fund's legal ceiling is reached (imposed by the legislature and currently at $20,000,000), no more money can be loaned until the ceiling is raised or money previously loaned out is repaid, and farmers must look elsewhere.[20] The most common sources are the Alaska Commercial Fisheries and Agricultural Bank (CFAB), commercial banks, and the Farmers Home Administration (a U.S. Department of Agriculture agency). All have higher interest requirements, with CFAB taking the major spillover loan business from the Agricultural Revolving Loan Fund.[21]

The Farm Credit System is the most common institutional provider of loanable funds to American agriculture.[22] Originated by the federal government and now owned by its farmer-clients, it does not have a significant presence in Alaska. Not only are its interest rates high, but its farmer-owners are unwilling to risk losses in the unproven area of Alaska agriculture.

Capital is also needed to develop an infrastructure—which includes transportation systems, marketing systems, and farm supply systems. In the case of the Delta project, a major source of capital for all three has been state government. Transportation includes the road system, which is government funded, and the Alaska railroad, a federally controlled entity. The railroad comes within 80 miles of the project, so incoming fertilizer and seed and outgoing grain transported by railroad must be hauled by truck between railhead and Delta. The railroad is an integral part of the marketing system, for agriculture generally lends itself to bulk handling and a railroad specializes in such movements. Currently there is a movement to transfer the Alaska Railroad from the federal to the state government and to extend its tracks to the Alaska-Yukon border in hopes of hooking on to an as yet unbuilt Canadian railroad connecting with the North American railroad system. The rail expansion at least to Delta for agriculture and possible forest and mining development seems to be an increasing possibility. Construction costs would be at least $1,000,000 per mile and borne by the state government. Such an extension should reduce transportation costs of farm supplies coming in and grain going out.

Marketing infrastructure refers to the grain elevator system. It has two central components, a country elevator complex adjacent to the Delta project itself and a terminal port elevator. The country elevator, owned and managed by the Alaska Farmers Cooperative and built with a $1,000,000 long-term low interest loan from the Special Projects Office, Office of the Governor, is necessary for conventional grain handling at the local level. The country elevator facilitates grading, cleaning, and handling of grain or oilseed. A transfer facility is required at railhead, twenty miles from Fairbanks, to move products from truck to rail or vice versa. This is an auxiliary facility which can be used for feed, seed or fertilizer transfer and temporary storage. Railroad extension to Delta, if it occurs, would remove the original need for the facility but local use such as livestock and dog feed manufacturing is expected to build up around the transfer point.

The port terminal elevator, a major component of the infrastructure, was funded by the state legislature in 1981. Site selection involved requirements of an adequate ocean port, access to both rail and truck movements, and cost as determining factors. The Alaska Agricultural Action Council selected the port of Seward, but controversy has surrounded this selection because the port of Valdez, without railroad access but much closer to Delta, is also vying to be the port terminal for Delta grain. Valdez, the southern terminal of the Trans-Alaska Pipeline, is trying to increase the movement of goods through its port for interior Alaska destinations. Grain from Delta could be considered a truck back haul for goods shipped from Valdez to Delta and Fairbanks. Thus, the City of Valdez has offered to build a grain terminal using its own funding sources.

Without the railroad extension, transportation costs are similar from Delta to Valdez or Seward. There is another factor, however. The only way the export grain terminal can be competititve with others along the Pacific Coast of North America is through high grain volume. Delta alone does not have enough grain producing land to support a port terminal of the necessary volume; but, Delta plus the Nenana project, a planned agricultural development that could include 300,000 acres of cropland, would likely produce enough volume to make the port elevator competitive.[23] Nenana is located adjacent to the Alaska Railroad, and it would be much more expensive to transport grain by truck from Nenana to Valdez than by rail to Seward. Wherever the port elevator is built, in its first years of operation, it will require a government subsidy to reduce the handling costs paid by farmers and to be competitive with similar facilities in southern Canada and the lower 48 states. The City of Valdez has offered to pay the operational subsidy for the proposed Valdez elevator, as has the state government for the Seward elevator. Of the two, the Seward elevator has the greater possibility of attaining sufficient grain volume to eliminate the need for this subsidy.

Marketing—In State

The Delta agricultural project differs from previous attempts at agriculture in Alaska, in that an integral part of its planning involves export marketing. This approach has received some criticism from people within Alaska who feel that inasmuch as so little food is produced in-state, it is unwise to design a project for outside markets without first supplying local needs. Taking an economic perspective, this assertion is generally true. Local markets have lower transportation costs associated with them. If farmers are fully aware of market prices, these lower costs will result in higher profit margins. Of course, if no export outlet is available, an unusually large supply of locally produced barley would drive down the price below that of grain brought in from outside the state.

Alaska, with its 400,000 widely dispersed people, is a very small market. The Delta project and existing crop lands in the Matanuska Valley and Delta areas could supply virtually all the feed grains for livestock, the cool season vegetables, and the milk used for domestic consumption. There are significant complexities in establishment and/or expansion of local processing for red meat and vegetables, however, and it would likely take five to ten years to accomplish. Without an export market, project grain farmers would share substantial uncertainties as to when and how much to expand production. To compensate for this uncertainty, the Delta project could be slowed down to allow markets to develop. This of course reduces the grain volume through the Delta country grain elevator, thus requiring a substantial operational subsidy to continue operation. If this subsidy is not available the elevator would be shut down, making in-state grain marketing very difficult. Grain sales outside Alaska will also face price fluctuation, but because the world market is so much larger, these fluctuations are likely to be much smaller than those caused by an in-state closed system.

The emphasis of agriculture could be changed from grain to other crops produced for the local market. Using vegetables as an example, only 2,500 acres would be required to satisfy Alaska's fresh, and processed market needs. The problem is that conventional size vegetable processing plants require far more acreage than is necessary to supply the Alaska market.[24] Even if smaller plants are economically feasible, the complexities of the business and efficient competition from outside the state suggest that vegetable processing calls for much more serious study before any action is taken. A recent announcement of the start up of a small potato chip factory in Anchorage may indicate one viable form of vegetable processing in Alaska. Alaska red meat processing is also being considered. A recent study indicated that a small efficient slaughter plant for swine and beef could cover all costs after eight years of operation.[25] Beef production would take much longer to develop than pork production because hogs lend themselves to single unit production from birth to slaughter and have a much higher reproductive rate. It appears probable that increased livestock production and slaughtering will occur in Alaska, but the process is complex and takes time. Alaskan grain production provides the feed necessary for red meat production, so initial emphasis on a healthy grain industry should facilitate expansion of in-state animal production.

Marketing—Grain and Oilseed Exports

Given Alaska's small domestic population, export markets must be considered if Alaskan agriculture is to work efficiently. The lower 48 and Canada, themselves major grain and oilseed exporters, cannot be viewed as prime market opportunities. Japan, however, because of geographical proximity and a strong economy is such a market, and is the prime potential market for Alaskan agricultural commodities.

Currently importing about 1,600,000 metric tons of barley and over 700,000 metric tons of rapeseed each year,[26] Japan has a large, growing economy, and is an industrialized society with a gross national product on a per capita basis comparable to that of the United States. It imports much of the food it consumes and, with the imposition of the 200-mile fisheries limit worldwide will need to import even more food products; for the 200-mile limit has reduced opportunities for ocean fishing. Japan's major protein source is fish, or seafood products, and when its fishing capability is restricted, it must find replacement sources. In this situation, Japan's particular development strategy is to buy feed and produce its own livestock, a situation which works to the advantage of grain exporting areas.

Canada and Australia supply most of Japan's barley requirements, and a new supplier like Alaska would have to be price and quality competitive. An interesting aspect of the Japanese market is that the government controls the purchase of barley; without government permission one cannot sell barley to Japan. Also, the major Japanese trading firms have segmented the barley market. There is a strong working relationship between the Japanese government and private trading firms, and establishment of close working relationships with both of these groups should facilitate sales of Alaska barley to Japan. In contrast, the importation of rapeseed, used as oil for cooking and as meal for livestock feed, is not controlled by the Japanese government. The mechanics of rapeseed sales to Japan are to find a buyer who would then contract with a trading firm to facilitate importation of the crop. The only marketing requirement is to be price and quality competitive with other suppliers.

Other nations in East Asia, particularly South Korea and Taiwan, are also potential markets for Alaska barley. These markets are more distant and potentially less reliable than Japan, but could be considered as residual market oppotunities.

IMPLICATIONS FOR DEVELOPMENT

The Delta project has already generated new agricultural projects in Alaska. The need for high grain volume to make the proposed port terminal elevator viable has led to the Delta expansion or Delta II project. This includes state lands just to the north and east of the boundaries of Delta I and across the Delta River to the west of the city of Delta Junction. Total acreage in Delta II after soil surveys are completed in the summer of 1981 could be 80,000 acres. The Alaska Agricultural Action Council has approved the project, and the land lottery is scheduled for Februray 1982.

Another development, in southcentral Alaska, the Point Mackenzie dairy project, is smaller and more controversial than any project to date. This project was put forward to help save the Matanuska Valley dairy industry, and was designed to add 3,000 producing milk cows to Alaska's present 1,200. This would provide greater volume through the dairy processing plant, thus allowing it to achieve greater plant efficiency.[27] Of the proposed thirty-one tracts in the 15,000 acre project, only nineteen were designated specifically for dairy use. The remainder could be used for any type of agriculture, with hay and vegetable production the leading uses identified. Point Mackenzie should already be underway, since the land lottery was held in March 1981. A court injunction, however, prevented the land transfer from taking place. The point of disagreement is whether the state government has the legal right to require farm development plans from those wishing to participate in the lottery before the lottery takes place. This was not done in Delta I because all twenty-two farm tracts were sold as grain farms. The Point Mackenzie case is before the Alaska Supreme Court, and the court must decide either to void the old lottery or to let the winners stand. The outcome of this court case is not known at this time.

A third development, in Nenana, has the potential of being the largest of all considered to date. It is located sixty miles south of Fairbanks, adjacent to the Alaska railroad. The project will be designed primarily for grain and oilseed production and should provide increased volume for the grain marketing system. Access is something of a problem in that three bridges are needed to cross water courses between the railroad and project lands, but transportation planning is continuing. Utilization of tree cover on the possible 300,000 acre project has also been of concern. There is substantial public sentiment within Alaska against clearing land by tearing down and then burning the tree cover.[28] Several approaches have been considered for tree utilization in Nenana, but these have become unnecessary, at least in the first phase. A forest fire which began in late May 1981 has burned over 100,000 acres of proposed project lands, including land possibly intended for offering in the lottery which is expected to be held in autumn 1982.

There are several other potential agricultural project areas in Alaska, but a primary factor in most is lack of access to the existing state road network. A study in 1974 indicated that Alaska might contain as much as 20,000,000 acres of arable land.[29] The Alaska Division of Agriculture, however, has substantially lower expectations, and suggests that 500,000 acres will be in production by 1990 (Delta I, Delta II, Point Mackenzie, and Nenana) and 1,000,000 acres by the year 2000 (mainly lands in the Tanana Valley and near the Yukon River).[30] It is difficult to assess whether this second goal can be achieved because of limited road access to Yukon River lands, but the first looks very possible.

Agriculture, from its meager beginning over 100 years ago, now has the potential to be a major economic force in rural Alaska. Its growth is dependent on establishing a highly efficient production and marketing system, a system which has begun with the Delta Project.

NOTES

1.   W. Burton, Creating a Northern Agriculture: Historical Perspectives in Alaskan Agriculture. Fairbanks: University of Alaska, Institute of Agricultural Science, Bulletin 43, 1976.
2.   R. Stern, L. Arobio, L. Naylor and W. Thomas, Eskimos, Reindeer and Land. Fairbanks: University of Alaska, Agricultural Experiment Station, Bulletin 59, 1980.
3.   P. Berton, The Klondike Fever: The Life and Death of The Last Great Gold Rush. New York: Knopf, 1958.
4.   C. Lewis and W. Thomas, "Expanding Subarctic Agriculture in the United States," Interdisciplinary Science Reviews. vol. 6 (in press) 1981.
5.   W. Thomas, "Agriculture in Alaska: 1976-2000 A.D." Alaska Review of Business and Economic Conditions. University of Alaska: Institute of Social, Economic and Government Research. vol. 13, no. 2, 1976, pp. 1-27.
6.   Burton, Creating a Northern Agriculture.
7.   Ibid.
8.   Stern et al., Eskimos, Reindeer and Land.
9.   Thomas, "Agriculture in Alaska."
10.   W. Thomas, An Assessment of Alaska Agricultural Development. Federal-State Land Use Planning Commission for Alaska. Report 13.
11.   J. Faris and R. Hildreth, Considerations for Development—Alaska's Agricultural Potential. Federal-State Land Use Planning Commission for Alaska, Report 14.

12. Alaska Department of Natural Resources, Division of Lands. Delta Land Use Management Planning Study. vols. 1-4, 1977-79.

13. W. Thomas, C. Lewis, F. Wooding, D. Carney, A. Epps, and E. Kern, "Potential Barley Production in the Delta-Clearwater Area of Alaska." Report prepared for the State of Alaska, Office of the Governor, 1977.

14. State of Alaska, Office of the Governor, Division of Policy Development and Planning. "Barley Production in the Delta-Clearwater Area of Alaska: Review and Recommendations." 1977.

15. W. Thomas and C. Lewis, "Alaska's Delta Agricultural Project: A Review and Analysis." Agricultural Administration. vol. 7 (in press) 1981.

16. Agricultural Experiment Station, Guidelines for Production of Rapeseed in the Delta-Clearwater Area of Alaska. University of Alaska, 1978. See also C. Knight, C. Lewis and F. Wooding, "Potential for Rapeseed Production in Alaska." Proceedings 29th Alaska Science Conference, 1978, pp. 149-158 and F. Wooding, "Continuation of Rapeseed Research in Interior Alaska." Progress Report, Agricultural Experiment Station, University of Alaska, 1979.

17. Thomas, "Alaska's Delta Agricultural Project."

18. These rights consisted of limited fee simple title, with the state retaining subsurface (mineral) and development rights. These restrictions, imposed by state law, are intended to prevent non-agricultural use of agricultural lands. All land sold in Alaska for agricultural development after 1975 must be sold with agricultural rights only.

19. Lewis and Thomas, "Expanding Subarctic Agriculture in the United States."

20. Limitation on loanable funds allows farmer application selection using quality determinations. This means that some farmers with readily financiable loan applications may receive a lower rating and not obtain the loan because of the imposed ceiling.

21. Farmers Home Administration does have a low interest loan program but it is limited to "smaller" farms. Delta project farmers could apply for Farmers Home Administration higher interest loans but their farms may be too large for its 5 to 7 percent interest program.

22. J. Penson, 'Financing the Development of Alaskan Agriculture." 3rd Annual Alaska Agricultural Symposium, 1981.

23. W. Thomas, K. Casavant and A. Gasbarro, "Transportation and Elevator Assessment for the Delta Agricultural Project." Report prepared by the University of Alaska, Agricultural Experiment Station.

24. Little Goldstream Associates, Vegetable Industry Report. Prepared for the City of Nenana, 1981. Export vegetable marketing is more problem filled than is export grain marketing.

25. Alaska Department of Natural Resources. Agricultural Briefing to the Committee on Natural Resources, Alaska State Senate, 1981. See also Featherstone Corporation, Nenana Livestock Report. Prepared for the City of Nenana, 1981.

26. D. Carney and W. Thomas, Alaska Grain and Oilseed Export Marketing: An Analysis and Suggested Approach. Alaska Department of Commerce and Economic Development, 1978.

27. C. Lewis, J. Harker, E. Arobio and W. Thomas, Potential Milk Production in the Point Mackenzie Area of Southcentral Alaska. University of Alaska, Agricultural Experiment Station, Bulletin 58, 1980.

28. This was also the subject of controversey in the Delta and Point Mackenzie projects.

29. Alaska Rural Development Council, Alaska's Agricultural Potential. Publication 1, 1974.

30. Alaska Department of Natural Resources, Agricultural Briefing to the Committee on Natural Resources.

4
The Future of Mining in Alaska

Charles Hawley

INTRODUCTION

Alaska has an abundant mineral resource base. It contains coal resources and reserves [1] that are significant on a worldwide scale and reserves of copper, lead, zinc, molybdenum, gold, nickel, silver, platinum metals, tin, fluorite and other mineral substances which are significant both nationally and for state employment. Because of its Pacific Rim location, the presence of coal and certain metal reserves is important internationally. The general course of mining development in the state seems destined to be upward, although there is uncertainty with respect to the rate of expansion because of economic and some environmental factors.

Critical factors to Alaska's mineral development include: 1) mineral commodity prices, 2) costs of energy, 3) cost of labor, 4) infrastructure—mainly transportation corridors, utilities, and development sites, and 5) timing of market availability. The latter factor is especially influential; because of the sparsity of developed infrastructure, it is difficult to assemble large mineral packages which can catch a current market cycle. A case in point involves Alaska coal: a definite potential market for subbituminous coal exists in Japan, Korea, and Taiwan; the potential suppliers include Alaska, South Africa, Western Canada, and Australia. All competitive sources, except Alaska, already have a developed export coal industry; Alaska would need to gear up in a rapid fashion to catch the next coal contract cycle. It is this type of uncertainty which precludes more than general forecasts of upward mineral development. On the other hand, it is prudent to forcast a two to three times constant dollar expansion of the industry in the next ten to fifteen years.

Past and present mining activity in Alaska is instructive in assessing the future. Prospecting activity started immediately after purchase of the Alaska Territory from Russia in 1867, and by 1880 significant mineral discoveries had been made. The development and production of these discoveries occupied Alaska until about World War II. From World War II until the mid-1960s when gold mining almost ceased entirely, there was continued production of platinum metals, mercury, and uranium; but the scale of mining did not at all compare with that between 1880 and 1942. Approximate production during the period from 1880 until 1960 was:

Major Metals:

Gold	20,000,000	fine ounces
Copper	1,400,000,000	pounds
Silver	16,000,000	fine ounces
Platinum	+ 200,000	fine ounces

Minor Metals:

Uranium	30,000	long tons
Mercury	20,000	flasks
Antimony	5,000	tons
Tin	2,000	tons

From about 1960 until the present, the dominant activity has been prospecting for new deposits. At the beginning of this era, total exploration expenditures were on the order of a few million dollars per year. They now total about $100 million per year.

Tangible results of exploration in this period were the detailed outline of coal reserves in relatively accessible parts of Alaska, and discovery of nationally significant deposits of copper, nickel, lead, zinc, molybdeum, tin, and fluorite.

ALASKA'S MINERAL RESOURCE BASE

Except for far northern Alaska and a few interior basins, most of Alaska potentially has metal-bearing mineral deposits. Major mineral regions include the Brooks Range and Seward Peninsula in northern and northwest Alaska, the area along the Yukon and Kuskokwim Rivers in Interior Alaska, the Alaska-Aleutian Range, Cook Inlet and Prince William Sound, and Southeastern Alaska (see Map 4.1). Types of important deposits represented include: 1) relatively large but low-grade or bulk deposits of copper, molybdenum, tin or tungsten minerals, 2) concentrated (massive sulfide) bodies of copper, lead, and zinc minerals, 3) concentrated and disseminated deposits of copper-nickel minerals, and 4) deposits of the precious metals gold, silver, and platinum of two types—lode or hard rock and placer. Historically, the exploited deposits have been the relatively easily mined placer deposits of gold and platinum, concentrated copper deposits, and in times of high prices, deposits of antimony, mercury, tungsten, and chrome.

Because of the sparsity of infrastructure in most of Alaska, only part of the mineral base can be produced economically in the near future. It can generally be predicted that in the next 20 years, Alaska will continue to produce precious metals; that it will begin to develop the large bulk deposits, if such deposits are close to tidewater or developed transportation routes; and that the higher-grade concentrated deposits will be gradually developed at remote sites. Deposits of specific current interest are scattered throughout Alaska (see Table 4.1).

The coal resources, especially those of subbituminous rank, are immense. In terms of deposits which can be exploited in southcentral Alaska, reserves would total several hundred million tons. In the remote northern Alaska field, Barnes estimated coal resources as 120,197 million tons, including about 20,000 million tons of bituminous coal.[2]

MAP 4.1

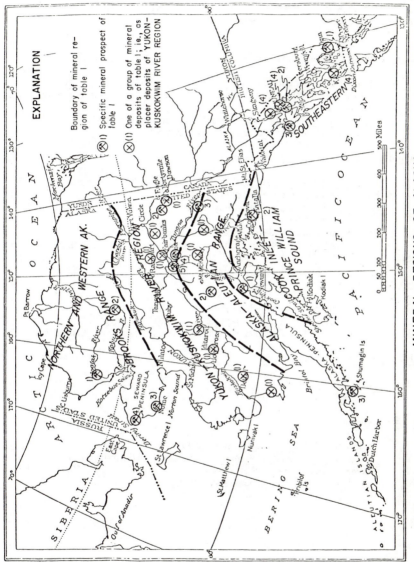

MINERAL REGIONS OF ALASKA

TABLE 4.1
MINERAL AREAS AND DEPOSITS OF CURRENT (1981) INTEREST
(Underlined if producing or in development)

Northern and Western Alaska (see Map 4.1)

1. Concentrated deposits of zinc and lead at Lik and Red Dog
2. Concentrated deposits of copper, zinc, and lead in Ambler River belt, Southern Brooks Range
3. Placer deposits of gold in and near Nome, Seward Peninsula
4. Disseminated tin-fluorite deposits, Lost River

Yukon and Kuskokwim River Region

1. Placer deposits of gold at numerous sites including Circle, Fortymile, Fairbanks, Livengood, Flat, Nyac, McGrath; Platinum placer at Goodnews Bay
2. Asbestos near Eagle
3. Concentrated sulfide deposits, Tok River and Bonnifield
4. Deposits of tin, tungsten, and molybdenum at several locations (not shown)
5. Coal field at Nenana

Alaska-Aleutian Range

1. Placer deposits of Chistochina and Valdez Creek districts
2. Concentrated sulfide deposits in Central Alaska Range
3. Epithermal lode gold-silver deposits of Unga Island and Alaska Peninsula

Cook Inlet and Prince William Sound

1. Coal field at Beluga
2. Coal field, Bering River

Southeastern Alaska

1. Disseminated molybdenum deposit at Quartz Hill
2. Concentrated zinc-silver deposit, Greens Creek, Admiralty Island
3. Disseminated copper-nickel deposits of Bohemia Basin, Yakobi Island
4. Numerous well-known precious metals deposits

SOME CONFLICTS IN THE DEVELOPMENT OF MINING IN ALASKA

Alaska has a land area of about 365 million acres. Although precise acreage ownership figures cannot be given, the approximate near term distribution of Alaska's land will be: 1) state of Alaska, 110 million acres, 2) Native villages and regional corporations, 45 million acres, and 3) federal government, 210 million acres. Private land, other than Native owned, is insignificant.

In 1980, the U.S. Congress passed Public Law 96-487, the "Alaska National Interest Lands Conservation Act." This act added about 44 million acres to the National Park System and created over 26 million acres of new National Wildlife Refuges. Combined with the old conservation units and additions to older units, over half of federal Alaska is now in conservation units which are withdrawn from entry to develop metallic and solid fuel energy minerals. Further, the distribution of the federal conservation lands and checkerboard pattern of federal-state and Native lands vastly complicate the development of infrastructure in the largely undeveloped state.

The attitude of individuals toward mineral development is as complex as the land patterns. Mining has been a major economic basis of rural Alaska since purchase. Small scale family mining operations (placer) currently total several hundred, and this type of mining, on an average, has been one of the main bases of rural employment since 1900. Except for some local environmental concerns, small-scale placer mining is relatively non-controversial. The attitude toward large scale corporate mining development, however, varies from one of support by some state and Native corporation leaders to uncertainty and even hostility in some rural areas. Although controversial in part, the larger corporate mining ventures offer the main opportunities for both rural employment and the production of significant amounts of resources for export.

In a recent survey, mining was estimated to employ 3 percent of the total rural resident labor force,[3] or about 1,500 people at seasonal maximum. Because of metal price increases, the level may have doubled, but it still is insignificant in terms of potential. Two or three large mines would employ about the same number of people on a long term basis, and would employ more during the construction phase. Thus far, mines planned for construction will employ at least 2,000 rural workers by 1986.

SUMMARY AND CONCLUSIONS

Alaska has a major resource base of subbituminous coal which is potentially valuable as an energy base for the Pacific Rim countries. The prospective development of this resource is being actively considered, and is likely, but it is not absolutely certain. In southeastern Alaska two hard rock mines are being developed—one for molybdenum, one for zinc-silver. In northern and interior Alaska, several major discoveries of rich concentrated deposits have been made and could be developed in the next ten to fifteen years. Geologically, Alaska has the potential for exploitation of precious metals; the common base metals copper, lead, and zinc; the alloy metals nickel, tin, tungsten; and a variety of other mineral substances.

Restrictions on development of over half the federal land in Alaska undoubtedly inhibit mineral development, both by direct withdrawal of the resource base and by the imposition of land barriers to transportation. Nevertheless, because of depletion of higher grade sources of minerals in the more accessible parts of the world and the gradual development of Alaska, Alaska's mining future seems assured. On a statewide basis, mining should be the main industry of rural employment, although locally renewable resources will be dominant. Total mining employment will likely total 10,000 by about 1990.

NOTES

1.   Resources include mineral materials that are currently non-economic or geologically likely; reserves are defined as the resources which can currently be mined economically or those where feasibility studies indicate they can be mined economically at the present time.

2.   F.F. Barnes,   Coal Resources of Cape Lisburne-Colville River Region, Alaska. U.S. Geological Survey Bulletin, 1242-E, 1967.

3.   C.C. Hawley and J.W. Whitney, The Economic Importance of Small Mining Businesses in Alaska. U.S. Geological Survey Bulletin, 1307, 1978.

5
Prospects for Trade Expansion in East Asia

Leon Hollerman

This is a propitious moment to discuss the Japanese solution to the problems of economic development in rural Alaska. It is propitious because of various favorable circumstances from an Alaskan point of view and various unfavorable circumstances from a Japanese point of view. I will consider the problem at hand from a Japanese perspective. An adversary relationship between the United States and Japan has been gathering force for quite some time. It is very urgent that this relationship be reversed. Alaska, and conditions with respect to the development of rural Alaska in particular, may provide a means of access to a solution.

What are the various difficulties that the Japanese face? If we perceive these difficulties, we may develop a better appreciation of how a solution for both Japan and Alaska might be devised. Japan obviously is enormously dependent on external resources which Alaska is in a position to provide. The dependence is becoming aggravated in that our long-term prospect is for depletion of natural resources throughout the world. Moreover, an adverse new development has appeared—the phenomenon of resource nationalism. The result is that there has been a great deal of protectionism with regard to natural resources, and many less developed countries which possess such natural resources have attempted to develop them independently rather than export them to Japan. Thus, there has been a collapse of resource possibilities for Japan. Alaska appears anxious to deliver raw materials to Japan without necessarily developing import substitution activities within the state.

One dimension of the U.S.-Japan adversary relationship is U.S. protectionism. The doctrine of fair trade versus free trade is one aspect of this new American protectionism. This doctrine also has been advocated by Western European nations in a form they call "organization of trade." It has given rise to plans for agreed specialization and allocation of activities to the members of the European Economic Community (EEC) group on a cartel-like basis. Thus, cartelism is a new phenomenon associated with the protectionist movement.

Japan also has been confronted with the world recession and the world inflation. By a peculiar and little understood mechanism, Japan's own recession is subject to being cured by an export promotion drive. This is rather ironic and counterproductive for a

---

A paper presented at a conference on "Developing Rural Alaska," held at the University of Alaska, Fairbanks, July 20-21, 1978.

good relationship between Japan and the rest of the world. The method by which the Japanese currently recover from domestic recession is different from the method adopted ten years ago during the period of the "economic miracle." During that period, it was possible for the government to relax its tight money policy, and an enormous flood of investment would then be released for purposes of capital investment. Capital investment in Japan in the earlier decades was the means by which recovery from the recession would occur. Today, Japan has a lower growth rate, and the rate of expansion of the Gross National Product (GNP) is much smaller than it was formerly (approximately one-half), so that the means for recovery from recession is an export drive. This practice compounds the world recession, for other countries are very resistant to receiving exports from Japan at a time when their own economies are in a state of recession. Here Japan faces another dilemma in the recovery process.

Japan now also faces competition from new industrial countries in the types of products that she has traditionally exported to the world—textiles, handicrafts, and labor-intensive goods. Japan is being forced into producing high technology outputs, a condition which has implications for instability. Notwithstanding her position as the third leading power in the world economically, Japan actually is a highly unstable and vulnerable economy. This can be seen in the great variability of Japan's economic statistics and also in the great difference in the level of performance of various sectors of her economy.

On the international plane, Japan has attempted to abide by the doctrine of separation of economics from politics. But it is becoming increasingly difficult for that separation to be maintained. Japan is being propelled into taking sides and crucial issues have arisen which, although they may not be of a long-term nature, are yet so compulsive and urgent that they may shift Japan's strategy of maintaining an economic separation from politics. For example, Japan may be compelled to line up with one side or the other in the controversy between China and Russia.

The institutional changes that are taking place domestically are another difficulty faced by the Japanese. Because of their recession, the lifetime employment system is now subject to pressure and is being gradually modified by means which are not at all agreeable to those who are exposed to this change. Workers are being forced to shift their employment from major companies to their affiliates, for example, and to take unattractive positions, or are being forced to retire prematurely with minimal wage settlements. These practices have caused considerable distress in Japan. Other institutional changes have taken place within the structure of the Japanese economy which reduce the degree of control that the government is able to exercise. For example, the fact that corporations no longer have a compelling impulse to invest in further capital investments means that they have accumulated vast funds which are lying idle in the banks. The independence of companies in finance means that they are less subject to control by the banking system which in turn is controlled by the government, and therefore, the government has less control over the activities of these corporations. Corporate independence means that the degree of government control over industry has decidedly diminished.

Another important difficulty and element of controversy between Japan and the United States is the so-called locomotive strategy that has been promoted by the United States recently. The Organization for Economic Cooperation and Development (OECD) developed the idea that the leading industrial powers should act as locomotives and haul the rest of the world out of the recession of 1975-76. The United States, Japan and Germany were designated as the locomotives, and the United States adopted that policy, urging Germany and Japan to do likewise. Germany and Japan were very resistant to the procedures implied by the locomotive strategy, namely policies of monetary and fiscal expansion. Traditionally, the Japanese have attempted to maintain a very restrictive and non-inflationary monetary and fiscal policy, as have the Germans. That Japan has been relatively more conservative in its monetary policies than the United States is now used as an argument by the United States against Japan. Washington says that Tokyo is dragging its feet and not cooperating in this effort to lead the way out of the recession. Also, Washington misinterprets the export surplus. In reality, at the present time Japan's export surplus is not a sign of strength, but of weakness—a point that is not at all perceived.

The export surplus is less a strategy than an involuntary reaction to the dynamics of the economy. The fact that the domestic market is weak in Japan requires corporations to seek to export their products, because they have a heavy obligation to life-tenured employees who are underutilized, which is inefficient for the corporation. During a domestic recession, the corporation must export even if it recovers less than the full price of the merchandise, but only a little more than the variable cost. This in turn leads to further troubles with trading partners who accuse Japan of dumping. In general, the Japanese have not been dumping. There is a vast wilderness of accounting problems involved, but the question of whether a nation is dumping depends, for example, on whether one includes research and development costs in the final price of the delivered goods. On the international plane, the Japanese may not include the cost of domestic research and development in their export product, and this may be legitimate. We have also accused the Japanese of industrial espionage, subsidizing their exports, and resisting imports in the form of non-tariff barriers. The Japanese, on the other hand, feel that they are being treated as scapegoats for the failure of the United States to solve its own domestic problems, which they identify as the basic reason for the American balance of payments deficit. They claim that the United States has adopted inappropriate monetary and fiscal policies in line with the so-called locomotive strategy, and that that has been the cause of the tremendous deficit in the U.S. balance of payments and the deterioration in the value of the dollar. The failure of the United States to solve its energy problems, and the failure of the United States to balance its budget (and the deficit financing of the budget deficit, which has resulted in an expansion of the money supply) have caused inflation and a relative incapacity of the United States to compete on the international market. Thus, there are two very strikingly antagonistic versions of what has caused economic maladies.

Internationally, the Japanese have further troubles. The United States has adopted a protectionist policy in retaliation for Japan's failure to cooperate, but in the last decade, under U.S. pressure, Japan has liberalized both its domestic and its international economies.

Also, on the international plane, Japan has problems with respect to north-south relationships, and east-west relationships. Japan faces difficulties in the north-south context with developing areas, for example Thailand. In the east-west relationships, Japan faces difficulties with the Soviet Union. Russia has denied Japan fishing rights, harassed Japanese fishermen on the Siberian coast, sent military patrols down to Etorofu Island, and buzzed Japan with military airplanes. This makes it particularly difficult for Japan to maintain the separation of economics and politics. The 200-mile limit on fishing has added to these problems.

Domestically, Japan has problems of pollution, environmental deterioration, and lack of sites for new plants. One of Japan's chief advantages in international trade was that its plant siting on the sea shore was very economical. Raw materials could be imported and processed on the seashore, eliminating the necessity for domestic transportation of the material; and products would be available for immediate export without inland transportation. Now, availability of such sites has practically disappeared, and it is hard to find locations for the construction of new plants.

Also, in addition three types of industries have declined in Japan. First, Japan is attempting to phase out energy consuming industries, such as petro-chemicals which use expensive oil. Aluminum refining is another expensive, raw material consuming enterprise. Second, Japan is attempting to phase out heavy industries, such as the open hearth furnace method of steel making. Third, Japanese textiles are subject to competition from the less developed countries (LDCs), particularly from the Republic of Korea and Taiwan. Retiring such marginal industries imposes responsibilities and burdens. On the one hand the Japanese government is expected to give aid to declining industries and to small and medium-sized industries, while on the other hand it does not make sense to do so economically. Most efficient economically would be to let declining industries go bankrupt and to give assistance to new high technology industries.

Where does Alaska fit in this situation? In the past, and probably in the future too, world trade will be concentrated in horizontal rather than vertical sectors. The largest component of world trade is the exchange of products among industrial countries within the manufactured goods category. This pattern of trade is influenced by the problem of free trade versus protectionism. Free trade seems to have a dismal future in the world, because of factors mentioned above, and because of the increased importance of horizontal trade. This horizontal structure of trade implies that the products involved in exchange will be more highly processed and more highly sophisticated, and that the trade itself will be subject to cartelization and to the decline of the so-called free trade philosophy. Countries will come to an agreement with one another as to the kinds of enterprises in which they will engage, and concerning the products they will buy and sell, in order to avoid the enormous expense of miscalculating investments and the prospects of economic warfare internationally. With the industrial countries developing into higher and higher phases of sophisticated activity, it is natural that they will come to some agreements about their relationships instead of fighting with each other for markets on a price basis, as has been characteristic of Japanese penetration of world markets in the past. This new configuration creates an enormous dilemma for Japan that is very ironic. Japan is temperamentally predisposed to finding such agreements congenial. In fact, this is what Japan Incorporated is supposed to signify. Japan has a long history of government controls and intervention; it is being asked by the United States to intervene now, to restrict exports to the United States. We have urged them to dismantle free trade, to circumvent their liberalized system.

In the category of industrial and highly sophisticated manufactured products, Japan has a great deal to lose by the disappearance of free trade in the world economy. With reference to raw materials, the situation is somewhat different. Japan does attempt to maintain diverse sources of raw materials. It attempts to play off one source against another in order to get cheaper sources of imports.

Alaska as a source of raw materials could perhaps contribute to salvaging the free trade system in this area. This does not mean that Alaska will necessarily be subject to a disadvantage as a free trade competitor, because presently the raw material suppliers are in the saddle. Japan has less of an opportunity to play one off against the other.

This is a sketchy design of the international trade picture, Japanese problems, and the Japanese point of view. The Alaska point of view introduces different considerations. First, one cannot just rely on the fact that Alaska is well endowed and Japan is not well endowed in terms of physical resources, thus expecting trade to occur naturally. There has to be trade promotion. At the moment, there are several very propitious factors from that angle. Because of the U.S. adverse balance of trade with Japan, an agreement was reached between the Japanese Minister of State for External Affairs, Mr. Ushiba, and Mr. Robert Strauss, then President Carter's Special Representative for Trade Negotiations. This agreement was signed in 1978, and it provided for the expansion of Japanese imports from the United States. Japan does not require American manufactured goods. What it does want is American raw materials and primary products, and these are what Alaska is in a position to supply.

The problems of the lower-48 are to the advantage of Alaska in this situation. The Ushiba-Strauss agreement is being monitored by the Subcommittee on Trade of the Committee on Ways and Means of the House of Representatives. Alaska's interests in expanding exports to Japan could be very constructively promoted within the framework of the Ushiba-Strauss agreement.

Another aspect of trade promotion is to avoid reliance on Japan alone. Alaska can play customers off against each other, as Japan has done in the past. In particular, the Scandinavians are very much interested in Alaska's fish, especially Denmark and Norway. In March, 1978, a Danish fishery inspection commission visited Alaska and at the end of May a mission was dispatched from Alaska to Norway. Also, the state government has opened a trade office in Copenhagen to strengthen ties with the Scandinavian countries.

A further point concerns the Native regional corporations which are excellent trade instruments, in that the Japanese prefer to do business with government agencies. The Native regional corporations could organize export departments which would make contact with the Alaska representative offices abroad, especially in Japan, and do business with the Japanese Ministry of Agriculture, Forestry, and Fisheries.

There are some problems which need to be overcome in the process of resolving or achieving development in the rural areas and developing Alaska's export potential. For example, most seafood products exported from Alaska are transshipped through Seattle where their identity is lost in the statistical process. In other words, the statistics on quantity of seafood exports from the state are inadequate. Another statistical problem is that presently there is no way to determine the extent of Japanese investment in the Alaska fishing industry. These statistical procedures need to be improved considerably so that current operations are understood as a basis for future planning.

A curiosity I noticed recently in a Japanese press report was that Japan maintains a ban on the importation of pollock caught by American fishermen. Alaska should insist that such exclusionary clauses be eliminated in its future contracts for supply of resources to Japan. Processing facilities need to be improved, too. With respect to the vertical structure, from production to transportation and export, it seems that Japanese investment in one level will lead to Japan's having a vested interest in making the whole vertical structure work. If Japan invests in an installation which depends on processing Alaska materials from the production to the export stage, Japan will commit itself to insuring that its investment is viable and that the vertical process is effective.

Rural Alaskans should be drawn into the political process by urging the state government to install an infrastructure. This cannot be done by private enterprise or by any of the regional corporations on their own. Also, the political process, concerning the regional corporations, should be the site of action leading to the removal of the economically unwarranted embargo on exports of oil to Japan from Alaska.

In general, the raw materials producers are in the driver's seat at the moment, and are in a position to exact favorable conditions in return for long-term commitments on the supply of primary products to Japan.

Part Two:
Development Organizations

6
Contemporary Rural Alaska and the Role of the Village Corporations

Michael DeMan

Approximately 60,000 Indians, Eskimos and Aleuts live in Alaska. Despite increasing urbanization, two-thirds of these Alaska Native people live in remote villages with predominantly Native residents. About half of all Natives live in the western and northern sections of Alaska where they constitute at least two-thirds of the population. The remaining one-third of the Alaska Native people live either in or near the state's urban centers of Anchorage, Fairbanks, and Juneau, where lifestyles more closely resemble the way of life in other states.

The median age for Alaska Natives is about 18, and the child population is larger than the population of those in the prime employment years. This, of course, creates a heavy burden of dependency on those who are of employment age. Rural Native families average nearly six people, and three of very eight village Native families have seven or more members. This factor, in and of itself, clearly demonstrates the support pressures on the rural Native adult. In the not too distant past, adults and children cooperated to support the family through their varied subsistence activities. Subsistence still plays a significant survival role, but increased external pressures have diminished the resources, and lifestyle expectations have inevitably evolved towards the U.S. norm. While hunting and trapping, fishing and gathering activities are still important both economically and culturally, cash has become a necessity. It takes cash to buy groceries from the village store, cash to buy heating oil, cash to buy gasoline for the snow machines now used for hunting and trapping. And cash comes from two basic sources: jobs and government support programs. Since it was the intent of Congress to stimulate economic independence with Alaska Native Claims Settlement Act (ANCSA) corporations, it becomes necessary to examine the current employment—or rather, unemployment—situation in rural Alaska.

THE EMPLOYMENT SITUATION

Unemployment in rural Alaska is impossible to view through conventional statistical methods used to determine the American norm. You are either employed or not, you are probably "looking for work" and thus registered. Rural Alaska cannot be viewed through the same lens. Although the economic system within which most Americans function is becoming more and more a part of rural Alaska, many rural Native villagers still rely on subsistence activities for a substantial portion of their livelihood. As a

A paper presented at a conference on "Developing Rural Alaska" held at the University of Alaska, Fairbanks, July 20-21, 1978.

matter of fact, subsistence has been and continues to be the single largest employer in the state. This mixed participation in dual economic systems confuses our efforts to define unemployment statistically in rural Alaska. It keeps many Natives out of the measurable job market altogether, and causes many others to limit their participation in the labor market to those times and places which will permit them to continue to participate in the traditional subsistence-type of economic activities.

Section 2(c) of ANCSA stipulated that a study of Alaska Natives and their relationship to federal programs be undertaken. Despite the fact that those who conducted the study were forced to rely on admittedly inaccurate and out-dated 1970 census figures, the data which they presented is still indicative of the position in which rural Native people find themselves. The section of this study which dealt with labor force participation is particularly relevant here:

> By usual U.S. standards, the Native labor force, as conventionally measured, is relatively small.... The Native civilian labor force is about 11,000 altogether, or about 40 percent of the Native civilian population 16 years old and over. This is well below the civilian labor force participation rate of 66 percent among non-Natives and about 60 percent for the U.S. population. Even among males, the Native participation rate is only about 50 percent.

> [FIGURE 7]–Civilian Labor Force Participation as a Percent of Civilian Population 16 Years Old And Over

	Male	Female
Alaska Natives	49%	31%
Alaska non-Natives	86%	49%
U.S. Figure	76%	44%

> The high rates for non-Natives reflect their concentration in prime working ages. The low rates for Natives reflect the constraints on their availability for employment.

> Even in the most urbanized regions, Native labor force participation is low.... In Cook Inlet in 1970 it was 54 percent; in Sealaska, 48 percent; in Koniag, 45 percent. In the rural regions of the west and north, it ranged from 25 to 37 percent. These are regions where village economic activities predominate.[1]

Numerous, if uncoordinated and contradictory, efforts have been made to measure rural unemployment more accurately. The State of Alaska Department of Labor, using figures adjusted from the consumer price survey (CPS), showed an 11.3 percent unemployment rate for the twenty-three non-urban census districts during 1977. In contrast, the overall state unemployment rate for 1977 was 9.4 percent. The same source indicated that the statewide figure for January 1978 was 12.6 percent. Although rural figures have not yet been broken out, it is safe to assume that rural unemployment followed the same upward trend.[2] There was a slight decrease in the overall state unemployment rate (11.9 percent) in February 1978, apparently reflecting increased activity in oil extraction and seafood processing industries along with a relatively stable situation in the transportation, finance, and service industries. This small overall growth in employment may also be reflected in rural employment, despite a continuing decline in the construction and trades industries.[3]

Figures from the Comprehensive Employment Training Administration (CETA) of the state's manpower division present a substantially different picture than that drawn by the State Department of Labor.

[Their figures] were derived by estimating the number of unemployed not counted by the Department of Labor and adding these to their projections for unemployed for FY78. This estimate of unrecorded unemployment was formulated by applying a fairly conservative participation rate of .51 to estimates of 1976 population by CETA region.[4]

The CETA unemployment figures are substantially higher than the state CPS adjusted figures as indicated below:

Region I	(Southeastern)	20 percent
Region II	(Interior)	21 percent
Region III	(Bering Straits, NANA)	11 percent
Region IV	(Bethel, Bristol Bay)	16 percent
Region V	(Anchorage, Mat-Su)	32 percent

CETA officials indicate that region III and IV figures are probably unrealistically low.[5]

Yet another picture is presented by the Tlingit-Haida manpower office which works with seventeen rural villages in southeast Alaska. Of the potential workers they estimate in their jurisdiction, 6,600 are age 16 or over, and are actually physically and mentally capable of working. Yet only 3,128 are actually employed giving an unemployment rate of 56 percent. Tlingit-Haida estimates that in some villages winter unemployment ranges between 70 and 90 percent.[6]

Whether we rely on the 1970 census data presented in the 2(c) study or the more recent but somewhat contradictory data, two conclusions are clear: 1) unemployment in rural Alaska is very difficult to measure, and standard methodologies for determining unemployment figures are inapplicable; and 2) whatever the method used to measure rural unemployment, it is cruelly and unacceptably high.

The authors of the 2(c) study put it this way:

Clearly, as the Alaska labor market is now structured, employment does not offer an escape route from Native poverty. . . .

All indications are that there is a chronic shortage of jobs for Natives. Unemployment rates of 20 or 30 percent are demoralizing, and act as a powerful disincentive even to look for employment. . . .

Shortage of jobs is peculiarly a Native affliction; it has not been characteristic of the Alaska economy generally. . . .[8]

Underemployment of the rural Native is another factor which needs—and defies—scrutiny. There simply are no hard data on underemployment in the rural Alaska economy. Nevertheless, it undoubtedly exists and is a problem. Two Alaska manpower specialists estimate that underemployment is a problem for 30 to 40 percent of those rural people who do have jobs.[9]

> There are many part-time jobs, and many seasonal jobs, but if you define under-employment as a full or part-time job that doesn't put a person above the poverty level—then underemployment is very common in rural Alaska.[10]

Part-time and seasonal jobs are typical of village employment. Common village jobs are teacher aides, health aides, day care workers, school maintenance personnel, and school culinary workers—jobs that by their very nature are not full-time. Seasonal jobs of one sort or another (trapping, commercial fishing, fire-fighting, construction, and snow removal, for instance) are also prevalent parts of the village employment picture. Seasonality has, of course, traditionally been the norm rather than the exception in villages, so the pattern is culturally comfortable but economically tenuous at best.

There has of late been much discussion about how the state's newly created permanent fund might be tapped to improve rural economic health. The possibility exists that very large sums of money from this fund will be made available for the development of businesses in Alaska. Despite good legislative intentions, this particular type of monetary injection could actually contribute to the current underemployment problem:

> Making capital cheaper and easier to obtain will undoubtedly have one effect which may be regarded as counterproductive: business will be given an added incentive to substitute capital for labor and the state's economy will tend to become more capital intensive than it otherwise would be. If investment policy is to be in any way directed toward "job creation," it must be highly selective and not simply a matter of lowering capital costs across the board.[11]

Although in some respects underemployment clearly does not present the immediately critical problem of unemployment, it is potentially at least as destructive. One cannot labor to provide for one's own needs and those of one's family, and continually fail to meet those needs without suffering some degree of discouragement. Two often the underemployed fall into a "why bother when I can't succeed?" syndrome—and this then leads directly, via self-fulfilling prophecies, to unemployment and usually dependence on welfare.

Unemployment and underemployment cannot be considered in a vacuum. In and of themselves they are meaningless without information regarding three additional factors: the income levels of village people, the village standard of living, and the real and potential growth of both the commercial and industrial sectors of the rural economy.

INCOME LEVELS IN RURAL ALASKA

The first of these factors, income levels, is another area where information is both scarce and imprecise. Figures available from the state's Department of Labor are for "wages," and are broken out by industry and by place of residence. Places of residence include Anchorage, Fairbanks, and Juneau, but do not include any information (either specific or generalized) regarding rural village circumstances. In addition, "wages" themselves are far more difficult to understand than the number of "wage-earners," and are given only as totals per industry.

Once again we are forced to rely on the 2(c) study. Recognizing that the statistical information on which researchers had to rely was inaccurate, and that the study itself is now out-dated, it is still the best source of information available. The chart below is taken from this study and is indicative of the inequitable distribution of income in Alaska.

[FIGURE 8]–Family Income And Size And Per Capita Incomes, 1970 [12]

	Native		Non-Native	
	urban	rural	urban	rural
Median Family Income	$10,172	$5,219	$12,582	$12,264
Mean Persons/Family	4.4	5.9	3.7	3.7
Median Income Per Capita	$ 2,312	$ 916	$ 3,671	$ 3,315

But even these income figures, dramatic though they may be, are empty without an understanding of the relative value of this income in rural Alaska. All commodities, from a case of canned milk to a new oil stove, are extremely expensive in the remote corners of the state. Not only is the cost of transportation high, but the ancillary costs of doing business in the rural areas are inflated; and these costs are, of course, passed on to the village consumer.

It is important to note that the rural villages included in the usual price indexes are Bethel, Nome, and Barrow: each of these communities is large in village terms (with populations in excess of 2,000), and each is accessible by both jet and barge. Food prices will be even higher in smaller, more remote communities not served by jet planes or even, in many cases, by barges.

Any consideration of income levels and the value of income in rural Native villages is confused by the continued, if diminishing reliance on subsistence activities to provide a portion of the food on the family table and fuel in the family fires. Conscientious efforts have been made to attach dollar values to subsistence activities.[13] Common to all of these discussions is a series of "ifs" and "buts": "If" it were a pure (i.e., closed) subsistence economy one might be able to draw some firm conclusions, "but" the subsistence resources are gradually diminishing and the lifestyle expectations are changing. There is no doubt that, at the moment, subsistence activities supplement village family incomes. But efforts to quantify the extent of this income supplement are imprecise, inconclusive, and rapidly changing as villagers participate more and more in the cash economy.

One additional factor must be included in this examination of village income levels: that of transfer payments. Despite the fact that it is difficult to get a firm fix on village incomes, it is patently clear that they are abysmally low. Given this fact, the presence of any measureable transfer payments will obviously have an impact. Given the additional fact that the typical village economy is cash-short, transfers assume even greater significance. A recent federal-state Land Use Planning Commission study on village life defines three types of transfer incomes:

First, there are direct government transfers such as old age pensions, aid to dependent children, unemployment payments, food stamps, boarding fees for school children, etc. These represent a substantial source of income in many villages. Second, there are what may be termed indirect transfers in the form of salaries and other expenditures associated with services paid for with funds which originate outside the region. These, too, can be an important source of cash flow in a typical small village, quite aside from their functional values, although the highest salaried positions are typically held by non-Natives. Finally, there may be in some cases a private remittance, money sent back to relatives by villagers now living more or less permanently elsewhere. Although, based on the experience of other poor and labor surplus regions, these payments may at times be quite substantial, we found no information about them.[14]

The study goes on to note that although in real dollar value these transfers may be "modest, they can be quite important in a small village, particularly because they are more dependable than other sources of money and can be counted on during the long winter, when the probably greater summer savings have been exhausted."[15]

STANDARD OF LIVING

A few decades ago the factors we have addressed above—unemployment, underemployment, or cash income levels—would have been irrelevant to Native villagers, and their standard of living would not have even been thought of as a "standard." It was simply a way of life—a way of life unlike that of most other U.S. citizens, but a way which was traditional and acceptable. This is no longer true. Contact with the outside world—either through direct experience of this outside world or via the media—has made what was once a traditional way of life an inadequate standard of living.

Our superimposed idea of a proper "standard" causes us to see village standards of living as extremely low. Their relatively new concepts of what a standard of living "should" be have caused them to see their way of life through a new lens—a lens which also defines their way of life as substandard. And the complex realities of change, of decreasing resources and increasing needs for cash incomes, have altered the situation dramatically. There is no longer a way or a reason to separate village and non-village perceptions of adequate standards of living. Village people have moved into late twentieth century America, and the standards applied to other American communities now apply to Alaska's Native villages.

High unemployment rates and low incomes are primary causes of rural Alaska's exceedingly low standard of living. These factors are compounded by extreme geographic isolation.

Prices

For most of the villages in the state, air transportation is the major means of travel, except when there is enough snow to allow snow machine travel or when the ice has left waters open to boats. This means that everything must come into the villages either by cargo flights or, in the summer, by barge (usually once a year). Consumer products are less prevalent and very expensive. For example, in the large rural communities of Nome and Bethel, food prices were 196 and 200 percent of Seattle prices respectively.[16] Both of these places are served by a number of barges in the summer, and frequent jet flights provide relatively inexpensive air cargo. Commodity prices in smaller, more remote villages are even higher. Considering that Seattle prices are already higher than those in most of the United States, it is not surprising to find foodstuffs and building supplies in Alaska's villages costing almost three times what they would cost in Washington, D.C. In comparison, Anchorage food is 118 percent of Seattle prices while Juneau's is 121 percent and Fairbanks' is 126 percent.[17]

Health Care

Geographic isolation also means limited access to health care services. Health care in most villages is provided by visiting doctors and dentists. In their absence, village health aides with various levels of training provide medical service, consulting with doctors either by radio or by the new village satellite telephones. Even with this system, access to hospital care in emergencies is by small aircraft, and in bad weather no such access is possible. As a result of these and other factors, mortality figures are high: the crude death rate for Natives is double that for other Alaskans, and the infant mortality rate is 28.5 per 1,000 births as compared to 19.8 per 1,000 in the rest of the U.S.[18]

Housing

The housing situation in village Alaska has been well summarized by the authors of the 2(c) study who, after surveying housing in the bush, concluded:

> Housing is the most serious and most intractable of the problems of infrastructure in Native Alaska, most especially of village Alaska. The harsh climates, the low level of income, the scatter of populations, and the uniquely high costs of transportation, construction, and heating have held down the quality of housing. At the same time it has placed obstacles in the way of programs to bring a supply of housing, which only begins to approach the U.S. standard in quality and quantity within the reach of Alaska Natives. Native housing is overcrowded and for the most part lacking in the standard amenities and facilities, including public water and sewer service. The same is not true of housing for non-Natives.[19]

Three major problems plague rural Native housing: poor quality, overcrowding, and inadequate utility services.

Poor housing is mainly the result of the extremely high costs of housing construction and operation. Extreme cold places a premium on small easily heated structures, while the low family income of most Native village families prevents the purchase of the materials necessary to build more adequate dwellings.

The 2(c) report, stating that "substandard housing conditions are endemic to Native Alaska," found that non-Natives in the same places did not share sub-standard housing, even if they had lower incomes than some poorly housed Native families:

> Whether urban or rural, above or below the poverty line, non-Natives live in better conditions, with less overcrowding and better facilities. . . . In fact, non-Natives below the poverty line (of whom there were few) are less subject to overcrowding and substandard conditions than Natives above it. . . .[20]

A housing study in Kotzebue found that:

> Four-fifths of all families live in homes that are sub-standard as shelter for one reason or another. These homes are physically inadequate by reason of unsound construction, dilapidation, poor insulation, poor ventilation, and similar physical

shortcomings. About 770 children are now spending their fomative years in these unfavorable living conditions.[21]

The study then evaluated all of the homes in the village:

> In May, 1970, Kotzebue had a stock of 302 private homes currently in use. <u>Of these homes, 264, or about 80 percent, were evaluated as sub-standard.</u> Thus, Kotzebue has a deficit of almost 250 homes of decent quality. At least that many additional standard homes are needed before the present population will be adequately housed.[22] [emphasis in original]

Overcrowing is nearly as serious a problem as poor quality of the houses. Both the Kotzebue study and the 2(c) report found that sixty percent of Native dwellings were overcrowded. In Kotzebue this meant that "about 575 children live in these overcrowded and unhealthy quarters."[23] The 2(c) study found that dwelling units, although small, accommodated on the average more than five persons. Sixty percent of Native dwellings were overcrowded by the standard of more than one person per room, and one-third contained more than two persons per room. Among Native families living below the poverty line, seventy percent lived in dwellings which were overcrowded and of those, half lived in dwellings that were severely overcrowded (two or more persons per room).[24]

Public services related to shelter such as electricity, sewer, garbage collection, telephone, and running water are not present in many Native dwellings. 1970 figures on the lack of these services taken from the 2(c) report, indicate:

[FIGURE 6]–Percentage of Population Living in Places Without Utility Services [25]

	Native	Non-Native
Telephone	26%	1%
Electric Power	18%	1%
Water	38%	20%
Sewerage	45%	7%

These conditions have improved somewhat in the last ten years, mainly as a result of the federal government's spending huge sums on village sewer and water programs. It is sad indeed that after the completion of hundred-thousand dollar projects, their management is assigned to villages which cannot afford to pay costs of fuel and wages for those who run the plants.

New construction of Native housing is almost impossible without substantial government assistance. Costs of even the most basic construction materials are inordinately high, and mortgage loans to villages are extremely rare. This is mainly because, from the banker's point of view, village residents are extremely poor risks for mortgage loans. First, it is frequently difficult to get an insurable legal title to land in rural Alaska. Second, all banks are reluctant to make construction loans in places where they do not have either an office or someone who can supervise the construction. Should the owner construct the house himself (which is frequently the case in the villages), bankers are even less anxious to grant a loan. (Owner-built homes have a bad reputation in the even less anxious to grant a loan. (Owner-built homes have a bad reputation in the Alaska banking community.) To all of these factors one must add Alaska's recent short supply of investment money.

Unfortunately, government programs to build housing in rural Alaska have been notable failures. Not only have houses been poorly designed for harsh arctic conditions, but construction has been shoddy, and supervision of quality frequently lacking. An Alaska State Housing Administration (ASHA) program to build scores of houses in "remote" villages has led to complex litigation which has continued for almost ten years.

Crime

Health and housing are not the only standard of living indicators to consider: crime in rural areas is a serious problem.

Current crime statistics in Alaska are not categorized by urban-rural areas, so we must depend for a description of rural crime on the 2(c) study:

> Within Alaska arrest records show a much higher rate of arrests of Natives than for non-Natives. For violent crimes Natives have a rate of 107.8 per 100,000, versus 29.3 for non-Natives. For property crimes, the rate was 447.9 for Natives and 197.8 for non-Natives. Alaska had higher-than-national crime rates for murder, forcible rape, and aggravated assault. Native arrest rates were significantly higher than those for non-Natives in each of these categories. The Native cumulated (1968-72) death rate by homicide was also quite high, 24.2 per 100,000 population, compared to the U.S. rate of 8.3 in 1970. . . .

> [T]he largest number of arrests are alcohol-related. Violent crimes account for 8.8 percent of adult Native arrests in 1970 but decreased to 6.9 percent in 1973.[26]

Education

Educational facilities, too, are both a major indicator and a determinant of standard of living. Up until the last few years, almost all of the education in rural Alaska was provided by either the Bureau of Indian Affairs (BIA) or the State Operated School System (SOS). Recently, rural education has been placed under the control of Rural Educational Attendance Areas (REAAs). They have inherited all of the facilities installed by government agencies over the years.

A recently decided state court case (Tobeluk v. Lind, also known as the Hootch case) mandated the presence of a high school program in villages which had nine or more eligible students. This decision necessitated a massive construction program for village high schools, and as of 1979 ninety-five have now been built.

Additionally, almost all of the village elementary facilities in some way fail to comply with the applicable codes. The state has received a report on 100 school and associated buildings in twenty-two villages in western Alaska. Of the buildings surveyed, not one met standards. As a result of this study the state has concluded that instead of the predicted thirty-year life expectancy, village school buildings may have a useful life of only five years. [27]

In discussing this study the Director of Facilities Procurement said that these changes would not improve the quality of life in the villages, and in fact were probably energy inefficient, adding to the costs of school programs.[28]

PROSPECTS FOR COMMERCIAL AND INDUSTRIAL DEVELOPMENT

We have considered the employment situation, income levels and standard of living in rural Alaska, but without an understanding of the real and potential growth of what the U.S. Economic Development Administration (EDA) refers to as the "commercial and industrial" sector, we can develop no real perspective.

The commercial and industrial sector is too grandiose a term for the type of businesses which rural villages can support. Because villages are small (most are under 200 people), isolated, rarely served by land transportation systems, and have virtually no internal cash economy, the commerce which the typical village can support is minimal.

Most villages have a single general store, selling groceries, gas, guns, traps, oil stoves, and snow machines. Inventories are usually limited, and toward the end of the winter stocks are frequently depleted. The stores are as large as they can be, but no expansion is possible—the limit to growth is the absolute amount of cash coming into the village in a year. These stores, and any other village business, face extreme problems. The seasonal nature of cash work makes the granting of credit mandatory, and, again toward the end of the winter, there is a long period when little or no cash flows back into the business. The distance from suppliers, and the high expense of transportation make it advantageous to develop a large inventory when the less expensive barge delivery is made. However, this requires a large amount of money in advance, and makes it impossible to control the store's inventory based on demand during the year.

Larger villages (like the hub communities of Bethel, Dillingham, etc.) offer opportunities for other types of businesses; but, again, they are limited to small trade and service organizations.

The lack of population growth in rural Alaska is the main limitation to business growth. The "snowball effect" of population growth encouraging business expansion which, in turn, leads to more population growth, is absent. In the place of the snowball effect is a "project orientation." Things are done once, to serve a particular need, and then people move on to something else. The limited market also acts to discourage competition and innovation.

The major "industry" in rural Alaska is thousands of years old. It is subsistence hunting, fishing, and food-gathering. This industry is now "failing." With the increase in Alaska's population, control and regulation of hunting and fishing, land use planning, placing public lands into private ownership, and other factors, the Natives' ability to subsist from the land is declining.

The preservation of subsistence is a battle that is being hotly fought now. Much attention is focused on public lands legislation, and through this process Native groups are attempting to preserve what they consider their right to subsistence activities. Limitations on subsistence affect strongly the economy of rural Alaska. For each pound of subsistence-gathered food which does not enter Native homes, a pound of food must be purchased—for cash. In cash-short communities this means sacrificing money which is badly needed for fuel or other essential supplies.

Growth in the commercial and industrial sectors of the rural economy is, at best, difficult to measure quantitatively. The Alaska Division of Economic Enterprise knows of no statistics or studies which will isolate the condition of the commercial and industrial sector in rural Alaska.

However, the Deputy Director has said:

Commerce and industry in rural areas is almost entirely restricted to small trade and service businesses. There is some slow growth, but it is not measurable. The largest single factor in encouraging growth in this area is the Native corporations, and any future growth will be closely linked to how they invest in their areas. The Native corporation's impact far exceeds that of any state efforts for businesses.[29]

VILLAGE CORPORATIONS

The Alaska Native Claims Settlement Act provided a hope for future change and a structure and methodology for a rural Alaska development strategy. The word strategy, however, inherently implies a unified direction and implementation, which has not "naturally occurred." Alaskans, residents of the "Last Frontier," are highly resistant to planners in Juneau or Washington, D.C., but central, dedicated support is badly needed to implement a rural development strategy.

Hope is present in the potential of the village corporations established under ANCSA. Under the terms of that act, profit-making corporations were established in each Alaska Native village (a total of 178 in all).

The Alaskan Native has been treated somewhat differently under the terms of this act than has any other aboriginal group in the U.S. In all other cases of aboriginal claim, sovereign title was granted to a small portion of the lands occupied by Native Americans. The balance was placed in the public domain and aboriginal title extinguished after payment of "fair" value to the aboriginal group.

Alaska was not made sovereign, but instead land was transferred to private ownership. In return for extinguishing Native Claims, the U.S. agreed to pay Native Alaskans $962 million and grant them 44 million acres of land (or approximately 12 percent of the state).[30]

Under the terms of ANCSA, there was to be a twenty year moratorium on taxation of any of these lands. The intent of the Congress was that during this twenty year period, the corporations established under the act would become economically viable entities in rural Alaska.

This entire notion, however, is a double-edged sword. While on the one hand the resources, in the form of cash and land, are provided to achieve economic viability for Native Alaskans, and indeed rural Alaska, the requisite managerial capability does not yet exist within these corporations.

At the time of ANCSA's passage, Native Alaskans were ill-equipped to understand or effectively deal with the many complicated provisions of the Act. Living in remote settlements which had only become permanently established in the last three or four generations, Natives were totally unfamiliar with the concepts of corporations, investments, and other attributes of a modern economy which the

Act thrust upon them. Even today, most Native Alaskans do not live in a cash economy as we know it in the Lower-48.[31]

Despite these problems, the corporations taken as a whole represent the most viable economic potential for rural Alaska. They possess not only capital, but significant assets, i.e., land. Further, they have access to a vast labor pool: village residents. No other entities exist in rural Alaska which have these qualities. The single most apparent deficiency of these corporations is the technical ability to manage successfully their assets in capital, land, and labor in a way consistent with traditional rural Alaska lifestyles and cultures and which is economically sound.

Contrast this change with the rural Alaska of only a short time ago. The economy was totally based on subsistence: hunting, fishing, and gathering provided all sustenance. Villages were non-existent. Temporary camps and settlements existed and changed depending on the season. Only a few short generations ago permanent settlements came into being, mostly at points of white contact. With those permanent settlements came the rapid transition from a nomadic subsistence lifestyle to the current mixed dependence on subsistence activities and cash economy. The transition has been rapid and difficult, and is still in process.

As villages have moved into a cash economy, they have, in effect, become conduits for this cash. Cash has come from three primary sources: the few relatively stable jobs which are common to most villages (postmaster, school custodian, health aid, etc.), transfer payments, and the income brought home by various types of seasonal, temporary, or sporadic employment opportunities (firefighting, construction of the pipeline and the like).

Because there is no significant commerce or industry in the villages, most of the cash which enters the village economy turns around and leaves it: with exception of the few foods, some fuel, and certain clothing materials provided by subsistence activities, everything else villagers need must be purchased outside. The school custodian, whose salary brings cash into the village, orders his family's clothing from a catalog and sends money out of the village to cover the cost of the purchase. The firefighter, who brings his summer's wages home, buys food at the village store—and the storekeeper buys his stock from an urban wholesaler. The examples are endless and the results are obvious: what cash does come into the village goes out again for imported goods and services.

A number of authorities believe that the rate of out-migration of villagers will continue to increase, in part because of the scarcity of local sources of income. If this occurs, village economies will suffer. Nonetheless, the villages are essential to those who are not willing or able to make the transition to urban life, and several recent studies indicate that many current village residents would prefer to remain in their villages. A survey conducted by the Alaska Native Foundation in Ruby and Galena found that most residents of these two villages not only wanted to continue living where they were, but that they would rather have jobs in the village than leave for temporary employment elsewhere.

Assuming, however, that those predicting an increased out-migration are correct, and that (as some fear) future village residents will be primarily the old, the young, and the unemployable, then it is essential that an infrastructure be developed to support these people. This eventuality presents an even greater challenge to corporate leadership if it is to avert despair and squalor which could lead to the complete collapse of village Alaska.

Whatever the future holds for the villages, one thing is certain: the village corporations hold the key to a private sector economy and therefore many will expect them to assume the responsibility of stabilizing the village economies.

At the risk of over-generalizing, we can define three types of villages, each of which can respond to the present challenge in a different way. Of course, there are villages which fall into more than one of these categories, and which therefore have greater options.

One group of villages has indigenous resources which are, or will be, in demand outside of the village itself. For instance, it is estimated that as many as 10 billion barrels of oil and 19 trillion cubic feet of gas lie beneath the surface of Native-owned lands.[32] These resources, and others, fall into the extractive category, and will be developed primarily at the initiative of large outside businesses that are interested in the particular resource. Such villages will most likely develop a rather conventional export-based economy. Their corporations can play reactive, passive, or accommodating roles: they can make land available, build facilities, and undertake training programs to enable village residents to take advantage of the local employment opportunities which may develop in the extractive industry. In such cases, there is little need for entrepreneurship on the part of the village corporation; but the potential for disruption of village life and the depletion or destruction of corporate assets is magnified, as are benefits if such development is successfully managed.

Another group of villages is favorably situated, has buildings of particular historic or aesthetic significance, or has a unique and commercially-valuable handicraft tradition. These assets may make such villages of interest to tourists—an industry which will create some employment and will inject varying amounts of cash into the local economy, depending, of course, on how the industry is developed.

However, the vast majority of villages do not and are unlikely to have a commercial economic base in the traditional western sense. Very few have items which can be exported on a competitive commercial basis and which would therefore create jobs for local people and bring cash into the local economy. The corporate management in these villages is faced with a different challenge, one which can perhaps only be met by the development of cottage-type industries which produce goods and services for local or regional consumption only. This approach would create local jobs and would keep more of the cash within the local economy. This approach has been described in the recent Federal-State Land Use Planning Commission study, "The Evolving Pattern of Village Alaska":

> The ideal industry for the region may be described abstractly: it should use local materials, it should produce output with a high value to weight ratio, it should be labor intensive, it should be capable of high productivity at small scale of operations (perhaps even cottage industries), and it should be counter-seasonal, to complement the higher levels of activity in the summer.[33]

We are, of course, referring to import substitution, the residual effects of which are obvious: each dollar not spent outside of the community remains within the community and has a multiplier effect.

Mathematically, the multiplier is the inverse of the propensity to import, so that if investment can improve the local economy's ability to provide locally what had previously been imported, each dollar that comes in from the outside will cycle longer within the local economy and provide more local jobs and income. In the developing countries, an economic strategy of increasing the multiplier has been called an import substitution strategy. If Village Alaska cannot devise exportable production, it can probably find ways to increase the local bang for the buck of its outside income by developing its capacity to serve its own population.[34]

The import substitution strategy can be applied to labor as well as goods; construction is a good example in Alaska. For instance, the state of Alaska has identified the need for rental or lease housing, overnight facilities, offices, warehouses, and laboratory space in a total of fifty-five rural villages.[35] No doubt this need will eventually result in contracts for construction, a service which could be provided by village corporations.

In March of 1978, the State Department of Administration requested proposals for the design, construction, maintenance and renting of facilities in eleven rural villages. This is another opportunity for village corporations. Such requests are common and contracts frequently are awarded to contractors from urban areas who bring work crews in with them. While this practice has some positive economic effect on the village, it fails to maximize potential benefits. Regardless of the type of village involved, the corporations have only one real choice: they must take full advantage of the opportunities which exist for their village.

There is potential for the development of a sound economic base in rural Alaska. Possibilities abound. Strategies need not be as sophisticated as those sometimes employed in the urban lower-48. The problems are different, the people are different, and the scale is certainly different. The addition of only a handful of jobs in a rural Alaska village can have a significant impact on the economy of that village. That theme, repeated throughout rural villages, can go a long way toward assuring a continued and healthy economy in rural Alaska.

Clearly solutions can be found. And they will be, if the new managers of the new village corporations are given the technical assistance they need to help them determine what kind of solution is appropriate to their village.

Finding the proper solution is half the battle won. The other half is making the solution into a lasting reality. Management expertise, accounting expertise, planning expertise—all these things can be bought, for a price. But the village corporation management itself must at the very least know how to select the right kind of experts, how to direct them, monitor their efforts, and evaluate the results. Given the current lack of experience in such matters, an immense effort is required. Management personnel and corporate board members must be given the kind of training which will make them capable of fulfilling their mandate and meeting the needs and desires of their shareholders—the village residents.

The approach we are suggesting requires policy decisions by the state of Alaska and the federal government to assist and build the village corporations in basic ways. Other groups, like the Alaska Native Foundation, may serve as the cutting edge of such programs, but the powerful weight of government must be applied to make a difference. Failure to do so will result in a continuation of present rural Alaska conditions and will require public, not private, development dollars; and that will increase the tax burden on everyone.

Of course, the corporate success itself must be two-pronged. The corporations must provide a return to their shareholders, most of whom are villagers and who therefore will spend at least some of their dividend earnings in the village. This influx of cash will serve to bolster the economy in much the same manner as any indirect income transfer. In addition, the corporations have an implicit responsibility to develop an economic infrastructure if they are to meet both Congressional intent as expressed in ANCSA and the obvious needs and desires of their shareholders. Both prongs of corporate success will have an impact on the village economy. In combination, the impact will increase geometrically.

The presence then of healthy, viable corporations means that, outside of benefits accruing to Alaskans (by themselves important enough to demand attention), trading partners, whether for import or export, have someone to talk to. More importantly, that someone knows what they want and is capable of executing, in an organized way, such agreements.

NOTES

1. United States, Department of the Interior. 2(c) Report: Federal Programs and Alaska Natives. Portland, Oregon: 1973, Task I, Part A, Sec. 1, p. 14.
2. Alaska, Department of Labor, Labor Force HIGHLIGHTS. Juneau, Alaska, April, 1978, p. 1.
3. Ibid.
4. Fred Ali, (Project Field Representative, CETA, Community and Regional Affairs Department, State of Alaska), telephone interview, April 20, 1978.
5. Ibid.
6. Richard McKinley, (Tlingit-Haida Manpower Office), telephone interview, April 20, 1978.
7. Alaska Native Foundation, Alaska Natives: A Status Report. Anchorage, Alaska: 1977, p. 5.
8. 2(c) Report, pp. 15-16.
9. Ali, op. cit., and McKinley, op. cit.,
10. Ali, op. cit.
11. Arlon R. Tussing, "Economic Considerations in Establishment of Alaska's Permanent Fund" (for the Alaska Legislative Affairs Agency). Juneau, Alaska: July 7, 1977.
12. 2(c) Report, pp. 17-18.
13. Alaska Natives: A Status Report, p. 7.
14. William Alonso and Edgar Rust, The Evolving Pattern of Village Alaska. Anchorage, Alaska: Federal-State Land Use Planning Commission for Alaska, 1976, p. 38.
15. Ibid.
16. University of Alaska Extension Service, Comparative Food Prices. Fairbanks, Alaska: 1977, p. 2.
17. Ibid.
18. Community Enterprise Development Corporation, Refunding Proposal, Anchorage, Alaska: 1976, p. 32.
19. 2(c) Report, p. 12.
20. Ibid., p. 13.
21. Alaska State Housing Authority, Kotzebue, Alaska, Comprehensive Development Plan. Anchorage, Alaska: 1971, p. 53.
22. Ibid., p. 55.
23. Ibid.

62

24. 2(c) Report, p. 12.
25. Ibid., p. 13.
26. Ibid., p. 10.
27. RoEn Design Associates, Inventory and Condition Survey of Educational Facilities. Fairbanks, Alaska: Alaska Department of Transportation and Public Facilities, 1978.
28. Roy Peratrovich, (Director, Division of Facility Procurement, Department of Transportation and Public Facilities), telephone interview, April 20, 1978.
29. James R. Deagan, (Deputy Director, Division of Economic Enterprise, Alaska Department of Commerce and Economic Development), telephone interview, April 20, 1978.
30. T.J. Smith, "Native Alaskan Economic Development: Issues and Recommendations"; Economic Development Law Project Report. January/February 1978, p. 22.
31. Ibid., pp. 27-28.
32. The Alaska Native Management Report, June 1, 1977.
33. Alonso and Rust, "The Evolving Pattern of Village Alaska," p. 37.
34. Ibid., p. 39.
35. Letter from B.B. Allen, Commissioner of Administration, April 5, 1978.

7
Rural Alaska's Developing Economic Institutions: The Entrance of Native Corporations into International Trade

Ronald Dixon

Rural Alaska's products are not new to the international marketplace. Goods from Alaska first entered foreign markets in the mid-18th century. For almost 100 years, Russian traders probed Alaska for furs to bring home. Following Alaska's purchase by the United States, traders from a dozen nations sought Alaska furs, and European markets paid high prices for fur seal, sea otter, and walrus hides.

An Alaska-Asian connection began in the early years of the 20th century when Chinese provided the labor force for the development of the cannery industry. Until World War II, cannery owners hired Chinese laborers from San Francisco to work in the canneries instead of hiring local labor. Japan played an active part in Alaska's development after the early 1950s when an organization representing Japan's timber industry approached U.S. officials in Tokyo, seeking to import timber from national forests in Alaska. This event initiated Alaska's modern connection with Asia, and Japan soon became Alaska's major natural resource customer. In fact, to the present, Japan has accounted for the majority of Alaska's exports (roughly 90 percent), and her interest has spread from the timber industry to Alaska's fish, oil, and natural gas resources.

This Alaska-Japan connection, and the growing Alaska-East Asian relationship in general, may prove even more important to the future economic development of rural Alaska. In this paper, we focus on the development of international trade opportunities as one strategy of economic change in rural Alaska. We begin with a brief historical review of the Alaska-Japan connection emphasizing the economic, political and geographical factors which have influenced the development of international trade opportunities. We then report the results of two surveys conducted in 1979 and 1980, which provide data on rural Alaska's current relationship with East Asian corporations. In this section, we examine Asian interest in rural Alaska's resources, the response of rural Alaska's Native corporations to this attention, and those internal and external factors which serve to limit the entrance of rural Alaska's developing economic institutions—the Native corporations—into the international marketplace.

THE ALASKA-JAPAN CONNECTION: AN HISTORICAL PERSPECTIVE

When Japanese traders visited Alaska in the early 1950s, they found few of the comforts they had grown to expect in other parts of the United States. Instead, they found a situation comparable to that of a "developing" nation, for rural Alaska was a capital-short area with little technical or managerial expertise and high rates of unemployment. It had none of the transportation, communication, or business systems found in modern America: there were no telephones, no means of sending a telegram, and few post offices; there were no roads or highways and in many cases the only transportation was by air charter or boat. The final and greatest inconvenience for these visitors was that many of the Americans in rural Alaska spoke not English, but Aleut, Inupiaq, Yupik, Tlingit, Koyukon, or Kutchin. The only significant difference from other developing nations in which Japanese businessmen were working was that Alaska was a part of the United States, and Alaska operated under American law.

Faced with these inconveniences, it is not surprising that Japanese businessmen and their corporations withdrew to Seattle where they based their headquarters for Alaska operations. In Seattle, the Japanese could deal with America as they understood it; but equally important, Seattle controlled much of the Alaska economy. The Japanese made their entrance into Alaska's fishing industry through Seattle. Their initial investments have grown considerably, and today the Japanese have investments in more than half of Alaska's seventy-five largest processing firms.[1] Alaskan processors welcomed the Japanese investment, for after years of weak salmon runs, they desperately needed venture capital to refurbish plants, to expand processing into new species, and to begin a search for new markets.

The influx of Japanese capital, and the heretofore untapped Japanese market allowed rural Alaskan fish processors to move into new sectors of the fishery—salmon eggs, herring roe, king crab, and snow crab.[2] This has been a decidedly beneficial impact of Japanese investment in rural Alaska. With such heavy investments at stake, the Japanese naturally assumed a more active role in rural Alaska fishing communities. They transferred technicians to Alaska to process the salmon eggs, herring roe and herring roe on kelp because, in their view, rural Alaskans were not skilled in the harvesting or the processing of these newly valuable products. As one Native corporation leader commented at the 1978 conference, Developing Rural Alaska: A Role for China and Japan?:

Before the Japanese provided a demand, we used to throw the salmon roe away—or feed it to the dogs. Now, the Japanese pay us for it. They taught us to make money from something we used to waste.[3]

However, in the opinion of many rural Alaskans, the Japanese have not trained individuals so that they could manage fishery enterprises by themselves. Rural Alaskans have been trained to perform the more menial processing and canning functions, but not in the more sophisticated fishery skills. Nevertheless, seasonal employment is plentiful. In some regions up to 90 percent of the able-bodied workers are employed during the two to three week salmon runs, and in one exceptional case, at Unalakleet, some Natives work twenty-four hours a day harvesting and processing salmon.[4]

Japanese investment in Alaska began with the incorporation of Alaska Lumber and Pulp in 1953. Since then, this investment has grown in response to the expansion of markets in Japan for Alaska's timber—to satisfy part of the construction material needs of the Japanese building industry and the Japanese paper industry's need for dissolving paper chips. In 1968 it was reported that there were Japanese investments or contracts for timber supplies in five Alaska locations.[5] The number of sites increased to eight by 1974, and would likely have been higher if there had not been fewer stumpage sales by the U.S. Forest Service and a waning timber market during the economic slowdown of the mid-1970s.[6]

In this sector, too, there have been both positive and negative impacts. In Interior

Alaska, one Native corporation which entered into a sales contract soon after receiving land conveyances complained that it was victimized by the Japanese corporation with which it traded.[7] The corporation president reported:

> We're still trying to figure out what went wrong. Perhaps we didn't have the self-discipline to wait, but I think our biggest problem was that we didn't know our partner. We signed timber contracts with the Japanese, and we didn't really know them. We couldn't communicate with them. We were never able to develop a working relationship as partners.[8]

A group of village corporations in southcentral Alaska provides a contrasting example. They formed a joint timber sales venture and seem pleased with their sales arrangements with the Japanese.[9] The need for expertise in international trade prior to ventures with international firms is apparent on the basis of the interior village experience. Whether or not this expertise is available, Native corporations are forming international business ties in increasing numbers, and Native timber is beginning to enter the international marketplace. Several villages started harvesting operations in 1979 and one regional corporation began operations in the latter part of 1980.

Active consideration of Alaska as a source of oil supplies for foreign markets began in 1965 when the president of Japan's Teikoku Oil inspected the Cook Inlet area, but U.S. government policy delayed the development of this interest. At first, the principle of reciprocity was applied; and since U.S. firms were not allowed to develop oil resources in Japan, Japanese firms were excluded from holding mineral rights leases in Alaska. Once this barrier was removed, Teikoku met other obstacles in its drive to import Alaskan oil supplies.[10] Fuel prices, currency adjustments, environmental problems and finally specific language in the trans-Alaska pipeline legislation made foreign participation in the development of this resource impossible.

While Japanese efforts to obtain supplies of Alaskan oil have been unsuccessful, natural gas has been a different story. Japanese firms have been able to participate in this sector of the Alaska economy, and are major customers for liquified natural gas and pilled urea from the Cook Inlet and Kenai natural gas fields.

Although Japan's demand for hard rock minerals is strong and growing, Alaska's resources have yet to make an impact on the international marketplace. Resource prices, extraction costs, the lack of transportation infrastructure, and the lack of resource surveys of Alaska's hard rock mineral potential serve to limit the development of this resource group. However, in 1981, Sun Eel Shipping Company, Ltd. of the Republic of Korea began mixing Alaskan coal with Australian and Colorado coal for testing in Korean power and cement plants. If these initial tests prove satisfactory, a long term contract between Sun Eel and Usibelli Coal Mine in interior Alaska is considered likely, marking the beginning of the export of hard rock mineral resources to Asia.[11] Obviously, the investment in hardrock minerals is in its infancy. The real impacts will come in the future, and it appears that foreign firms may serve as an impetus for the development of this rural Alaskan resource.

To the present, benefits to Alaska Natives from these international trade developments have been minimal. The cash economy of rural Alaska improved slightly as some residents gained employment in the timber and natural gas industries, and as others gained seasonal employment in the fisheries. However, the early developments were controled by non-Alaska corporations. Native corporations participating in the international market now differ from these earlier developers, in that they must balance their need for profit with other equally vital non-economic needs of their shareholders.

RURAL ALASKA'S DEVELOPING ECONOMIC INSTITUTIONS

In the mid-1960s, a new source of power arose in rural Alaska. Alaska Natives, statewide, joined together to seek a resolution to their land claims which neither the U.S. Congress nor the state of Alaska had extinguished. Their efforts resulted in the passage of the Alaska Native Claims Settlement Act (ANCSA) in 1971, which included the ingredients to improve the economic status of Alaska's Native people: capital and land. This legislation was more than a settlement of aboriginal claims. It also created over 200 village corporations and 12 regional corporations—new institutions which would own land and the resources of the land in rural Alaska, and institutions with which the Japanese could negotiate for their natural resource supplies. More important-ly for the rural residents of Alaska, the Native shareholders in the Native corporations could now determine for themselves which strategies of development they would pursue. Native corporations became the sole entity in rural Alaska with the capital, the land and its resources, and the manpower to create production, employment, and income opportunities in rural Alaska. For this reason, we have limited our study of rural Alaska's international trade potential to the interaction of Native corporations with potential Asian customers.

The land settlement, or more specifically, the resources of the lands selected by Native corporations, have put these institutions in an advantageous position. But more importantly, it is Native shareholders and their corporate leaders who will make the decisions regarding the development of their resources. In 1971, Morris Thompson, then area director for the Bureau of Indian Affairs, said:

> To me there are a couple of basic elements necessary to expand opportunity for Alaska's Native people. One is to adopt a self-determined policy that is explicit in regard to distribution of economic activity . . .[so that Natives] will be able to use their resources in an efficient and coordinated manner.[12]

He spoke then of the economic development aspect of self-determination. He saw the need for a coordinated strategy by the Native corporations in the development of their economic potential, but he also emphasized the importance of having Natives control the decision making process. Moreover, he and other Native leaders, then and now, thought Native corporations should be concerned with more than the profit motive which had characterized the behavior of non-Alaska corporations in their dealings with rural Alaska. To Native leaders, the Native corporations had to balance the social, cultural, and environmental needs of their shareholders with the need for profit. Income to improve village lifestyles, jobs and job training, and considerations of the effects of development on the subsistence pursuits of village residents, were just as important as the need for profit.

RURAL ALASKA-EAST ASIA: A MARRIAGE OF CONVENIENCE?

The interest of foreign nations in Alaska's resources has grown as the world's natural resource stocks have declined. Industrial nations, such as Japan, need resource supplies to maintain their industrial machine, and thus many commentators have pro-posed a "marriage of convenience" between rural Alaska and the developed states of East Asia. This would seem reasonable, as the economic interests of the two regions are complementary. East Asia needs natural resources. Alaska holds an abundance of these resources; and Native corporations, the largest private landholders in Alaska, own, or will soon own, land containing many of these resources. Additionally, as the U.S. balance of trade deficit increases, Alaska becomes even more attractive to those U.S. trading partners with a favorable balance of trade.

Alaska's geographical location also makes it an attractive trading partner for Asia's industrial nations. Anchorage, and more recently, Fairbanks, are stopover or refueling points for international flights between Asian and Europe and the U.S. east coast. Alaska is convenient for ships traveling the Great Circle route to Asia, and it is a politically stable trading partner when compared to many other resource suppliers throughout the world.

Rural Alaska's need for venture capital, for technical expertise, and for management assistance might be met by Asian corporations, particularly Japanese firms which have already played roles as development agents in Third World countries. Although Congress intended the $962.5 million cash settlement of the ANCSA legislation to provide the initial capital for the economic development of Native communities in rural Alaska, much of this has gone to meet other vital needs of the corporations, such as funds to meet the ANCSA deadlines, for day to day corporate operations, and for lengthy court battles to resolve those questions left unanswered in the legislation. Most of the cash settlement has now been distributed to the corporations, but only some have been able to invest a part of their settlement in economic undertakings. As a result, there remains a serious need for development capital in rural Alaska, and Asian firms appear willing to provide this.

ANCSA left unanswered the question of technical and managerial expertise for the Native corporations. There was no ready pool of technicians or managers in rural Alaska in 1971, and corporations were forced to turn to managers hired from outside of Alaska, to consultants, and to the few local managers available to oversee daily operations and implement the objectives of the shareholders and their corporate leaders. Although the Native corporations have made great progress in developing and training a local cadre of technicians and managers, Asian corporations might offer further assistance in these efforts. Notwithstanding the legislative intent of ANCSA, rural Alaska still needs venture capital, managerial skills, and technical expertise—needs which can be met by Asian corporations.

RURAL ALASKA-EAST ASIA: THE CURRENT RELATIONSHIP

These political, economic, and geographical factors seem to facilitate the development of international trade between Alaska and East Asia. To determine what relationship had developed between these regions, two surveys of native corporation leaders were conducted in 1979 and 1980. The first was a mail survey of the approximately 180 village corporations created under the Alaska Native Claims Settlement Act. Sixty-one percent of the leaders of these corporations responded to our questions. The second survey, by mail and telephone, collected data from twelve of the thirteen regional corporations. While we recognize the limitations to the use of survey research methodology, we believe that the information presented below reports reliably the current attitude toward the new "international frontier" of rural Alaska.

East Asian Interest in Native Corporations

Based on their previous economic activities, it appeared likely that Asian corporate interest in rural Alaska's resources would expand to include Alaska's Native corporations during the late 1970s. A 1966 study by the University of Alaska's Institute of

Social, Economic and Government Research (ISEGR) noted:

> It is not surprising that customers are actively seeking a source of supply rather than vice versa. Rural Alaska lacks capital, large scale business organizations and the technical and managerial skills that go with them. The initiative for development and marketing of rural Alaska's resources is coming from large outside firms—mainly Japanese.[13]

Thus our first concern was to determine whether foreign nations had expressed an interest in the village and regional corporations. Our data show they have, and that fifteen years after the ISEGR study little had changed. The initiative for the development and marketing of rural Alaska's resources still comes from "large outside firms— mainly Japanese."

As indicators of Asian interest, we selected three variables: visits by Asian representatives to the village or regional corporation, phone calls or letters from Asian representatives received by the corporations, and trade-related meetings outside of the village or regional corporation headquarters. As an additional variable indicating both Asian and Native interest, we included visits to Asian nations by Native corporation leaders. The results are shown in Table 7.1.

TABLE 7.1
EAST ASIAN INTEREST IN NATIVE CORPORATIONS

Expression of Interest	Village	Regional
	(percent)*	(percent)*
Visits by Asian representatives	14%	58%
Asian letters or phone calls	14	58
Meetings "outside"	22	42
Visits to Asian countries	5	33
	N=107	N=12

*Total exceeds 100% as many corporations received more than one type of expression of interest.

Source: Native Corporation Surveys, 1980.

Only five village corporations and four of the larger regional corporations sent representatives to visit potential customers or investors in Asia. In contrast, Asian companies appear greatly interested in rural Alaska's Native corporations. When we aggregated the number of village and regional corporations receiving some type of Asian attention, we found that one-third of the villages, and two-thirds of the regional corporations had been contacted by Asian firms.

Where village corporations were concerned, Asian firms appeared interested in their renewable resources. Of course, under the terms of ANCSA, villages are conveyed only the surface rights of their selected lands, and timber and fish are currently the primary surface resources. As we noted above, Asian development in the past focused on both these industries. Villages where Asian firms had previously operated were paid much more attention than were those villages with no previous Asian connections. Given the emphasis on timber and fish products, it is not surprising that Asian firms were far more interested in tidewater locations. Interior villages, and especially those villages distant from transportation routes, attracted little Asian attention.

Asian firms were very interested in those regional corporations with hardrock mineral, oil, and natural gas potential. Despite the past difficulties of the Japanese in gaining access to supplies of these resources in Alaska, their obvious value continues to draw the attention of Asian firms. Seven of the regional corporations contacted by Asian firms reported a hardrock mineral potential, and five believed they had oil and gas reserves on the lands they selected.

Joint Ventures and Contracts with Asian Firms

Having determined the extent of Asian interest in Native corporations, we wished to ascertain the Native leaders' response to this interest. The answers to questions regarding resource sales contracts and participation in joint venture arrangements provided us with this information. Asian corporate interest in Alaska's Native corporations and their resources has not been reciprocated to any great extent. As seen in Table 7.2, Asian firms have yet to penetrate very deeply into rural Alaska's Native corporations, but firms seeking resource supply contracts were more successful than those seeking Native partners.

TABLE 7.2
NATIVE CORPORATIONS WITH ASIAN CONTRACTS OR JOINT VENTURES

Type of Agreement	Village Corp.	Regional Corp.
Joint Ventures/Partnerships	5%	8%
Resource Sales Contracts	10%	25%
	N=107	N=12

Source: Native Corporation Surveys, 1980.

Five village corporations reported entering into joint venture arrangements with Asian firms, while one regional corporation followed this route to the international marketplace. In contrast, eleven village corporations and four regional corporations had signed contracts for the sale of resources to Asian firms. Timber and fish were again the primary resources of interest, but village corporations also reported contracts for reindeer antlers and seal products. Japanese firms were the primary customers for Native timber and fish, but Korean interest is growing, and two village corporations have contracts with Korean firms. One village leader also reported a sales contract with a company from Hong Kong.

Simple economics may explain this apparent preference for contracts over joint ventures or partnerships, but it may also reflect Native corporations' desire for local control of their resources.

Local Control

We asked two questions regarding the importance of local control and creation of local jobs compared to the corporations' economic benefits (profits). In both instances, respondents felt local control was much more important than profits, 61 percent to 9 percent favoring jobs, and 44 percent to 25 percent favoring management control over profit. Native corporation leaders have developed critical attitudes toward exploitation of the resources they possess, and they appear to be influencing the terms of development to benefit local shareholders and local corporations. Native leaders felt that Native-held corporations were much more likely to provide local jobs and local management control than would other corporations operating in the village.

The entrance of Alaska's Native corporations into the international marketplace as yet has made little impact on foreign markets or the general economic development of Alaska's rural communities. But then, very few Native corporations have risked entry into the international arena. As the vanguard corporations reported in this study succeed and as their numbers increase, the impacts will be greater. Our findings suggest that foreign interest in rural Alaska continues, and that this interest is directed increasingly toward the developing Native corporations. However, these institutions have yet to respond to this interest to any great degree.

CONSTRAINTS ON INTERNATIONAL TRADE DEVELOPMENT: INTERNAL FACTORS

We selected three factors as potentially influential in constraining a Native corporation's entry into the international marketplace: first, the existence of a resource to market; second, willingness to develop that resource; and third, willingness to work with others, particularly foreigners, in the development of the resource. Responses to our questions regarding these constraints are summarized below.

Resource Potential

Native corporation leaders were optimistic about their corporations' resource potential. Only 10 percent of our respondents felt their selected lands had no available resources. However, few villages have conducted resource surveys, and our findings in Table 7.3 reflect "best guess" estimates by the corporate leaders.

TABLE 7.3
RESOURCES OF VILLAGE AND REGIONAL CORPORATIONS

Potential Resource	Village Corp. (percent)*	Regional Corp. (percent)*
Timber	42%	67%
Fish	69	83
Sea mammals	20	42
Oil and gas	25	58
Hardrock minerals	28	92
Agricultural lands	29	58
Tourist interest lands	44	83
No resources available	9	
	N=104	N=12

*Total exceeds 100% as many corporations claimed more than one potential resource.

Source: Native Corporation Surveys, 1980.

As expected, Native corporation leaders indicate that timber and fish are their most abundant resources. Resources with a presently unknown potential for Alaska's Native corporations are oil, natural gas, and hardrock minerals. Both national and foreign interest in these resources is high, and most of the regional corporation leaders believe they are potentially available on their lands. However, Congressional prohibitions on the export of strategic resources may severely limit efforts to develop many of these resources for the international market.

Village and regional corporations alike, reported that they had agricultural and tourist-interest lands—two relatively untapped sectors with potential for rural Alaskan development. Although garden plots and small truck farms have produced vegetables since the arrival of the first Euro-Americans, large-scale agriculture in Alaska has been limited to the Matanuska Valley and the large state-assisted project in the Delta Junction area. For the present, most Native corporation agricultural interest is directed to import substitution economics on a small scale in rural villages.

Little attention has been paid to tourism potential in rural areas. Most tourist-related development by Native corporations thus far has occurred in Alaska's urban areas and previously established tourist sites in rural Alaska such as Barrow, Nome, Kotzebue, and southeastern Alaska.

Attitudes Toward Development

In the past, resource development efforts adversely affected a significant number of rural Alaska Natives. Some saw conflicts between resource development and maintenance of their subsistence lifestyle. Many Native leaders thought that the two values were not inherently incompatible,[14] however, and a growing number of Natives are increasingly interested in developing employment opportunities in their own communities. A recent study reported that: "seventy percent of the residents favor more jobs in the community, but only if outsiders do not move in as a result of this development."[15] Our data support this finding. Over 60 percent of our village leader respondents favored development of available resources. Only 3 percent were not interested in development, and the remaining corporate leaders and their corporations were undecided as to the future direction of their communities. This question was not asked of regional corporations, because our research strategy accepted a development attitude as a given for these larger Native-held firms.

The Receptiveness of Village Corporations to Outside Corporations

Our third constraining influence was the corporate leaders' receptiveness to outsiders in business roles. This question asked whether leaders would work with outsiders of different nationalities in increasingly closer relationships. We selected three roles for use in the scale—customer, investor, and partner.[16]

The 1968 study of Alaska-Japan economic relations stated:

> With very few exceptions, Alaska public opinion is favorable to the involvement of Japanese industry in the state's economy. The exceptions are Kodiak and some Bristol Bay communities. In most other communities, the Japanese seem welcome either as a possible source of income, or to help keep U.S. packers honest.[17]

Thirteen years later, the opinion of Native corporate leaders was also favorable to Japanese involvement in the rural Alaska economy. Although the mode of our inquiry, a mail survey, did not permit detailed and sensitive estimates, we found no material opposition to Japanese involvement, as can be seen in Table 7.4.

TABLE 7.4
ACCEPTABILITY OF "OUTSIDERS" IN BUSINESS ROLES
(Percentage of respondents expressing a willingness to work with groups of various business roles.)

Role	Other Americans	Japanese	Chinese	Norwegians
Which of these groups are you willing to work with as business customers?	75%	83%	47%	62%
Which of these groups are you willing to work with as business investors?	69%	53%	30%	45%
Which of these groups are you willing to work with as business partners?	69%	51%	27%	41%

N=12

Source: Native Corporation Surveys, 1980.

Native leaders were most receptive to Japanese in the role of customers. Eighty-three percent of the respondents accepted the Japanese in this role, and Japanese were favored over non-Native Americans. Of course, Japanese firms have actively pursued trade with Native corporations, while other American corporations have taken a wait-and-see approach in their dealing with them. Also, as world prices for resource materials have risen, Japanese industrial firms have consistently outbid competitors for resources.[18]

Native leaders were less receptive to Norwegians or Chinese, but neither of these groups has made inroads into rural Alaska, and many Natives are simply unfamiliar with them. They may be viewed more favorably as they take a more active role in rural Alaska. It is quite likely that Native leaders were registering a preference for groups with which they were familiar rather than expressing a prejudice against any of these groups. Northern European interest in rural Alaska is a relatively recent occurrence, and although our study emphasized Alaska-East Asian connections, we did notice perceptions of Northern European interest in rural Alaskan resources.

In those roles requiring the closest interaction—investors and partners—"other Americans" were by far the most accepted group. In this case, too, groups with which Native leaders had interacted in the past appeared more acceptable. Also, some Native leaders may have been reluctant to accept foreigners in these roles because they were unfamiliar with their methods and corporate structures.

This review of internal factors suggests that the preconditions for the development of international trade have been met. Native corporations hold, or will hold, resources of interest to East Asia and other nations. The majority of the Native corporations favor developing these resources to some degree. Finally, Alaska Natives appear willing to work with international firms in the development of these resources.

CONSTRAINTS ON INTERNATIONAL TRADE DEVELOPMENT:
EXTERNAL FACTORS

To date, few Native corporations have responded to East Asian trade initiatives, even though the internal forces for entry into the international frontier appear to be in place. We now consider those external factors which might limit the response of Native corporations to these initiatives.

Three factors external to these developing institutions have limited rural Alaska's response: the limited land conveyances to date and the lack of development capital; the lack of leadership by the state and the regional corporations in assisting in the development of international trade opportunities, and finally the lack of a comprehensive plan for international trade development.

The Land Settlement

Resource ownership and working capital are keys to the expansion of international trade opportunities. In rural Alaska, the slow pace of land conveyances has seriously retarded development of these opportunities. Although ANCSA in 1971 had called for the expeditious conveyance of lands selected by village and regional corporations, when we conducted our survey eight years later, only 16.5 million of the 44 million-acre land settlement had been conveyed, and much of this only during the winter of 1979 and 1980.[19] Forty-nine percent of our village respondents and 50 percent of those regional corporations entitled to surface estate acknowledged that they had received no lands. This has caused a financial hardship for these institutions, and it has further served to retard the economic development goals expressed in the ANCSA legislation. As the pace of conveyances increases, we expect an increase in the number of Native corporations entering the international marketplace.

This slow pace of land conveyances has also had an effect on the availability of working capital for these corporations. Without land and its resources, smaller village corporations and to some extent the regional corporations have been limited in their investment opportunities. Without income from the sale of resources or from other investments, they have had to use their ANCSA cash settlements for day-to-day operations rather than for investment purposes. This has left insufficient working capital to make the sunk costs required in trade expansion.

The Role of the State

The state of Alaska has expressed an interest in expanding the role of international trade in the state's economy. The Delta barley project is the most recent state development in this arena, and state officials anticipate international sales of the barley from the project. Based on the amount of public information from state agencies, we expected that Native leaders would perceive a state interest in Native corporations and their international trade development efforts. This did not prove to be the case.

Only 3 percent of the village corporation respondents reported that they had received any help from the state. We expanded this area of questioning in the regional corporation survey. Again, we found little perception of any state initiative in assisting the development of international trade opportunities. Only one regional corporation felt the state had helped it contact potential East Asian customers or investors. While some corporations acknowledged that they had used the Alaska trade office in Tokyo, others were unaware that such an office existed. Four regional leaders reported receiving international trade information from the Department of Commerce and Economic

Development, but five of the twelve corporate leaders expressed the opinion that the state was not interested in helping Native corporations. The state's proclaimed interest in international trade appears to have had little impact on Native corporation leaders.

Village corporation presidents viewed their regional corporations as even less helpful than the state. Only two villages found their regional corporation supportive in international trade development efforts. At the same time, the regional corporations were unaware of the interests of their village counterparts. Over half were uncertain as to whether there was any interest in foreign trade at the village level. Although many regional corporations have made development of international trade opportunities a corporate objective, they appear to have offered little assistance to villages interested in developing these same opportunities. Only one regional corporation offered technical assistance to villages, and none of the regional corporations had yet developed a means of communicating international trade information via workshops or seminars.

Of course, regional corporations have just entered the international arena themselves. Their perceived lack of support thus far may speak of their lack of familiarity with the international arena. One regional corporation president stated: "We're just now getting into this area because we were leery of foreign controls which might be placed on us."[20] Our information suggests that there is a beginning to international trade activities by regional corporations. One president reported that his firm now had a full time staff member working on international trade development, while others have assigned foreign trade responsibilities on a part-time basis to some of their staff. The regional organizations are in a position to provide information, facilitative assistance, and leadership in development efforts. Such activities on their part seem likely to increase.

The Lack of Comprehensive Planning

The lack of leadership by the state and the regional corporations is one factor held to be responsible for the slow pace of international trade development efforts. It may be, however, that this is due more to a lack of comprehensive planning than to willful negligence. At a 1978 statewide conference, Developing Rural Alaska: A Role for China and Japan?, commentators questioned whether Alaska had an international trade policy. Alaskans, Native and non-Native, spoke of the need for comprehensive planning and stable policy. A banker said, "We have no clear, defined policy; maybe we should begin by establishing what our true attitudes are." Another commentator noted, "We have stayed put; the Japanese trade companies are leaving Alaska because there is nothing for them to do. We have no defined policies from the state of Alaska." A regional corporation leader commented,

> Alaska's policies toward Japan fluctuate dramatically. We are in a ball game where state policy affects us dramatically. If we are to sell any coal to Japan, we need a stable, stated policy to allow us to go through the whole process. There is an interest, but with all the hurdles to get over, it is difficult to even consider it.[21]

Obviously, before the state or regional corporations can assume a leadership role they need coordinated planning and clearly defined policies. Perhaps the business community and the government should work together on such a plan. Then and only then, will the state and regional corporations become active and aggressive international trade conduits for rural Alaska's resource development.

THE INTERNATIONAL FRONTIER: A SUMMARY

East Asian firms are interested in rural Alaska as a resource supplier, and they are turning to Native village and regional corporations as the brokers of these resources. Nearly one-third of the village corporations and two-thirds of the regional corporations have attracted East Asian attention and interest, but only a few Native corporations have responded to this interest.

The entrance of Native corporations into the international marketplace has made little impact internationally or on the general economic development of rural Alaska communities. As with most early economic endeavors, the benefits are likely to come in the future. For now, a few jobs have been created in the fishery, timber, and reindeer herding industries, and some foreign capital is flowing into Native corporation coffers. But, only a few corporations have entered the international arena.

Perhaps the best example of the potential for Native efforts in the international trade arena comes from Sealaska Corporation, the Native regional corporation for southeast Alaska that has just joined Fortune's list of the 1000 largest American corporations. In October 1980, the president of Sealaska Timber Corporation (STC), Frank Roppel, discussed the impacts of logging by Alaska Native corporations. STC is a wholly owned subsidiary of Sealaska Corporation which is developing and marketing the timber resources of the corporation (at present, primarily for the Japanese market). Mr. Roppel commented to the Alaska Loggers Association:

> The future of logging by Alaska Native corporations and its effect on the economy of Alaska, especially southeast Alaska looks very promising . . . .In 1980 alone, more than $12 million will be injected into the economy with an impact of 200 new jobs. Most importantly, the profits stay in Alaska—a new concept considering the history of development in Alaska.[22]

He further emphasized that Alaska Natives are being trained to perform the various jobs in the logging industry.

Development of exports for international markets is one strategy of economic development for rural Alaska, but it is not a strategy for every corporation. Some have no natural resources; others are not inclined to develop those resources they have; and still others of these developing institutions have yet to set the course for their corporations. Some of the corporations identified in this study are vanguards in the sense that they seem to feel that the cash settlement from ANCSA is insufficient to support economic development within their communities, and they are turning to international trade to support these efforts. One president summarized his company's attitude as: "We will consider all proposed ventures, but we will undertake only the most beneficial."

Alaska's developing economic institutions, the Native corporations, stand poised to enter the international frontier. It seems likely that they will enter the international marketplace, but only if they feel such involvement will benefit their communities.

NOTES

1.   W.P. Daugherty, "Japanese Seafood Investment Climbs," Alaska Fisherman, October 1978, p. 1.
2.   Ibid.

3.   Proceedings of the Conference: "Developing Rural Alaska: A Role for China and Japan?", July 20-21, 1978, unpublished transcript. Fairbanks, Alaska: University of Alaska.

4.   Ibid.

5.   Arlon R. Tussing et al., Alaska Japan Economic Relations: A Study of the Potential Contribution of Trade with Japan to Alaska's Economic Development, Fairbanks, Alaska: University of Alaska, Institute of Social, Economic, and Government Research, 1968, pp. 100-103.

6.   Alaska Department of Commerce and Economic Development, Japanese Investment in Alaska. Juneau, Alaska: August 1974, pp. 17-19.

7.   Tundra Times, June 21, 1978.

8.   "Developing Rural Alaska," op. cit.

9.   Tundra Times, June 21, 1978.

10.   Tussing, Alaska Japan Economic Relations, pp. 115-116.

11.   The Alaska Economic Report, Anchorage, Alaska: January 12, 1981, p.1.

12.   U.S. Senate Hearings, Committee on Public Works, Subcommittee on Economic Development, 92nd Cong., 1st sess., April 17, 1971.

13.   Alaska Review of Business and Economic Conditions, University of Alaska, Institute of Social, Economic, and Government Research, October 1966, p. 7.

14.   Cooperative Extension Service, Proceedings of the Alaska Rural Development Council, July 13-14, 1977, p. 20.

15.   Institute of Social and Economic Research, Agricultural Experimental Station, Yukon-Porcupine Planning Study. Fairbanks, Alaska: 1978, p. 8-1.

16.   Approximately 15 percent of our respondents had difficulties with the questions, so our findings require further study. For those who did respond, we found that acceptability declined as the intensity of interaction increased.

17.   Tussing, Alaska Japan Economic Relations, pp. 19-20.

18.   Japanese Investment in Alaska, p. 11.

19.   Alaska Business News Letter, Anchorage, Alaska: August 15, 1980, p. 2.

20.   Native Corporation Surveys, 1980.

21.   "Developing Rural Alaska," op. cit.

22.   Sealaska Corporation, Sealaska Shareholder. November 1980, p. 6.

8
The Role of Regional Native Corporations in Alaska's Rural Development

Dean Olson
Bradford Tuck

INTRODUCTION

Passage of the Alaska Native Claims Settlement Act of 1971 (ANCSA) was foremost a settlement of long-standing land claims of Alaska Natives. Beyond settlement of land claims, however, was the implicit hope that the Act would also serve as a vehicle for the achievement of a degree of economic self-sufficiency, or economic independence of Alaska Natives. Less clearly stated, but also implied, was the notion that the Act might lead to the more general economic development of rural Alaska. Whether or not these expectations were real, it is of interest to consider the economic consequences, both past and future, of the implementation of ANCSA.

In carrying out this task there are two interrelated dimensions that must be considered. First, if the Native corporate structures and the cash and land settlement are to play a central role in the process of economic development, we must look at these entities and their newly acquired assets in the context of their ability to achieve development aspirations. Success or failure will, in part, be dependent upon the internal workings of the new corporations and the difficulties of actually acquiring the assets promised by the Act.

Of equal concern and importance is the second dimension of our analysis. Economic development of rural Alaska, at least as such development is judged by American economic standards of production, employment, and income, had not occurred prior to passage of the Act. Many reasons could be advanced for the lack of such development, but the underlying difficulty was the absence of any economic justification for development. Where such development did occur, such as that related to fisheries or sporadic mining, the activity was not of a magnitude or nature to induce or support a process of sustained economic growth.

While significant oil and gas activity has occurred in one part of rural Alaska, economic conditions in most of rural Alaska remain today much as they were prior to passage of the Act. Thus, our analysis must consider the economic sphere within which the Native corporations are expected to have their impact. In short, the study attempts to look at both the internal problems of the corporations and the general economic environment within which the corporations must function.

Revised edition of a policy recommendation to the Joint Federal-State Land Use Planning Commission for Alaska, May 30, 1979.

The remainder of the study is divided into several sections. The first part reviews those sections of ANCSA of economic significance. In the second part we consider possible overall economic impacts of ANCSA implementation, primarily from a regional economic perspective. The third part focuses specifically on the regional corporations and deals with major problems encountered in implementation of the Act, as well as an assessment of regional corporation performance. The fourth part provides an overview of future prospects, while the last part contains conclusions and recommendations for change.

ANCSA PROVISIONS OF ECONOMIC SIGNIFICANCE

The economic thrust of the Act was threefold. First, Section 17(d)(2) provided for the withdrawal of up to 80 million acres of unreserved federal lands for possible inclusion in National Park, National Forest, and National Wildlife Refuge Systems, as well as for possible classification under the Wild and Scenic Rivers program.

Because of extensive treatment of the issue elsewhere,[1] we do not deal in depth with the subject here. However, the conclusions of our analysis can be briefly summarized. In general, the negative economic consequences of (d)(2), both at the state and national levels, appear to be negligible. Some specific geographic areas, and some particular economic interest groups may be adversely affected. At the same time, the possibility of positive economic benefits is very real.

The second dimension of the Act of economic interest was Section 17(c), which prevented Native land selections within transportation and utility corridors withdrawn under existing authority of the Secretary of the Interior. This effectively resolved the problem of Native land claims blocking the Trans-Alaska Pipeline System (TAPS) corridor and construction of the pipeline. As events worked out, other impediments to the granting of the corridor developed that further delayed construction.

The third, and central dimension of the Act for the present analysis is the array of provisions related to settlement of Native claims. In its broadest context the Act provided for a cash payment (over time) of approximately one billion dollars and for selection and other rights to what has amounted to about 44 million acres of land, generally including both the surface and subsurface estate.

The cash settlement provisions of the Act are set forth in Sections 6 and 9. Section 6 provides for the creation of the Alaska Native Fund (in the U.S. Treasury). A total of $462,500,000, in specified annual amounts, was to be paid into the fund over an eleven year period by the federal government. In addition, $500,000,000 was to be paid into the fund by the federal government and the state of Alaska. These funds were to be derived from the lease or sale of mineral resources in Alaska under the control of either the state or federal governments, as set forth in Section 9.

In general these revenues were to be derived from a 2 percent royalty on production, and 2 percent on bonuses and rentals. Federal OCS revenues were not included. In actuality, the bulk of these revenues will probably come from production of Prudhoe Bay oil and gas. Barring prolonged shutdowns of the pipeline, these monies should be paid by 1985.

Distributions of the Fund balances were to be made on a quarterly basis to the regional corporations established under the Act, where the share to each regional corporation was in proportion to Native enrollment in the corporations, compared to total enrollment. (Section 6(c).)

Additional provisions for distribution of the Fund are contained in Section 7. Section 7(j) states, in part, that 10 percent of the Fund disbursements to the regional corporations shall be distributed on a proportionate basis to stockholders of the corporations for the first five years following enactment of the Act. Furthermore, 45 percent of the Fund disbursements to the regional corporations shall be redistributed among the village corporations for the first five years, and after that 50 percent. Section 7(j) also contains provisions for similar distributions of revenues received by the regional corporations under Section 7(i) and other net revenues.

Section 7(i) is of particular significance. The section states that 70 percent of the revenues derived from the timber resources and subsurface estate patented to a regional corporation pursuant to the Act shall be distributed to the twelve regional corporations on a per capita enrollment basis. The intent of the provision was to ensure some degree of equity in the distribution of resource wealth resulting from the Act.

The second major aspect of the settlement was the establishment of selection rights to some 40 million acres of surface and subsurface estate. Both village and regional corporations were granted certain selection rights, but the regional corporations retained the entire subsurface estate.

There are other provisions that need to be mentioned in regard to the settlement. Section 7(h)(l) makes stock of the Native Corporations inalienable for a period of twenty years from the date of enactment. In particular, this meant that the stock (or attendant dividends and other payments) could not be sold, pledged, or otherwise alienated. It should be emphasized that no such restrictions were placed on the sale or alienation of the lands conveyed pursuant to the Act.

Section 21 also contained significant provisions with regard to taxation of the settlement. Distributions from the Fund were not taxable, nor was the transfer of lands from the federal government to the Natives. In essence, the cash and land settlement was to be an untaxed transfer of assets. Furthermore, Section 21(d) provided for a twenty-year exemption of any form of state or local property tax on the real property interests conveyed pursuant to the Act, so long as these lands remained in an undeveloped status. Land commercially developed or leased would be subject to taxation. Rents, royalties, profits, or other revenues derived from development of the real property interests would be subject to taxation in accordance with Federal and State laws.[2] While there are other provisions of the Act that may be of consequence, the above appear to be those of particular significance.

ECONOMIC IMPACTS OF ANCSA IMPLEMENTATION

The description of economic consequences of ANCSA is complicated by the fact that there is no single measure of economic activity that adequately describes the benefits accruing from such activity. Furthermore, when the focus of the analysis is Alaska Natives, the problem is more complex because of a cultural dimension. At the risk of oversimplification, however, we can suggest a set of measures that will be indicative of at least some of the potential economic impacts of ANCSA.

First are measures of aggregate economic activity, such as employment, production, and income. Second, measures relating to individual economic well-being must also be considered, such as per capita income, individual employment opportunities, and the stability and permanency of such employment. Third, the distributions of income, or more generally, the distributions of economic benefits among individuals, is of vital concern.

Finally, the relationship of economic change to the general amenities of life must be addressed. This is a particularly significant variable in a situation where the traditional organization and implicit values of economic activity are reflections of one society, but prospective participants in the activity are of a different cultural background.

The history of the Act is too short, and the data too sketchy, to arrive at definitive conclusions regarding the economic impacts, or lack thereof, of ANCSA, but there is certainly enough information to suggest some of the probable consequences.

With respect to the impact of the Act on aggregate economic activity to date, we need largely to consider only the cash settlement portion of the Act. Table 8.1 summarizes annual disbursements from the Alaska Native Fund to the twelve in-state regional corporations.

In assessing the impact of these disbursements on the state's economy, it must be recognized that these funds were transfers of assets, and that only a portion of these monies would actually enter the income stream. The primary ways in which this would occur would be through the operating expenditures of the corporations, direct investment in new construction or acquisitions of new plant and equipment, or in direct payments to shareholders.

Distributions to shareholders under the "10 percent rule" and the "at large" provisions amounted to about $18 million in 1973. Operating expenditures and direct investment injected additional amounts into the economy, but a substantial proportion of the disbursements remained as portfolio investment with no direct impact on the level of income. In other years, the impact on the aggregate level of income in the state was substantially less. In short, the disbursements from the Fund have been of minor significance to the Alaska economy as a whole.

With respect to regional and rural economies, the picture is less clear. Some direct investment in Kotzebue, Barrow, and Glennallen has occurred, and undoubtedly the same is true elsewhere. Such projects do have a short-term impact due to construction activity, and a long-run impact in terms of more permanent employment opportunities, but in the aggregate it appears that this type of investment activity has been quite limited to date.

What has occurred much more frequently has been the acquisition of existing enterprises (with no major economic impact) sometimes in the rural regions of the state, but much more frequently in the urban areas of Alaska. This has been a reflection of the lack of existing investment opportunities in rural Alaska. It is clear that passage of the Act has in no significant fashion altered the underlying structure of rural Alaska's economy.

The second way in which corporate expenditures might be expected to influence rural economies is through the direct operating expenditures of the corporations (both regional and village). In some areas, this may have been of marginal significance over the short run. In the longer run (when payments from the Fund are exhausted), such activity will be dependent upon the ability of the village and regional corporations to generate a stream of ongoing revenues and profits from their investment and development activities. In the aggregate, to date, the impacts have been limited.

It is also appropriate to consider the possible impacts of Fund redistributions to individual Natives. Table 8.1 indicates the general magnitude of payments. Of greater

TABLE 8.1
SUMMARY OF DISBURSEMENT TO THE 12 REGIONAL CORPORATIONS
1972-1978 (Millions of current dollars)

Year	Disbursements	Village Corporation Implicit Share	Stockholder Share (10%)	"At Large" Share
1972	$ 6.999	$ 3.150	$ 0.700	$ 0.262
1973	130.704	58.817	13.070	4.901
1974	71.347	32.106	7.135	2.676
1975	61.294	27.582	6.129	2.299
1976	37.548	16.897	3.755	1.292
1977	34.461	17.231	--	1.445
1978	65.904	32.952	--	2.763
TOTAL	$408.257	$118.735	$30.789	$15.638

Source: Computed from data provided by the Department of the Interior.

interest is what these represent on a per capita basis. In 1974, Native enrollment was approximately 78,000. Of these, some 60,000 resided in Alaska, while 18,000 resided outside the state. Of the 60,000 enrolled in Alaska, about 6,540 were "at large" enrollees.

Using these figures, the "10 percent" provision, for 1973, would result in a distribution of $167.56 per Native enrollee. The 6,540 "at large" members would have received an additional distribution of $754.06, or a total of $921.62. If we consider the average annual distribution for the first five years of the Act, the "10 percent" provision would result in a payment of $78.94 per year. For the "at large" members, there would be an additional payment of $355.26 per year, or a total annual payment of $434.20. The net result of these computations is to suggest that the cash distributions to individual Natives are of only marginal consequence in terms of raising their economic status.

It is possible to speculate on the impact of these funds on rural Alaska. The above enrollment figures suggest that about 53,500 Natives are residents of villages. Assuming that there are 205 villages (the number listed in the Act), the average village population would be 261. Since only the "10 percent" share went to village residents, the average village income originating from this source would be about $20,600 per year, over the first five years of the Act. It is difficult to see how this could have any perceptible impact on the level of overall economic activity in rural Alaska.

The same type of calculations can be used to suggest the average annual distributions to village corporations. For the village of 261, the village corporation would receive annually $92,723. How much of this would actually be spent directly, or invested directly in the village is impossible to determine. It is clear, however, that a substantial proportion of these funds probably never entered the village income stream.

There are two reasons for this. First, Section 7(1) provides that the village disbursements "may be withheld by the regional corporation until the village has submitted a plan for the use of the money that is satisfactory to the regional corporation." These plans may require the village to participate in joint ventures with other villages or with the regional corporation itself. Thus, substantial portions of the funds may end up as part of the regional corporation's investment funds.

The second reason is that the village corporation itself may choose the security of investment in urban areas or in portfolio investments. In either case, the economic benefits of the disbursements will occur at some future date, if at all.

In summary, it is clear that the cash distributions from the Fund have had, at most, a minor impact on the rural Alaska economy. Furthermore, the economic well-being of the individual Native, as measured by the cash distributions, has been only marginally affected. If the Act is to have any long-run significance in terms of increasing the economic well-being of Alaska Natives, or in terms of stimulating economic development in rural Alaska, it will have to occur in the future, either as a result of present investments based on the cash distributions or from development of the resource base represented by the land dimension of the settlement.

The analysis of the regional corporation's performance to date is considered in substantial detail elsewhere. Based on that analysis, it is clear that the regional corporations, in the aggregate, face some very great difficulties. Cumulative distributions to the regional corporations, as of 1978, amounted to about $189 million. The accumulated net worth of the corporations is about $142 million for the same period. Accumulated retained earnings show an overall loss of some $43.3 million. While several of the corporations have been modestly successful, the overall picture is bleak. In short, the results to date suggest that the future success of the regional corporations is heavily dependent upon the successful development of the land and resources to be conveyed under the Act.

If this is the case, what can be said about the prospects for Native controlled resource development? With the exception of the timber resources of southeast Alaska, the prospects for sustained yield management and commercial harvest of timber resources are not good. We should not rule out the possibility, however, of timber "mining" in some instances. In essence, this amounts to a one time cut and the conversion of assets from one form to another. Such activity clearly does not provide the basis for any sustained economic development.

Analysis of the potential for hardrock and industrial minerals suggests that such developments will not occur for a substantial period of time, if at all. Furthermore, to the extent that such activity does occur, the economic impacts are highly localized. While such activity may be of local economic significance, it clearly does not provide a basis for general rural Alaskan development.

Development of energy resources appears to be somewhat more promising. In at least one instance, the prospects for developing Native-owned coal exist, although the timing is highly uncertain. Several of the regional corporations have selected lands with potential oil and gas reserves, although to date no significant discoveries have occurred. But again, the direct impact of such development would be highly localized.

Under provisions of Section 7(i), resource development would also provide some indirect economic impacts. The rules of redistribution are presently a matter of litigation, but if we assume that the intent is to redistribute 70 percent of the net revenues, then we can at least speculate on the potential significance of the provision. In the case of hardrock minerals, coal, and timber developments, the impact would most likely be negligible due to the marginal economic nature of such developments.

Oil and gas development would have greater consequences. For purposes of illustration, assume that one of the regional corporations is successful in developing a 100,000 barrel per day field (which by non-Prudhoe Bay standards is a significant level of production). If we further assume a 1/8 royalty and a wellhead value of $5 per barrel, then annual after tax royalties might be on the order of $12 million per year. Of this, $8.4 million would be distributed on a per capita basis to the twelve regional corporations. Assuming an enrollment of 73,000 (excluding the thirteenth region), then the per capita distribution would be $115.06. This distribution would be to the regional corporations, and not the individual shareholders. In turn, 50 percent of the funds so distributed would be redistributed to the village corporations and "at large" members.

It is clear that the impact of such revenues for individual Natives is almost nonexistent. Any real benefits would have to accrue through the activities of the regional or village corporations which received the funds. But in the aggregate, such benefits could not exceed the initial distribution of $115.06 per individual. This does not suggest a particularly dynamic basis upon which to increase individual economic well-being or to spur sustained economic development.

The foregoing discussion has attempted to illustrate some of the overall economic dimensions of implementation of ANCSA, both in terms of enhancing the economic well-being of individual Natives and with respect to promoting rural Alaskan economic development. In both instances, the effects have been quite limited to date. The future prospects are not much better.

In part, these conclusions are derived from the analysis of regional corporation performance. More significantly, however, the conclusions stem from the fundamental economic conditions of rural Alaska. In short, rural Alaska has not, and probably will not exhibit the necessary conditions for sustained, diversified economic growth as traditionally defined. This does not necessarily mean the failure of ANCSA. It does mean that it is essential that we redefine our concepts of economic development, or more generally, our perceptions of development in general.

It is important to distinguish between "development" and "economic development." "Development" is a broader concept and should be measured, and in all other ways considered in the context provided by the people whose living condition is the object of interest. The necessary conditions for rural development must then include:

1. the institutional or other processes which tend to reduce rather than increase the dependence of rural people upon government transfer payments and the import of necessities;

2. the institutional or other processes which tend to encourage the self-reliance of rural peoples; and

3. the institutional or other processes which are controlled, that is "paced," by the people themselves and through which intelligence can be funneled and hence brought to bear on rural development opportunities.

The degree to which rural development will be influenced by ANCSA corporations depends importantly upon how effectively these corporations discard conventional "economic" models and focus upon import substitutions, self-reliance, and intelligent control over the pace of change. Corporate spending, particularly by village corporations, may have a decided impact upon development, if it proceeds along the lines described below and in recognition of how little we know about rural needs.

1. The period of the "big projects" is over. It is quite probable that massive projects affecting interior rural areas will be increasingly rare. Coastal areas may grow with fish processing and offshore oil developments, and energy projects close to urban concentrations may "mature," but interior Alaska is unlikely to be the site of large mineral extraction or transportation developments.

2. The prospect of meaningful increases in the recreation industry which may attend development of national parks and other withdrawn areas, is at most too distant in time and far too speculative in its nature to serve as a basis for current investment spending and employment planning in interior Alaska.

3. While the creation of the Permanent Fund and the Renewable Resource Development Fund may hold out the prospect for developmental capital of adequate scope, the imagination and creativity required to channel these funds to rural areas and into projects which have meaning to rural residents

has yet to manifest itself. In all probability, the major near term beneficiaries of development capital from these sources will be the coastal fishing and forest products industries. Little activity can be expected in interior areas until a certain level of basic intelligence about interior economics is achieved.

Our level of understanding about economics in interior areas is obscure. It is distorted by the "big project," export market orientation, and the pervasiveness of public sector spending. We know very little about small rural community private sector employment, spending, and commodity flows. Certainly, we can only guess at employment and spending multipliers and hence we can only approximate the potential for rural import substitution industries and the direction we need to move to enhance rather than diminish the economic self-reliance of people in small rural communities.

As ANCSA village corporations receive land title and begin the task of seeking ways to promote local development, the absence of knowledge about development processes in small communities will move to the front as the leading obstacle to practical investment spending designed to increase human effectiveness and reduce the cost of rural living.

Accordingly, the necessary condition for ANCSA corporations to influence rural development is for these corporations to serve as the conduit, the channel, for bringing greater insight, a deeper understanding, to development processes which match the abilities of the people those processes are meant to sustain and enhance.

It is very unlikely that the residents of any rural community in Alaska could ever achieve absolute economic self-reliance. Even those who argue with great conviction for the preservation of the "subsistence lifestyle" must, upon reflection, realize that rural living is an accommodation of wants and needs that can only partially be met through "hunting and gathering" activities. Once the "dual economy" nature of rural living is confronted, the widespread dependence upon government transfer payments to provide the means for meeting the modern requirements of rural living must also be confronted and dealt with.

The basic task of rural development is to use local resources creatively to reduce the need to import goods and services from outside the local economy, and hence to reduce the dependency upon government transfer payments. While absolute self-reliance is unachievable, we can produce from local resources many of the basic requirements now imported. To do so must be the goal of any village development program. A development program might contain the following basic features in a given area:

1.   production of agricultural products (vegetables, grains) for local consumption;

2.   production and local consumption of poultry and livestock to the extent possible using locally produced feed stock in (1) above;

3.   production and local consumption of dairy products from (2) above;

4.   production of craft and building products from wood fiber and clay resources;

5.   production of fuel products from wood fiber resources, again for local consumption;

6.   consumption of local fuel products for home, dry kiln, and greenhouse heating;

7.   use of the fishery resource to produce fish meal concentrate for fur ranching; and

8.   use of local wood fiber resources for limited craft and furniture manufacture.

The local production of basic energy, building materials, and food products is the cornerstone of the development program. Obviously, in some areas there will be more opportunity for local industry than in others. In some areas, small hydroelectric sources may provide the basic energy to drive the industry system. In other areas, soil conditions may simply not provide the minimum conditions for local agriculture.

The key ingredients to success in the program will surely be imagination; a willingness to work on a small scale, the resolve to remain committed to a higher order of self-reliance in spite of temporary setbacks, and a willingness to experiment and change. The central preoccupation in the program is that, while certain products (poultry, furs, crafts) may have an export potential, the principal criterion is to select industry components which are interrelated (the by-products of one activity are the raw materials of another) and whose products reduce the reliance of local residents upon products imported from outside the local area.

These are the necessary conditions for rural development. There is no short-cut. ANCSA village corporations can serve as the instrument of change, meaningful change, along the lines suggested above. However, it appears that these corporations are instead more likely to follow conventional models, building lodges, acquiring air charter operations, etc. This is less an indictment of village management than a reflection upon the advice they receive from planners, economists, and the like.

To summarize, the conditions under which ANCSA corporations could influence rural "economic" development are:

1.   that the level of understanding about rural development processes is itself improved to the point where ANCSA corporations can serve as constructive agents of change ;

2.   that the management of village corporations seize the opportunity to develop integrated import substitution industries;

3.   that state and federal agencies whose task it is to study and seek to apply "alternative technologies," coordinate and channel ideas, approaches, etc., with and through ANCSA village corporations; and

4.   that ANCSA corporations are able to attract and keep committed development agents as employees.

THE REGIONAL CORPORATIONS

We have considered the broad economic sphere within which the regional corporations must function. The present section of the paper turns to a consideration of the regional corporations themselves. Before turning to an analysis of corporate performance, it is helpful to consider, on an a priori basis, a general model of corporate decision making for the regional corporations, and to then relate this to the various regional corporations.

The component parts of any corporate decision model are:

1. Goals—broad statements of general intent (sometimes rather specific, often quite vague). For example, one regional corporation seeks to achieve (a) profitable operations which (b) employ shareholders, and which (c) provide for management control by Native corporations.

2. Policies—more specific guidelines laid down by the board of directors which management is to follow while seeking goal fulfillment. For example, the corporation with the profit, employment, and control goals mentioned above would have at least the following policies:

   a. investment—any project or proposal which yields returns in excess of passive portfolio yields, with prudent attention to risk premiums required;

   b. market penetration—projects conforming to (1) above but which are situated geographically so as to provide employment;

   c. personnel—shareholders first, if qualified, with provisions for training, OJT, such that the ultimate craft and management positions are filled by Natives; and

   d. organization—joint-ventures, partnerships, wholly owned subsidiaries, with provisions that majority control is retained by the Native corporations.

3. Procedures—more specific guidelines which "flesh-out" policy statements. For example, requiring feasibility studies containing detailed analysis as a precondition to decisions about investments.

Each ANCSA corporation has some elements of the above three components. The degree to which a given decision conforms to written (or oral) tradition depends upon the decision actors, their personalities, tolerance for organization, and general influence over the decision process. Intuitive processes often short-cut one or more components of the written procedures/policies/goal model. Expectations from shareholders, the perceived need of leadership to "get something going," and the economic pressures provided by inflation, can serve to create an environment intolerant of the time it takes to plan carefully. Hence, several corporations proceeded to make investments of significant size before setting goals. In effect, these decisions determined the "type" of corporate goals and policies then applicable. These corporations became what they acquired. Bering Straits Native Corporation (BSNC) and Cook Inlet Region, Inc. (CIRI) are examples of this "backing into identity" model. Both corporations moved quickly and without attention to the resultant inflexibility introduced to goal setting, policies required, etc.

The Northwest Arctic Native Association, Inc. (NANA) serves as a good example of an "open decision" model. The pace of development in critical policy areas is controlled by the elders who have direct access to the president and the chief executive officer. Bristol Bay Native Corporation (BBNC) serves as a reasonable example of a "closed decision" model. Shareholders are not allowed to attend regular board meetings. Decisions are made after prior study and on the basis of factual variables.

The range of decision models is more along a continuum of participatory v. non-participatory, rather than the conventional rational v. social continuum. In other words, for NANA management to engage in a selective participatory/open decision process, is quite rational. To regard rationality as attention to fact (quantifiability) is to suggest that sociocultural elements are not facts, which of course they are indeed for any corporation. It is more a matter of the weight applied to each factual input and the permeability of the process to all variables.

Placing the corporations along a participatory continuum is a matter of judgment in which several knowledgeable observers of corporate behavior should engage, rather than merely one. Furthermore, corporate positioning will change with each leadership recombination. It is not unreasonable to expect a more broadly constructed goal structure for corporations with more open decision processes.

Before turning to a review of financial performance, it is worth discussing one other point with regard to corporate decision making. It has been a fairly commonly held notion that because the corporations are organized "for profit," under the laws of Alaska (Section 7(d), ANCSA), the corporations are thereby obligated to maximize profits or otherwise seek profits. This simply is not so. There are no provisions in ANCSA or in State of Alaska statutes which require that a business organized "for profit" must maximize, optimize, or even sustain an "acceptable" profit level. This is a non-issue.

Corporate enterprise must be managed according to the procedures in the by-laws. The Secretary of the Interior reviewed this document for fairness (Section 7(e)). Consistent with the voting provisions contained in the by-laws, ANCSA corporations are organizations governed by the will of the shareholders. If the shareholders determine their interest is furthered most by directing the corporation to pay annual dividends which equal annual after-tax income, for example, it is within their right and power to cause management to respond accordingly. The shareholders own the corporation and, subsequent to the stock alienation restriction (Section 7(h)), could liquidate the corporation if the procedural guidelines of the by-laws are adhered to.

Corporations are vehicles which serve the needs of their owners. Disposition of earned surplus or other corporate resources need not conform to the abstract morality of the economist-lawyer. We turn now to a review of the financial performance to date.

To survive, ANCSA corporations, like any business, must reach and sustain sufficient levels of profitability to safeguard and effectively manage corporate assets. But ANCSA corporations also aspire, with varying intensity, to enhance the employment opportunities and the economic diversity of the rural areas where their shareholders reside. Some ANCSA corporations also strive to strengthen indigenous management talent and to extend Native control into the management decision processes which influence the social and political features of rural living conditions.

In the following pages, we have included a brief narrative for each of the twelve corporations, for the years 1975-78. For Cook Inlet Corporation and Bering Straits, the period covered is 1975-77.

MAP 8.1

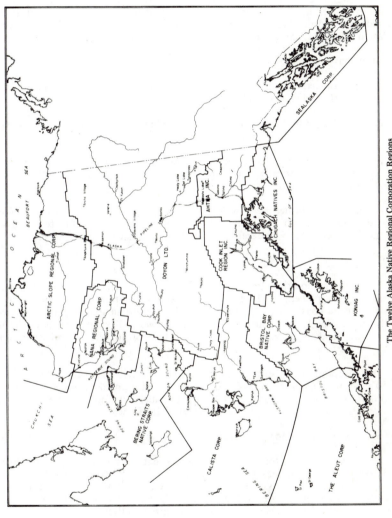

The Twelve Alaska Native Regional Corporation Regions

Ahtna, Inc.

This corporation is the smallest of the twelve in-state regional corporations. Over the 1975-78 period, the primary source of revenue for the corporation has been pipeline construction and maintenance contracts. With the reduced opportunities for contracting now available to the company, management has turned its attention to alternative models for diversifying the local economy in the Copper River Basin (where the corporation is located) and reducing its reliance upon pipeline contracting.

Ahtna has acquired two physical assets:

1.   construction facilities and equipment designed to undertake gravel and earthmoving work; and

2.   a thirty-room lodge in Glennallen which it owns with the eight village corporations in the region.

In addition, the firm has acquired an ownership position in UNICORP-United Bank Alaska. The balance of corporate assets is in a portfolio of government and corporate bonds.

Ahtna has performed very well in the past, but now faces major decisions as management seeks to make a transition into new activities. Fortunately, corporate borrowing has been held to moderate levels and the settlement estate is intact.

Aleut Corporation

The Aleut corporation derives the bulk of its revenues from fishing (80 percent) and freighting (13 percent). The corporation has not yet attained profitability, in spite of the heightened coastal activity in and around the Aleutian area. Fishing is carried on with the M.V. *Aleut Pride* and the M.V. *Aleut Princess*. Two other vessels, the M.V. *Aleut Provider* and the M.V. *Aleut Packer*, form the core of the firm's freighting business.

The corporation has suffered from internal conflict. Litigation costs for 1978 were 10 percent of gross revenues for that year. A new board of director election has been ordered by the Court as a result of a suit brought by certain shareholders. Subsequent goals and policies for this corporation will rest with the reconstituted board.

Arctic Slope Regional Corporation (ASRC)

The bulk of revenue for this corporation has in recent years been derived from oil and gas lease options and leases. This source provided 65 percent of gross revenue in 1977 and 31 percent in 1978. Contracting services provided through the firm's partnership with Alaska General (Arctic Slope Alaska General Construction Company) produced 31 percent of gross revenue in 1978 and, given continued field development on the North Slope, this activity should continue to be important in the future.

Litigation over Section 7(i) of ANCSA continues to obscure the prospective dependability of this stream of revenue to the corporation. But management seems to be developing its competitive location advantages (i.e., contracting services) to the maximum and hence is reducing initial corporate reliance upon resource revenue. The ANCSA estate is intact and the corporation is well managed.

Bering Straits Native Corporation (BSNC)

This corporation has been technically insolvent since 1977. A rapid and imprudently implemented series of investments executed over the 1974-76 period has cast doubt over the continued viability of the firm. Over the 1976-77 period, management has "written off" nearly $20 million in discountinued operations in its attempt to establish a sustainable operation and restructure debt obligations. The corporation has necessarily borrowed heavily against future ANCSA receipts in its effort to recover.

Bristol Bay Native Corporation (BBNC)

BBNC derives the bulk of its revenues from fish processing. This source accounted for 96 percent of revenue in 1977 and 81 percent in 1978. In its efforts to diversify, the corporation acquired the Anchorage Westward Hotel in April 1977. Hotel revenues provided 16 percent of gross earnings in 1978.

Banner fish harvests in 1977 and 1978 coupled with declining market acceptance of canned fish products encouraged high levels of finished goods inventory. The corporation has borrowed heavily to finance growth and now seems to be faced with a period of adjustment until its cash flow stabilizes.

The future ANCSA estate has been in part employed to finance current investment spending.

Calista Corporation

The management of this corporation has not as yet determined how best to employ the assets conveyed to it under ANCSA. Investments to date range from a highly sophisticated computer services company, to land development within the Anchorage area, to fishing and construction. Major commitments have been made to the development of a 1,200-acre site near Anchorage (Settlers Bay Properties, Inc., $10 million) and to the construction of a 15-story hotel in Anchorage (Sheraton Anchorage Hotel, $40 million). Both activities will require considerably more support prior to achievement of self-sustaining operations.

The future ANCSA estate has been in part employed to finance current spending. Accumulated deficits for the corporation exceed $14 million.

Chugach Natives, Inc.

The principal source of 1978 revenues for this company is its joint ownership (with Ahtna, Inc.) of a pipeline maintenance contractor. Some 63 percent of revenues were from that source. As is the case with Ahtna, this company is studying alternative strategies to achieve sustaining operations. Recently, the firm acquired an Anchorage office building, an ownership position in UNICORP-United Bank Alaska, and fish processing facilities in Cordova.

Cook Inlet Region, Inc. (CIRI)

This corporation has emphasized investment into hotel and rental properties and banking. Early difficulties in implementing land selections have been overcome and management seems to be developing corporate resources in an orderly, planned manner despite the efforts of a dissident group of minority shareholders.

Doyon, Ltd.

Doyon management has proceeded carefully, to first inventory its substantial land estate and second, to study investment potentials in basic industry sectors. The corporation is well managed. The financial estate is preponderantly in a portfolio of marketable securities of varying maturities (1978—$17 million; 60 percent of total assets).

Koniag, Inc.

This corporation has been plagued with extreme difficulty in implementing the village eligibility and land selection terms of ANCSA. Costs have been high. Revenues from investments are principally accounted for by merchandise sales (Shelikof Net Company, 85 percent) and from rental properties (13 percent). Management continues to focus considerable attention upon prospective offshore oil exploration and development.

Northwest Arctic Native Association, Inc. (NANA)

This corporation has moved forcefully into several activities. The principal revenue sources for 1978 are shown below:

Activity	Percentage of Total Revenue
Fuel Sales	14
Construction	52
Contracted services	9
Camp and hotels	12
Catering	2
Total Shown	89

Major investments of this well managed firm include a hotel/theatre in Kotzebue, and oil field support services such as drilling equipment and a camp housing facility.

Sealaska Corporation

Revenues for this corporation are derived primarily from building materials sales and freighting (Alaska Brick, 91 percent) and from portfolio earnings (7 percent). The corporation has been conservatively managed. Major investments include an Anchorage building materials supply firm and a Juneau office building. These investments constitute a modest fraction of the total resources available to this, the largest of the Native regional corporations.

In addition to reviewing the financial performance of the regional corporations, it is also appropriate to comment briefly on their performance with respect to stimulating economic development in rural Alaska. We have already suggested that their impact to date has been limited, but would add the following.

ANCSA regional corporations are neither fish nor fowl. Due to the "pass through" requirement legislated in the Act, the corporations are not well-suited as repositories of earnings accumulated and reinvested for the ultimate improvement of shareholder wealth. As decision making units, ANCSA regional corporations are awkward, clumsy, and costly to operate and to govern. General economic activity must be very accommodating for these corporations to maintain profitability while meeting revenue-sharing obligations; acquiring, defending, and eventually developing the land endowment; and keeping shareholders both informed and meaningfully involved.

ANCSA village corporations constitute a more promising structure for development, if the managerial talent and basic notions about the definitions of development can occur at the same time and place. At the present time, village corporations seem to be following one of three basic strategies:

1. do nothing—some corporations have no regular meetings, do not keep routine records, and have allowed basic incorporation documentation to lapse;

2. take over existing village businesses—such as air charters, grocery stores, fuel distribution outlets, etc.; and

3. avoid the problem through merger or consolidation of the management function—several villages have (and are) joined together in a variety of frameworks designed to share the costs and responsibilities of the Act.

Very few village corporations have moved forward due to an internal momentum. It is more a case of being pulled into activity by opportunity or by the requirements of the Act.

The review of corporate performance has suggested that major problems exist. Some of these were undoubtedly expected. However, other serious problems of an unanticipated nature have arisen in the process of implementation that do handicap both the regional and village corporations as they struggle with an already difficult task. While these problems do not justify the lackluster performance of many of the corporations, they certainly have not helped.

To begin with, ANCSA implementation placed unprecedented burdens upon government agencies to first, understand the terms of the Act; second, to achieve unusual levels of inter-agency coordination; and third, to respond with clarity in an environment containing a variety of special interests and interpretations of certain terms of the Act. In addition to this general problem, several specific items also should be noted. Some have been discussed in detail elsewhere in this paper and are mentioned in the following only by topic.

1. Problems related to the conveyance of lands selected, and the interrelated problems of easements.

2. Difficulties with respect to interpretation of Section 7(i), the "shared wealth" provision, and delays in distribution of 7(i) revenues.

3. Internal Revenue Service rulings on certain types of "income" related to resource exploration. (These apparently have been resolved by legislation.)

4. Village-regional relationships—several provisions of the Act specify these relationships, but have been interpreted differently by various parties involved; e.g., does Section 7(j) require a regional corporation to share

revenue which it earns through its own efforts with village corporations? Sections 7(l)-7(m) raise questions regarding the responsibilities of a regional corporation which is managing a joint portfolio containing village funds. In one case, village funds were used as collateral for regional corporation borrowing, and later actually expended without village board approval. What is the responsibility of the Secretary of the Interior in such a case? Finally, Section 14(f) requires the consent of the village for regional corporation exploration, development, or removal of the subsurface estate underlying the village-owned surface estate. Just what will happen should a village be adamant about withholding consent, particularly in the core township? What is the Secretary's responsibility should serious conflict occur?

5. Village corporation reconveyance responsibilities under Section 14(c)(1)-14(c)(4)—village corporation leaders are in large measure still working through the terms of the Act. There has been little effort to this point in developing uniform methodology, file systems, and so on, which will be required to execute reconveyance in an orderly fashion. There is no clearinghouse type organization, yet one will be clearly needed to avoid widespread confusion. Village leaders are already being confronted by specialized state and federal agencies, each with its particular land reconveyance documents. The Section 14(c)(3) provision shows every possibility of being completely confusing to village people.

6. Finally, we should mention the substantial costs, to the regional and village corporations, of attempting to achieve what they feel is promised by the Act. There has been an inordinate amount of litigation surrounding implementation, between regional and village corporations and the state and federal governments, and between corporations themselves. In addition to major litigation costs have been the costs of seeking congressional resolution of problems. Such costs have not been quantified, but it is clear that they represent an unanticipated burden of substantial magnitude.

FUTURE PROSPECTS

There are two dimensions that must be considered in the analysis of future economic prospects resulting from implementation of ANCSA. The first relates to the success of the Act in stimulating rural economic development. The second addresses the future viability of the corporations.

If the objective of ANCSA is to provide Native Alaskans with the basic tools (organization, land, money) for the achievement of self-reliance, there is small probability of widespread success in village areas. The organization seems unnecessarily complex and ill-suited for the purpose; inflation of unexpected severity has greatly impaired the real value of the financial settlement; and the land remains in a vague interim management status fully seven years after passage of the Act.

But the greatest obstacle to the emergence of self-reliance is the absence of intelligence, of understanding, about development in small communities. Self-reliance is impaired by the export oriented models which emphasize conventional quantitative growth. Self-reliance is aided by import substitution, perhaps in the context provided by a network of villages engaging in complementary production and exchange. Such development will not just happen upon delivery of the tools. We first must know what is needed.

We do not need complex corporate structures which require accountants and attorneys merely to run an annual meeting. We do need "linkages" and institutional relationships which make conventional investments (hotels, restaurants, etc.) more effective, and which also bring common sense to development issues.

For example, the success or failure of rural hotel/restaurant/bar properties into which ANCSA corporations have invested heavily, depends importantly upon linkages which must be created between these new properties and existing, well entrenched tour wholesalers and transportation companies. These linkages must be developed because profitability depends upon it, or an entirely new tour packaging entity must be created, the latter requiring substantial capital investment. In other words, Native facilities will not by themselves produce the needed institutional changes to the established pattern of commerce. These changes will require concerted effort beyond the means of all ANCSA corporations, politically and economically. It is fair to say that if the state seriously desires to broaden the economic base to include rural areas, the linkages between the rural and urban, Native and non-Native must become issues of importance and consequence.

Rural development will not occur when the ANCSA tool kit is in place. There must be the opportunity to "learn through doing." This opportunity does not exist sufficiently in ANCSA, due to the abbreviated, fast-track time frame encompassed there. Rural development, more correctly the success or failure of progress toward achieving development, must be assessed in the context provided by progress toward establishing the institutional and intellectual linkages which will make ANCSA corporations effective as tools for rural development. ANCSA is not unlike attempts elsewhere in the Third World, where economic planners have sponsored a large dam or rural factory in the honest expectation that the absence of such tools is the crucial obstacle to development. Ultimately non-Natives from outside the area operate the tools while the local resident continues as before. It is then understood that the tools were not appropriate to the task of development because the people, whose living conditions are the focus of development attention, do not understand and lose interest in the tools. There is high probability that ANCSA corporations are tools not "sized" for the people and hence not useful in the attempt to achieve enhanced self-reliance.

The use of ANCSA corporations for rural development may be possible but will require fundamental changes in the framework within which the corporations operate. Some of these changes are listed below:

1.   income earned from rural projects of a developmental nature should be free of federal and state taxes for at least twenty-five years from project initiation;

2.   the property tax provisions of the Act should date from development (i.e., twenty-five years without payment required) for rural development projects;

3.   land unused for development should be "banked" until required for development. Local agricultural use should not be regarded as development;

4.   a statewide development organization should exist with sufficient funding to serve ANCSA village corporation needs for technical, administrative, and educational assistance for at least a decade. The organization should focus its resources on:

a.   implementing local (village) industry development which is resource efficient and reduces import dependency;

b.   establishing uniform accounting, legal, and operating standards;

c.   gathering and distributing development intelligence, information, methods, and experiences; and

d.   becoming involved in secondary and adult education in all rural areas, with the emphasis upon understanding change, what it is, and how it can be controlled.

If the objective of ANCSA is to provide Alaskan Native people with a regional corporate structure through which shareholder wealth can be enhanced by increased net worth, the initial years indicate uneven accomplishment.

The future prospects for a Native (or any other) corporation which is "tied into" unproductive resources are bleak indeed. The sequence of events will be:

1.   corporate borrowing beyond sustained coverage from investment earnings;

2.   land resources are found to be marginally productive but costly to preserve, monitor, and otherwise manage;

3.   the fixed costs of debt are not met; and

4.   the corporation defaults.

In concluding this section, it is worth reemphasizing some key problems to be faced by the corporations. Under terms of the Act, undeveloped real property interests become subject to state and local property taxes twenty years from the date of the Act. The inexcusably long period that has elapsed without conveyance of selected lands significantly reduces the value of the tax exemptions. Proposed amendments that would provide for property tax exemptions for twenty years from date of conveyance seem warranted.

Given the massive acreage of undeveloped lands that may ultimately be conveyed, however, the tax exemption may provide only interim relief. There is clear public interest, as well as corporate interest, in ensuring that these lands, which were to meet both economic and traditional needs, not become an intolerable financial burden upon the corporations. At present, the resolution of the problem centers upon proposed amendments for the creation of a land bank. In essence, lands "deposited" in the land bank would be exempt from property taxation.

A third item of concern relates to future alienability of the stock of the corporations. It is entirely possible that at least some of the corporations would be prime candidates for takeover by non-Native interests.

The right of the individual shareholders to "cash out" their interest in the corporation is of vital concern. At the same time the implications of non-Native takeover are equally serious in the broader context in which the regional corporations were established. Existing law provides a means for dealing with this problem by allowing the corporations "right of first refusal" on the sale of stock by shareholders, and by providing for the creation of special classes of stock such as non-voting stock.

Existing law, however, requires unanimous consent of shareholders participating in "right of first refusal" agreements. Whether or not proposed amendments to ANCSA that would require participation in such an agreement upon a majority vote of the shareholders will be legal is apparently a matter of question.

Furthermore, while corporations may issue both voting and non-voting classes of stock, there is a general requirement that all holders of a given class of stock be given equal treatment. The proposed amendment that would restrict voting rights of a given class of stock to Natives, thus denying voting rights to non-Native purchasers of the stock, would appear to violate a variety of state and federal laws. The problems that arise with this provision are perhaps illustrated by an analogous situation in which a corporation initially issues stock that can only be voted by white owners, and if the stock is sold to a black, the black could not vote the stock.

The intent of the proposed amendment, retention of control of the Native corporations by Natives, is understandable, but there are probably better means for accomplishing this. One possibility is the creation of a trust, holding a controlling interest in the corporation, where the trust, in turn, is controlled by Natives.

The proposed amendment also raises serious questions with respect to the value of an individual shareholder's stock. The placement of restrictions on the disposal of shares, particularly the "no non-Native" vote provision, means that the stock will necessarily sell at a discount to non-Natives. An equally serious problem is that the proposed amendment would insulate existing management from some pressures for efficient management. If sale is restricted to Natives (without a discount penalty) the dissatisfied shareholder's only recourse is to organize other shareholders, either through proxy solicitation or through litigation. Both are costly processes.

CONCLUSIONS AND RECOMMENDATIONS

The foregoing analysis of the economic implications of ANCSA has focused on two general concerns; the ability of ANCSA to enhance individual economic well-being of Alaska Natives, and ANCSA as a vehicle for rural development in Alaska. The results to date suggest that neither of these objectives has been achieved.

The disbursements to individual Natives from the Alaska Native Fund (and some limited dividend distributions from some regional corporations) have not significantly altered the income of most Natives. Furthermore, the regional corporations, in their role of "wealth builders," have not established a very good performance record.

Whether or not it was realistic to expect ANCSA to have an effect on rural development, the impact to date has been negligible. Per capita injections into the rural income stream have in no way been sufficient to lead to sustained economic development, nor are the injections of a permanent nature. Furthermore, investment in import substitution related activities has been negligible, and major investment in economic base expansion has not occurred. The absence of such activity is largely a reflection of underlying economic conditions, and these conditions are likely to persist for some time to come.

If development is to occur, it will have to be of a different nature than that suggested by traditional economic growth processes, and it will require a reorientation both in our perceptions of development and in the institutional arrangements within which such activity can occur. In particular, it has been suggested that the regional corporations will prove to be largely unworkable as an instrument for such development. Rather, much of the burden for development will fall on the village corporations. If they are to be successful, certain conditions probably must be met.

1. The level of understanding about rural development processes must itself be improved to the point where ANCSA corporations can serve as constructive agents of change.

2. The management of village corporations must seize the opportunity to develop integrated import substitution industries.

3. State and federal agencies whose task it is to study and seek to apply "alternative technologies," must coordinate and channel ideas, approaches, etc., with and through ANCSA village corporations.

4. ANCSA corporations must be able to attract and keep committed development agents, as employees.

There are no instant answers to rural Alaskan development, nor can ANCSA be the vehicle for assured economic well-being of Alaska Natives. There are changes that could be made, however, that might enhance the chances of ANCSA contributing to the achievement of these objectives.

Because much of the rural economic activity that will occur through the development efforts of ANCSA corporations is of a highly marginal nature, it is appropriate to provide some assistance for such endeavors.

1. Income earned from rural projects of a developmental nature should be free of federal and state taxes for at least twenty-five years from project initiation.

2. The property tax provisions of the Act should date from development (i.e., twenty-five years without payment required) for rural development projects.

3. Land unused for development should be "banked" until required for development. Local agricultural use should not be regarded as development.

4. A statewide development organization should exist with sufficient funding to serve ANCSA village corporation needs for technical, administrative, and educational assistance for at least a decade. The organization should focus its resources on:

   a. implementing local (village) industry development which is resource efficient and reduces import dependency;

   b. establishing uniform accounting, legal, and operating standards;

   c. gathering and distributing development intelligence, information, methods, and experiences; and

   d. becoming involved in secondary and adult education in all rural areas, with the emphasis upon understanding change, what it is, and how it can be controlled.

The performance of the regional corporations as wealth builders is also of concern. There is no substitute for efficient internal management of the corporations, nor can such efficiency be legislated, but some changes might be of assistance. These changes would serve to improve the chances of successful corporate performance and at the same time protect the real interests of the individual shareholders as well.

Proposed amendments (discussed above) to the Act that provide for property tax exemptions from date of conveyance and that establish a land bank for undeveloped lands both seem to be clearly in the interests of the corporations and the shareholders.

The previously discussed amendment regarding alienability of shares presents serious problems, especially with respect to the rights of individual shareholders. We recommend that alternative means of achieving the intended objectives be pursued. In particular, it is suggested that the establishment of a trust, holding a majority of the corporation stock, be considered. The trust would be under control of the Natives of the region or village, and could thus retain control of the corporation. At the same time, remaining shares of the corporation would be freely alienable, without restrictions on sales or voting rights. Control of the corporations by Natives would be assured, but the marketability of remaining shares would be greatly enhanced, protecting the interests of individual shareholders.

Our final recommendation deals with the responsibility of congress and the Secretary of the Interior to ensure compliance of the corporations with terms of the Act, and more broadly, to protect the interests of individual Natives in the settlement.

Congress saw fit to "lock in" Native shareholders until 1991, by providing for the inalienability of shares. To date, however, no meaningful governmental responsibility for protection of shareholder values has been assumed. In the present situation, the only way a Native can show his dissatisfaction is by political action or litigation. Both courses of action are difficult (and expensive) for individual shareholders, particularly in view of the highly diversified ownership of shares.

As a first step, the Secretary should ensure that corporations are in technical compliance with the Act before disbursing funds from the Alaska Native Fund. The Secretary should further monitor redistributions of these funds by the regional corporations to ensure that village corporations and "at large" shareholders are receiving payments in accordance with terms of the Act. Such monitoring might prevent a repetition of the situation in which village funds held by a regional corporation were expended by the regional corporation without authorization by the village.

A second step would involve either Secretarial or Government Accounting Office review of corporate decision making and management practices when corporate performance became unacceptable, as judged by profitability, growth, or other predetermined standards. The foregoing financial analysis would indicate that the Aleut, Bering Straits, Calista, and Koniag Corporations would all require review and actions to protect the interests of locked in shareholders.

In the event that the Secretary or congress is unwilling to assume such a burden, then congress should legislate immediate alienability of shares. Those shareholders seeking to minimize future losses could then search out a buyer. Corporate management would have to perform better or find new owners in the boardroom.

NOTES

1. See especially these previous studies of the Joint Federal-State Land Use Planning Commission for Alaska: Study 10 (Krutilla and Brubaker), Study 22 (Tuck), Study 32 (Engelman, Tuck et al.), and the "d-2" book.

2. The descriptions of the various sections of the Act are sufficient for our purposes. They would probably not satisfy a lawyer.

9
Non-Profit Organizations in Rural Alaska Development: The Role of RurAL CAP

Philip Smith

INTRODUCTION

The Rural Alaska Community Action Program, Inc. (RurAL CAP) is an organization designed to eradicate the causes and conditions of poverty in rural Alaska. Carrying out that mandate requires a sensitivity to rural people and to the events which control their lives.

These are troubled times. Racism, alienation, insecurity, isolation and despair are commonplace realities experienced by many Alaskans. The tragedy of these conditions is compounded for those with the most to lose. Alaska's Native cultures, rich in such values as integrity, a genuine sense of community, respect for the natural environment, and community self-reliance and self-sufficiency are strong. But they are under assault. Rapid change is sweeping rural Alaska, leaving in its wake uncertainty and confusion and, for too many, human misery characterized by the many manifestations of poverty.

The state's treasury, bulging with petro-dollars, fails to automatically compensate for this erosion of human values. There is a pervasive selfishness in some segments of our society; a cowardly tendency to "blame the victims" of inequity, lack of opportunity, poor nutrition, alcohol and drug abuse, and the host of other ills which, for so many, define the realities of Alaskan life in the 1980s. This situation frustrates the efforts of those who desire equity and opportunity for all Alaskans—efforts which could, in part, be realized by applying Alaska's financial resources to that end.

In the summer of 1980, President Carter said, "We must be prepared, both as individuals and as a society, not only to deplore poverty, injustice, and the smothering of human aspirations, but to change them." RurAL CAP is committed to that change. This report is dedicated to those Alaskans who have given the most, whose sense of history is most critical to chart the ways of the future, and whose continued well-being is sought by us all.

HISTORIC OVERVIEW OF RurAL CAP

The United States can achieve its full economic and social potential as a nation

---

The author is Executive Director for RurAL CAP, and this paper, in expanded form, was published as a report by RurAL CAP in 1981.

only if every individual has the opportunity to contribute to the full extent of the capabilities of such individual and to participate in the workings of our society. It is, therefore, the policy of the United States to eliminate the paradox of poverty in the midst of plenty in this nation by opening to everyone the opportunity for education and training, the opportunity to work, and the opportunity to live in decency and dignity.[1]

With these words in 1964, the United States of America declared unconditional War on Poverty. In assessing the plight of the poor then, Congress and the administration determined that new approaches would be needed to break the cycle of poverty in America. In the first place, there was a recognition of the fact that the poor were frequently victimized by programs and policies designed to serve them, primarily because they had no controlling influence over the scope and the workings of those programs and policies. The services being received by the poor were, for the most part, totally inappropriate, no matter how well-intentioned the providers. Secondly, Congress and the administration realized that the poor lacked access to the institutions shaping the public and private economic and social policies of America.

These failures of control and access led to alienation, distrust, and other ills afflicting the poor, ills which could not be treated successfully by merely increasing transfer payments and other forms of income support. And so community action became the cornerstone of the War on Poverty. With program delivery controlled by the recipients of services, and with a new structure through which to address the public policy process, it was believed that the disadvantaged might well gain at least a measure of control over the institutions which controlled their lives.

For rural Alaskans, this approach has worked. Following the passage of the Economic Opportunity Act in 1964, RurAL CAP was created to serve all areas of Alaska outside the Municipality of Anchorage and the Fairbanks North Star Borough. Since then, RurAL CAP has been instrumental in developing the leadership skills of scores of Alaskan Natives, has provided a multi-disciplinary pre-school experience for thousands of children and their parents throughout the state, has met the challenge of escalating energy costs and dwindling fuel supplies in villages by weatherizing more than 2,000 homes and providing fuel loans to more than 150 villages, has provided counseling services to hundreds of rural Alaskans and their families who have suffered from alcoholism and other forms of substance abuse. . . and the list goes on.

Perhaps, even more significantly, the impact of RurAL CAP's program can be measured by the institutional development it has fostered and the institutional change that has resulted from its community organization and advocacy efforts. Throughout rural Alaska, strong and independent organizations have been created and are thriving, largely due to the commitment of RurAL CAP in the early 1970s to assist in the creation of organizations controlled by village people. Today, these Native associations and other groups provide tens of millions of dollars of services to village people throughout the entire state.

Beyond that, these organizations have formed the cornerstone of community organization and advocacy efforts assisted by RurAL CAP. The impact of this effort can be seen in state statutes related to transportation and telecommunications, education, health, natural resources management, alcohol and drug abuse, local government, rural justice, state energy policy development, and a variety of other public concerns.

RurAL CAP has not always been popular, for any successful effort to provide access to the distributive political decisions of the state and federal governments will inevitably upset the status quo and therefore its proponents. Yet, RurAL CAP has been responsible and respected. The depth of its roots, and its accountability to its constituents have earned it an important role in the struggle to "eliminate the paradox of poverty in the midst of plenty."

ADMINISTRATION AND ORGANIZATION

Board of Directors

More than any other single factor, the success of RurAL CAP can be attributed to the quality of the twenty-seven members of the Board of Directors. That individual quality is enhanced by the unique structure which brings them together. One-third of the twenty-seven member board is composed of elected public officials, while fourteen "target area" board members represent the poor. The remaining seats are held by private organizations whose activities and interests parallel those of RurAL CAP.[2]

Meeting quarterly, representatives of these organizations and public officials come together to manage the affairs of the corporation. As RurAL CAP is a private, non-profit corporation, organized pursuant to Title X of Alaska State Statutes, all legal authority for the activities of the corporation is vested in its board. In order to facilitate its business, the board has established standing committees in program policy and planning, natural resources and subsistence, health, education and social services, and administration and finance. A six-member executive committee conducts the business of the board between the quarterly meetings.

Internal Administration and Organization

The RurAL CAP staff numbers more than 200, 75 percent of whom are stationed outside of Anchorage. The staff is directed by the executive director, the deputy director, and the controller; all three are hired directly by the Board of Directors. Financial, personnel, travel, and property management is provided by the controller. The deputy director is responsible for the overall coordination, implementation, and evaluation of the activities of the four program departments of natural resources/subsistence, alcoholsim, energy, and child development.

Funding Sources, Amounts and Purposes

As Figure 9.1 illustrates, RurAL CAP's funding sources are varied, as are the purposes of those funds. Most noteworthy is "local initiative" funding, granted by the federal Community Services Administration. This versatile and flexible source allows RurAL CAP's board to define the essential characteristics of the agency. These funds are distributed throughout the entire RurAL CAP administrative and programmatic structure, reflecting the board's emphasis on a balance among programs.

All other funds fit within a specific program department and serve one or more of the overall objectives of service delivery, community organization and advocacy.

Administrative Advocacy

Government provides grants and contracts to private non-profit corporations for the delivery of certain services to targeted populations. Evidence of this can be found in the existence of RurAL CAP and dozens of other organizations throughout the state

FIGURE 9.1
FY 1981 GRANTS AND CONTRACTS ADMINISTERED BY RURAL CAP

GRANT/CONTRACT	SOURCE	AMOUNT	DEPARTMENT	PURPOSE
Local Initiative	CSA	$1,056,000	All	Basic Administrative & Program Support; Regional Programs
Community Food & Nutrition	CSA	155,000	Subsistence	Community Organization and Advocacy
Crisis Intervention	CSA	400,000	Energy	Energy Assistance, Fuel Loans, Planning & Research
Weatherization	CSA	78,000	Energy	Solar/Wind Demonstration
Energy Advocacy	CSA	42,000	Energy	Alaska Regional Energy Association
Fuel Assistance	CSA	419,000	Energy	Fuel Loans/Transportation Grants
Fuel Loans	State of Alaska	1,500,000	Energy	Fuel Loans
Weatherization	USDOE/State of Alaska	300,000	Energy	Weatherization
Alcohol Counseling	USDHHS/IHS	123,000	Alcoholism	Counseling, Community Education
State Office of Alcohol & Drug Abuse	State of Alaska	61,000	Alcoholism	Supplement to Counseling, Community Education Program
State Office of Alcohol & Drug Abuse	State of Alaska	82,000	Alcoholism	Statewide Community Action Training and Advocacy
Basic Head Start	USDHHS/ACYF	1,283,000	Child Development	Comprehensive Early Childhood Program
Head Start	State of Alaska	606,000	Child Development	Comprehensive Early Childhood Program (supplemental)
Head Start	USDHHS/ACYF (Cook Inlet Native Association)	98,000	Child Development	Comprehensive Early Childhood Program (supplemental for Native Services)
Head Start Training	USDHHS/ACYF	62,000	Child Development	Training Services to Head Start Staff
Head Start Handicapped	USDHHS/ACYF	90,000	Child Development	"Special Needs" of Head Start enrollees

KEY: CSA—United States Community Services Administration;
USDOE—United States Department of Energy;
USDHHS—United States Department of Health & Human Services;
IHS—Indian Health Service;
ACYF—Administration on Children, Youth and Families.

Source: <u>RurAL CAP</u>, Anchorage, Alaska: Rural Alaska Community Action Program, 1981, p. 10.

which, collectively, administer tens of millions of dollars of public funds. A disturbing reality, however, is that the funding agencies themselves are frequently part of the problem, imposing unnecessary burdens by virtue of statute, regulation and policy. The variety of these impediments to good management and common sense creates a continuing challenge to the management and accounting staffs of non-profit corporations throughout the state.

In recognition of these problems, RurAL CAP has taken the lead in establishing the non-profit financial association. This group, composed of finance officers from Native associations and other non-profit corporations within the state, has identified problems with such administrative concerns as indirect cost negotiation and allocation, cost-reimbursable contracts, etc. The association has designed a series of reforms for consideration by the administration and legislature during the coming year.

PROGRAM ACTIVITIES

Natural Resources and Subsistence

Although at one time RurAL CAP provided direct food supplements to villages, it soon became obvious that the real threat to human nutrition in Alaskan villages was the potential destruction of subsistence resources and loss of access to them. Accordingly, the department of natural resource and subsistence concentrates its efforts on organizational and advocacy activities designed to create a framework of state and federal laws and regulations to protect the options of rural Alaskan people so that they might continue the cultural, economic, social, and nutritional imperative of subsistence.

Although subsistence is the most difficult and controversial public issue facing RurAL CAP, the protection of subsistence resources, and historic access to them, is the most frequently voiced concern of village people. And so, RurAL CAP responds.

Community Organization and Advocacy. A cornerstone of the RurAL CAP effort is the Rural Alaska Resources Association (RARA), a group composed of representatives of eleven Native associations and non-profit corporations from all around the state. RARA meets periodically to forge consensus positions on public policies related to natural resources. Each organization represented in the association maintains a regional program, providing for a direct flow of information between RurAL CAP, the regional organizations, and the villages (and vice versa).

Some RurAL CAP work is contracted to regional groups which are directly responsive to village concerns. Extending actual activities of the organization to the regions has balanced state-wide activities. During the 1981 fiscal year, the department administered contracts with:

- Mauneluk Association (for the organization of local fish and game advisory committees).

- Kodiak Area Native Association (for impact analysis and organizational activities on Kodiak Island related to Outer Continental Shelf (OCS) oil exploration and development).

- Nunam Kitlutsisti (for a wide range of information sharing, organizational, and advocacy efforts related to the ecosystem encompassed by the Yukon/Kuskokwim Delta area).

- The North Pacific Rim Native Corporation (for the compilation of a subsistence use data base and village organizational activities).

- Kawerak, Inc. (for necessary organizational activities related to the Eskimo Walrus Commission).

- Tanana Chiefs Conference (for training and organizing the Koyukuk River Trappers Association).

The issues surrounding the exploitation and conservation of Alaska's resources are manifold. A partial list, with which the RurAL CAP natural resources and subsistence department is directly involved, includes the following:

- Marine mammal protection (related to organizing a consensus from various regions throughout the state on the best approach to proposed amendments to the Marine Mammal Protection Act).

- Alaska national interest lands legislation (concerns include both subsistence protection (Title VIII) and land use/conservation provisions).

- Migratory Bird Treaty Act (supporting efforts to legalize traditional Native hunting of migratory waterfowl during the spring).

- Outer continental shelf and coastal zone management concerns.

- Protection of the habitat of the Porcupine caribou herd and continued access to it by subsistence-dependent Alaska Natives.

- Alaska Department of Fish and Game regulatory practices, including implementation of Alaska's subsistence law (HB 960-Ch. 151, SLA 1978), development of appropriate management plans for various species upon which subsistence people depend, and the organization and training of viable local fish and game advisory committee structures.

As mentioned above, subsistence and natural resources issues are volatile and potentially divisive. Resolving these concerns in a manner consistent with the expressed wishes and desires of rural Alaskans will remain a major priority of RurAL CAP.

Alcoholism

Alaska's number one health problem, alcoholism, appears to have no respect for geography, ethnicity, sex, or age. Alcoholism and alcohol abuse have reached near-epidemic proportions in Alaska, but statistics about alcoholism fail to show the fact that alcohol abuse is robbing strong and independent cultures of their self-respect, their identity, and their ability to survive.

Answers to the problem are not to be found in Washington or Seattle or Juneau or Anchorage, although grants and programs may provide tools to help. Answers will only be found in the spirit and the determination of the village peoples.

Counseling Services. The RurAL CAP program does not impose any one treatment or prevention formula for alcoholism. Three counselors (stationed in their home villages of St. Paul, Iliamna, and Copper Center) work with alcoholics and their families, maintaining a case load of over 200 clients. More significantly, these counselors work with the total community to deal with the problem of alcoholism. The community approach does work with successful results, such as village donations of "safe homes" for the protection of children and spouses of alcoholics, the ability of a village to remain "dry" in the face of stiff economic opposition, regional efforts to come up with local solutions to spouse and child abuse, and a variety of other successes.

Community Organization and Advocacy. But success has occurred only in three villages, and the program is scheduled to "spin off" to respective regional associations at the end of the 1981 fiscal year. To continue and to expand the "community action" approach to the problem of alcohol and other substance abuse, RurAL CAP's alcoholism department has begun a series of educational workshops in various regional centers throughout the state. Although still young, the effort has been enthusiastically endorsed by representatives of regional organizations, by other organizations devoted to reducing the human misery associated with alcoholism, by health agencies, and by workshop participants. It is hoped that, provided with the right tools and motivation, Alaskan villages will be soon able to develop their own solutions to their own problems.

It will not, of course, be easy. But the effort must be made if Alaska's future is not to be trapped within a bottle.

Rural Energy

Fossil fuel costs throughout the world continue to rise at unchecked rates. For residents of Alaskan villages, these costs are much higher than for other Alaskan citizens. Geographic, economic, and political impediments complicate the problem-solving process. The survival of Alaskan villages is threatened. RurAL CAP's energy department is in the forefront of state-wide efforts to design appropriate solutions to problems created by inappropriate energy economies. In dealing with these realities, RurAL CAP is responding in four areas.

Energy Conservation and Weatherization. Using funds appropriated by the Congress to the United States Department of Energy and "passed through" to RurAL CAP from the State of Alaska's Department of Commerce and Economic Development (Division of Energy and Power Development), RurAL CAP has engaged in a major program of weatherizing homes of low-income families in rural Alaska. Since the program began in 1975, weatherization has been completed on almost 40 percent of inadequate rural Alaskan housing. Although the actual cost-to-benefit ratio varies according to climate, fuel costs, and housing conditions, the average "pay back" from weatherization occurs in less than four years.

During 1980, over 900 homes were weatherized in six geographic areas of the state. The state-wide policy advisory committee for weatherization has called upon the state legislature and the administration to appropriate a dollar-for-dollar match against the federal weatherization funding in order to provide greater flexibility in program operations and to extend the service to a broader public.

Fuel Loan and Grant Program. Winter fuel supply is a recurring problem, as many villages either run out of fuel or anticipate running out of fuel before normal summer resupplies are available. Accordingly, RurAL CAP has responded with a unique fuel loan program, making loans available to village councils, corporations, Indian Reorganization Act councils, or any other locally identified entity for the purpose of purchasing fuel products for local consumption.

In instances in which a village is in a "crisis" situation and anticipating that it will run totally out of fuel, thereby requiring that fuel be transported by air rather than less costly surface transportation, the RurAL CAP program provides a grant for the difference between transportation costs.

Most of the funds loaned under this program go to communities to purchase an annual fuel supply during spring and summer months. These funds are a result of an appropriation of $1.5 million by the 1980 Alaska legislature.

Planning and Research. Energy planning, which requires an appropriate data base, and alternative technology development are also functions of the rural energy department at RurAL CAP. Although the weatherization and fuel loan programs meet immediate or short-term needs, it is obvious that more appropriate energy sources must be identified and developed.

To this end, RurAL CAP has developed a state-wide data base, included in which are costs of fuel, transportation and electrical power in most Alaskan locales. The department also works closely with the Alaska Energy Center, the Alaska Center for the Environment, the State Division of Energy and Power Development, and regional non-profit corporations concerned with the development of appropriate energy technologies for villages in their areas, and with such national organizations as the National Center for Appropriate Technology. Together, these organizations provide training and information to village people to help them make informed choices about their energy economy.

Community Organization and Advocacy. Related to all other programs is the on-going effort of community organization and advocacy which serves as the cornerstone of RurAL CAP's overall activities.

Through contracts with five regional organizations, the energy department is directly involved with communication between regions and villages as well as with the rest of the state. The contracts and their varied purposes are listed below:

- Bristol Bay Native Association (for devising an overall energy plan for the thirty-five villages in the region).

- The North Pacific Rim Native Corporation (for devising an appropriate data base for the exploration of alternatives to the present energy economy).

- Central Council, Tlingit-Haida Indians of Alaska (for establishing a regional energy planning office to serve the seventeen Southeast Alaska villages).

- Upper Tanana Development Corporation (for activities related to energy development impact mitigation; i.e., the construction of the Alaska Natural Gas Transportation System).

- Mauneluk Association (for a demonstration wood heating project).

Additionally, the Alaska Rural Energy Association (AREA), sponsored by RurAL CAP, represents numerous Native associations and non-profit development corporations from all around Alaska. AREA performs the important function of coordination and information sharing at a state-wide level. Member organizations include Native association in almost all regions of the state.

In conjunction with AREA, a major effort is continuing to inform the administration and the legislature of the many problems related to energy in rural Alaska. During the 1980 legislative session several new programs, including a state fuel supply loan program modeled after the RurAL CAP effort, were initiated.

The Board of Directors of RurAL CAP has established the effort to obtain appropriate energy policies and technologies for Alaskan villages as RurAL CAP's number one priority. Until the energy problems of villages are solved, it will remain so.

Child Development

A society's most important expectations of its own future can be found in its commitment to the wellbeing of its children. For young Alaskans, Head Start is an important part of that hope, centering on the family. The RurAL CAP child development effort is committed to building strong family units throughout the state.

More than 750 Alaskan children and their families from small rural villages to the municipality of Anchorage, receive comprehensive services through Head Start in one of its three models. In the center-based model, three to five-year-old children congregate daily; in the home-based model, the same age group is served through home visits; and parent-child programs stress the role of parents as teachers through home visits to families with very young children (age six months to three years). Common to all Head Start delivery models is the comprehensive nature of the program, which includes these components.

Parent Involvement. Parents do far more than merely serve as classroom aides. Parents make all policy decisions at the local level, comprise more than half of the members of the statewide child development policy council, and serve on the RurAL CAP Board of Directors. Head Start provides ongoing parent training through village activities and conferences.

Nutrition. Good nutrition is the cornerstone of a child's health. Through workshops, parents learn more about the importance of good nutrition, how to plan and prepare meals, family economic and nutritional needs and cultural preferences.

Head Start provides training for teachers and cooks as they plan meals and prepare foods to meet one-third to one-half of the children's daily nutritional requirements. Children in Head Start programs participate in cooking activities and are encouraged to develop good eating habits. Staff are urged to include local foods in Head Start meals.

Children in Head Start center-based programs receive breakfast and lunch daily. In Head Start home-based and parent-child programs, parents and children are involved in planning and cooking nutritious meals within the home.

Health. RurAL CAP coordinates local, state and federal health services to ensure that children receive a complete health care program. Children are given dental and physical examinations, vision and hearing tests, immunizations and screening for possible developmental or speech problems. If any problem is found, followup treatment and services are provided. Parents, health professionals and health agency representatives serve on the Head Start health advisory committee to coordinate and improve the delivery of health services to Head Start children. The health advisory committee reviews problem areas and recommends solutions.

Education. Education in Head Start programs includes a variety of activities that reflect the cultural heritage of the children and their communities. Many of the RurAL CAP Head Start programs are bilingual, and all programs in Alaska are multicultural.

Special Needs. Through initial health examinations, developmental screening and observations, Head Start staff and parents identify children's special needs. Any child thought to have a special need is referred to the local school district or to child development specialists for thorough evaluation. Parents, staff and specialists then plan a program of learning activities for home and classroom to meet the special needs of each child.

Social Services. Family problems affect children and can interfere with their education, growth and development. Every effort is made to help families of Head Start children identify their own needs and to help them find solutions to their problems.

Head Start staff work closely with community and state agencies to link services to children and families. Families needing assistance and support in times of crisis are able to turn to Head Start for help. Staff at Head Start refer families to local community agencies for assistance, then coordinate the follow-through services the family needs.

Career Development. Head Start staff have many opportunities for personal career development. All teaching staff can enroll in a competency-based early childhood training program that will improve their skills in working with young children and their families. This program includes on-site training, workshops, written assignments and formal college classwork. Enrolled staff may receive college credit for courses they complete and for their ability to work effectively with children.

In addition, specialized training is given on-site for cooks and maintenance specialists in subjects such as food preparation, nutrition, carpentry, health and classroom safety.

The RurAL CAP Head Start staff development committee is the advocate for the expressed training needs of staff, by establishing training policies and recommending allocation of funds for training.

Community Organization and Advocacy. As it performs its mandate to provide the comprehensive services mentioned above, RurAL CAP has chosen to involve itself, through the child development department, as a catalyst for the development of public policies to coordinate services to children within the framework of a holistic approach to the well-being of families and children.

Head Start staff and parents have served as key members of the State and Indian Health Service team in battling otitis media, an ear disease common to many young children in Alaska. Because this disease may cause permanent damage to eardrums, children may suffer hearing loss, language delays and permanent impairment of speech. RurAL CAP, the Indian Health Service, the Department of Health and Social Services, parents, and community health aides have joined together to fight this disease. The battle against the disease continues through parent and community education, preventive health measures, diagnosis, treatment and training.

When the child's primary language is not English, screening tests in different languages are necessary. One such test, the Yupik Sequenced Inventory of Communication Development (the Yupik SICD) was produced cooperatively by the Lower

Kuskokwim School District and RurAL CAP Head Start. This Yupik language test is the beginning of the development of language screening tools and texts that will assure that bilingual children in Alaska are not discriminated against.

Dental problems also threaten Alaskan youth. RurAL CAP has initiated a model preventive dental program, using the services of a staff dental hygienist, to provide comprehensive community and parent education on nutrition and environmental factors which lead to dental disease in the very young. In addition to education services, the hygienist works with the children by providing fluoride treatments and instruction in proper brushing and flossing techniques. Dental health professionals want to expand this effort state-wide during the 1982 fiscal year.

Knowing that one organization, acting alone, cannot achieve the goal of providing leadership and services needed for all of Alaska's pre-school children, RurAL CAP has worked to expand the coalition of concern around children's issues by forming the Alaska Head Start director's association. This group is a consortium of representatives from fourteen organizations and programs.

Working together, the association meets periodically and takes positions on such concerns as the funding and administration of pre-school programs throughout the state, governmental response to children's needs, training concerns, and a variety of other issues.

If the care, love, concern, and commitment made by the child development department of RurAL CAP could be duplicated and expanded to all of Alaska's young children, the future would be bright indeed.

CONCLUSION

In 1978, the RurAL CAP Board of Directors adopted the following statement of philosophy:

> The causes and conditions of proverty in rural Alaska must be eliminated. Any attempts to do so, however, must be sensitively and imaginatively planned in order to assure the ability of rural Alaskan peoples to gain control of the changes affecting their lives. A broad range of activities, including assistance in organization and advocacy, direct delivery of services, and coordination with other agencies and organizations is the most appropriate way to accomplish this goal.

A brief report cannot adequately express the full range of RurAL CAP's activities, nor can it measure the full extent of the commitment of the RurAL CAP Board of Directors and staff to that philosophy. It is not only space which limits a full measuring of this commitment, but also the fact that community action is a people process, one which serves to reinforce the intangible values of community self-reliance and self-sufficiency, participatory decision making, and over all community well-being.

NOTES

1.   U.S., Congress, House, Economic Opportunity Act of 1964, 88th Cong., 2d sess., H. Rept. 1458, preamble.
2.   A list of these officials and organizations will be found in RurAL CAP, Anchorage, Alaska: Rural Alaska Community Action Program, 1981, pp. 6-7.

10
Government-Assisted Development in Rural Alaska: Borough and Regional Quasi-Governments

Gerald McBeath

INTRODUCTION

The questions of rural development in Alaska concern both values and goals of development and the effectiveness of alternate development structures and organizations. The first question involves the very definition of development itself. Should developing the economy of rural areas of the state take precedence over reducing the tensions and conflicts of sociocultural change, for example through protection of traditional cultures and life styles? And, following this, when one speaks of development, does one imply the change and transformation of individuals or of social and cultural groups? In rural Alaska, there is no agreement on the basic definition of terms, and the values of individual economic well being compete with community preservation and enhancement. Given the absence of consensus over values and goals of development, it is understandable why there is little agreement about the mechanisms and organizations in rural Alaska through which development, however defined, should proceed.

The purpose of this article is to explore some of the questions raised concerning development in rural Alaska, and to interpret the progression of development since Alaska's statehood in 1959. We will describe briefly the context of change and then outline the parameters of development assistance. Then we will turn to a description of government-assisted development on Alaska's North Slope, through the activities of the borough government. From this, we will investigate alternate models of governmental assistance through what may be called regional "quasi-governments." We conclude the paper by discussion of some emerging patterns of rural Alaska political development.

THE CONTEXT OF DEVELOPMENT IN RURAL ALASKA

The term "rural" in the Alaska environment is defined customarily as comprehending all areas of the state outside major population concentrations—that is, outside the state's three chief cities of Anchorage, Fairbanks, and Juneau. The land area of rural Alaska encompasses almost 90 percent of America's largest state. While some part of this territory resembles land in agricultural areas of the lower-48 states, such as that

---

An expanded version of a paper presented at the conference, "Theory and Practice of Rural Development: An International Symposium." Fresno, California, April, 1981. I thank Thomas Morehouse and Peter Cornwall for their review and criticism of the manuscript.

in the Matanuska Valley and Delta where agricultural developments have occurred in recent years, most parts do not. Land forms vary, including mountainous terrain, glaciers, tundra, elaborate riverine systems and deltas, and in southeast Alaska, forests. Climatic conditions vary too, but the northern latitude of the state means that for all sections north of the panhandle, winters are harsh with short days and conditions generally inhospitable for man.

Those who were native to Alaska—the Eskimo, Indians, and Aleuts who today are referred to collectively as Alaska Natives—still comprise most of the population of rural areas. Caucasian immigrants have settled in several communities outside the major cities, mostly near resource extraction sites (e.g., mining, timber, and fisheries resource areas). But permanent communities of Caucasians are few and sparsely populated. Over 200 Native settlements are located throughout rural areas, most being homogeneous by ethnic group. One can identify regions, too, that are ethnically homogeneous, where individuals share a common language, customs, and habits. The rural scene, however, is characterized by its sparse population (fewer than 100,000 people populate the over 350 million acres of rural Alaska), its sociocultural diversity, its political and economic underdevelopment.

The resources which are elemental factors of production in rural Alaska are distributed unevenly, as is typically the case. Riverine and coastal areas contain fish, and include, in the Bristol Bay area, one of the world's richest fisheries. Sea mammals are also found in Alaska's coastal waters—for example, seal, walrus, and migrating whale species which have been harvested by Inupiat Eskimo for centuries. Southeast Alaska and some sectors of the southcentral region contain large stands of timber. Fisheries and forests are renewable resources that have been developed over a century, and, in the opinion of some resource economists, have nearly reached their maximum sustainable yield.[1] Vast areas are suitable for agricultural production, but the shorter growing season, relatively poor soils, and distance from agricultural markets of these areas have discouraged agricultural development except where subsidized by the federal or state government.

Non-renewable energy resources—oil and gas, hard rock minerals, and coal—have placed Alaska on the world's energy map in the last decade; but these resources are not distributed evenly, and in exploring for and exploiting them serious obstacles of terrain and climate, and problems of transportation to market, have been encountered.

Several resource surveys have been made in rural Alaska,[2] but our knowledge of the potential for development is still inexact. The public policy issues that arise from the existing distribution of population and resources, however, are unlike those of other rural areas of the United States. First, most rural Alaskans, particularly the Native population, live in villages and regions without resources sufficient to sustain their livelihood beyond the subsistence level. While estimating the number of such residents is hazardous, most of the populations of rural areas of the state fall into this category at some point in the year. The issue that arises is supporting such individuals economically, providing them income to purchase goods and the social services to which they are entitled in the American welfare state—education, housing, medical care. In actuality, this is a plural issue, for it involves not only the provision of a certain level of support for all rural Alaskans, but it also entails the redistribution of support where there are few established social service agencies.

Second and related to the above is the issue of preserving those resources— economic and cultural—which have sustained the Native population historically. This is an issue with a statewide impact, pitting Natives of rural Alaska against urban Caucasians.[3] It concerns "subsistence"—the claim of Natives that they depend economically upon animal and fish species for survival, and that the survival of their culture requires subsistence hunting, fishing, and whaling. This claim, no matter how indifferently it has been supported by the state and federal government, has been used to justify special preference rights for Natives in game and fish habitats of the state. Moveover, it has been used in Native regions to enter objections to resource development activities that, it has been argued, would harm habitats.[4]

A third issue of rural policy is the rate and management of economic development activities. The speed at which developments such as oil and gas exploration and exploitation occur influences many Native Alaskans who would prefer a cautious strategy observing traditional land uses. But, simultaneously, speed is of the essence to Natives without other regular means of livelihood; and the issue has major statewide ramifications, for the state's revenues are dependent on oil exploration. The coordination of resource development, particularly the degree of involvement in planning and implementation of local people who experience the impact of development, is another aspect of this issue.

Income and services, subsistence (implying the culture, lifestyles, and identity of Alaska Natives), speed and manner of resource development—this is the policy context of rural Alaska development. And these are issues that must be addressed in the arena of government.

THE PATTERN OF DEVELOPMENTAL ASSISTANCE IN RURAL ALASKA

Capitalist Development

Much of the growth in twentieth century rural Alaska has stemmed from private, profit-making activity. (Capitalist development was not characteristic of Native communities before their contact with western society, and it can be argued that capitalism is not harmonious with much economic life in such communities today.)

Upon contact in the eighteenth century and until the 1970s, economic growth of rural regions of the state, in fact of the state as a whole, was dependent upon a succession of resource extraction booms—in fisheries, timber, trapping, and gold. These activities brought immigrants to rural Alaska, which resulted in the development of towns and enclaves, such as Nome, Skagway, Ketchikan, and regional development centers such as Fairbanks. Industrial development did not occur, however, and as resources were depleted, economic activity contracted. Moreover, little of this activity benefitted Native village Alaska.

The oil and gas discovery at Prudhoe Bay in 1968 changed this trend substantially. Although the oil bearing lands were state-owned, the leases were purchased by private, transnational oil companies which formed a transportation affiliate (Alyeska) to construct the oil pipeline from Prudhoe Bay to Valdez. This resource, too, is of limited life (oil production is expected to peak by 1986), but two factors make it potentially more conducive to long-term state growth.[5] First, additional discoveries comparable to the newly developed Kuparuk reservoir (about 1 billion barrels) seem likely, which will extend the life of the oil economy. Second, the value of this resource is correspondingly greater than that of any previous discovery. To the present, Prudhoe Bay has had a very limited direct impact on Native income and economic development in rural Alaska. Few Alaska Natives worked on pipeline construction,[6] and an even smaller number are part of the industrial work force at Prudhoe Bay.

However, oil and gas development has had a substantial indirect effect on rural Alaska. Before development could proceed, Native leaders (joined ultimately by the state government) demanded that aboriginal land claims be settled.[7] The resolution of these issues in the Alaska Native Claims Settlement Act (ANCSA) of 1971 changed fundamentally the rural landscape. First, Natives received clear fee simple title to over 40 million acres of land in Alaska, becoming the largest private landowner in the state. Second, Natives received nearly 1 billion dollars in a cash settlement, which was capital available for development. Third, the managers of land and money as well as the conduit for their development were new private profit-making corporations at the regional and village levels.

Today, the single most important "private" agency in most villages of Alaska is the ANCSA village corporation. The organization which now defines regions as well as directs development within them is most likely to be the Native regional corporation. However, in the opinion of specialists, most regional and village corporations have yet to make a substantial impact on the economic development of their areas.[8]

In short, the assistance that capitalist development has provided has been primarily indirect or through the public sector (i.e., taxes and royalties on oil properties assessed by the state and local governments).

Public Sector Development

Public sector development in rural Alaska, unlike private sector development, increased gradually up to the 1970s at which time it accelerated dramatically. During the territorial and early statehood period, the federal contribution obviously was considerably more significant than that of the territory or state. Initially at least, federal programs were directed at those who were "federal wards"—the Alaska Native population. Through the agency of the Bureau of Indian Affairs (BIA), Natives were provided educational and limited income support assistance; through the Public Health Service (USPHS), Native health needs were addressed in a limited fashion. When Alaska became a strategic area during and after the Second World War, the federal impact was greater. Military installations changed the complexion of some rural areas, and military construction (e.g., the DEW-line) provided jobs for many rural Alaskans.

The growth of the federal welfare state, especially at the onset of the War on Poverty in the mid-1960s, had a more general impact on rural regions. The popularization of a universal minimum income standard and the advocacy focus of many programs (for example, VISTA, RurAL CAP, and the Alaska Legal Services programs reached a larger number of areas than had theretofore been involved in any program, public or private.

State assistance to rural development was limited by revenues, which characterized all state programs until the late 1960s. Before Prudhoe Bay, the state was primarily a "pass through" agency, and this had different effects in rural areas of the state which were unorganized for governmental services than in urban, organized areas.

The Constitution of Alaska provided for two types of local government organization—cities and boroughs. Cities could be of several classes, varying by population size and type of function assumed. Boroughs were designed to be area-wide or regional governments. They were to be the chief structures for the state functions of education, planning and zoning; and they were empowercd to assess and collect taxes locally.[9] Although the Constitution and statutory law seemed to facilitate the organization of boroughs, there was little interest in organizing regional governments and assumption of local taxation responsibilities. In fact, there was open opposition. Consequently, in 1963 the state legislature passed the Mandatory Borough Act which organized populous areas with relatively great concentrations of resources and capital and which contained populations experienced in westernized forms of self-government. By the end of the first decade of statehood in 1969, over two-thirds of the people of the state lived within such jurisdictions. Although simpler in form and function and somewhat more auton-omous, they resembled county-type governments elsewhere in the United States.

The rest of the state was unorganized for area-wide government purposes. In some of the larger villages and towns, there were first-, second- (or, until these classifica-tions were eliminated by the legislature in 1972, third-, and fourth-) class cities which could manage government functions. Also, there were traditional village councils, some of which were incorporated under the Indian Reorganization Act of 1936 (IRA), but none of which then (or today) was a local government recognized by the state as a legal entity which could draw up ordinances and be responsible for the decentralized admin-istration of state programs. Thus, the most basic state services essential to development efforts—provision of public education, development of local transportation systems, hospitals, courts—were developed fully only in those few municipalities that were organized cities. Elsewhere they were provided in a limited way by the state and federal government.

What changed this pattern was the improved financial picture of the state as oil and gas were developed at Prudhoe Bay and the state's resource wealth changed atti-tudes of state leaders. Notwithstanding the enormous resources becoming available for development, however, local areas still lacked resources, capital, and skills; and the state lacked any means of making a sustained impact in rural regions. Administrators and the state legislature in Juneau were limited by distance from and lack of knowledge about rural conditions statewide. The formation of a rural borough and rural quasi-govern-ments, to which we now turn, has helped to overcome this lack on the part of Juneau.

BOROUGH GOVERNMENT-ASSISTED DEVELOPMENT IN RURAL ALASKA: THE CASE OF THE NORTH SLOPE BOROUGH

Since statehood in 1959, only one regional government has been created that is authentically "rural," and this is the North Slope Borough. As the state's largest rural borough, the North Slope government is obviously atypical; nevertheless, it serves as an illustration of the possibilities of development through the public sector in rural Alaska.

The North Slope was incorporated in 1972 in response to the development of oil and gas exploration in Prudhoe Bay, on the one hand, and the enactment of ANCSA on the other. Unlike the other "oil borough" of the state (Kenai), however, the North Slope Borough is Native-controlled, for 85 percent of the resident non-industrial popula-tion is Inupiat Eskimo. Unlike urban areas in the state, the borough's formation brought about the opposition of oil companies which saw the borough's taxation and planning and zoning powers as a threat to the profitability and control of their Prudhoe Bay properties. The state administration was not supportive of the formation of the borough either, for the borough taxed oil property for local uses, removing income from state coffers and statewide distribution.[10]

The borough's jurisdiction today encompasses all of Alaska's Arctic Slope, and

MAP 10.1

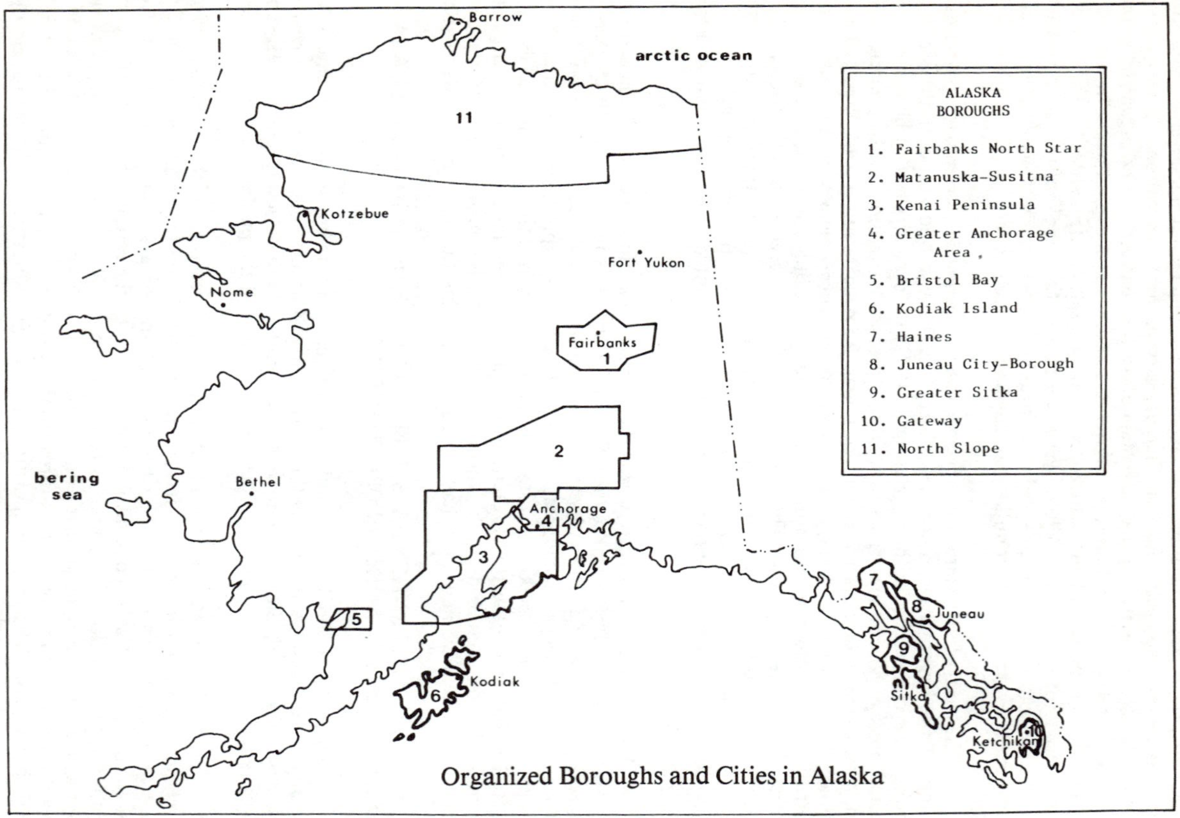

ALASKA
BOROUGHS

1. Fairbanks North Star
2. Matanuska-Susitna
3. Kenai Peninsula
4. Greater Anchorage
   Area.
5. Bristol Bay
6. Kodiak Island
7. Haines
8. Juneau City-Borough
9. Greater Sitka
10. Gateway
11. North Slope

arctic ocean

Barrow

Kotzebue

Nome

bering
sea

Bethel

Fort Yukon

Fairbanks
1

2

Anchorage
4
3

Kodiak

6

5

7
8
9
Sitka
Juneau
Ketchikan

Organized Boroughs and Cities in Alaska

includes the Prudhoe Bay industrial area, five original Inupiat villages (Barrow, Point Hope, Wainwright, Kaktovik, and Anaktuvuk Pass), and three new villages formed since the passage of ANCSA. The total population of this region is some 4,300 individuals who are permanent residents, and the highly mobile non-resident workforce of Prudhoe Bay. We will trace the borough's role in development in the three issue areas of income and services, subsistence protection, and regulation of resource development.

Income and Services on the North Slope

The most significant impact of the North Slope Borough on regional development has been through the creation of jobs, providing income for residents that is earned and not a transfer (or welfare) payment from the federal or state government. The formation of the borough government, and the development of an independent school district on the North Slope, have created over 1,000 jobs. In July 1980, some 450 individuals were general government employees of the borough; an average 200 workers were employed in borough construction projects; and another 420 individuals were employed by the school district. These jobs comprised over half of the resident civilian labor force on the North Slope.[11]

A survey of borough residents in 1977 showed that 55 percent of adults had worked for the borough on some occasion previously.[12] In studying employment opportunities, researchers have found that the borough has created an employment system that is congenial to the Native life-style (offering opportunities for subsistence leave during whaling season, for example, and work near employee's residences). Borough salaries are as high as those offered by the regional corporation.[13] These employment opportunities have helped reduce unemployment among North Slope residents to less than 5 percent of the work force—a lower rate than that found anywhere else in the state.

A second impact of the borough has been the creation of a massive social infrastructure on the North Slope, which has made the services available to residents begin to approach those in urban areas of Alaska and the lower-48. Within two years of the formation of the borough, leaders had drawn up five-year Capital Improvement Projects (CIP) which they proceeded to fund through general obligation bonds based on the taxable property at Prudhoe Bay. Oil companies challenged the borough's financing strategy in court, and the case was not resolved in the borough's favor until 1978. Thus, the first four years of the CIP were characterized by fits-and-starts. Presently, however, the borough CIP is unimpeded by oil company or state suits as to its legality. The total package of projects calls for the expenditure by 1985 of $511 million dollars.[14] The CIP includes:

- new secondary schools in all large villages and the upgrading or new construction of primary schools

- public housing construction in all villages of the North Slope

- construction of health clinics in all villages

- fresh water, waste removal, and sanitary facilities

- construction of roads and airports

The construction of new facilities and the hiring of borough employees to deliver educational, health, and general governmental services has significantly "modernized" the conditions of social life for Alaska's North Slope Inupiat, and this is entirely the result of government action.

Subsistence Protection on the North Slope

Traditionally, Inupiat Eskimo have depended on two species for subsistence. Coastal Inupiat have hunted whales which migrate to the Arctic Ocean each spring, and inland villagers have hunted caribou. A second major effect of borough government has been the protection of Native use of these species through creation of an institutional buffer between Native subsistence users and the state and federal government. The borough has also served as an advocate of the Native subsistence position in the state-wide and national political arenas.

Challenges to Native subsistence on the North Slope began well before the borough formed. In fact, one event that led to the formation of the Arctic Slope Native Association (the first effective regional organization on the North Slope and the association out of which the borough grew) concerned a threat to Native hunting of waterfowl.[15] For several reasons, including a reported decline in species populations and an increased capability on the part of state fish and game (ADFG) enforcement officials, such threats increased in the 1970s. The state fish and game board, responding to reports of declines in the Western Arctic caribou herd, imposed a ban on caribou hunting in 1976. And, in the following year, the International Whaling Commission (IWC), responsible under international treaties for the management of subsistence whaling, proposed a moratorium on the hunting of bowhead whales, the species most widely hunted in Arctic coastal waters.[16]

Although these challenges concerned different species, the response of the borough was essentially identical: it mobilized opinion of North Slope Natives against external forces; it formed new organizations; and it provided these agencies the staff support and financing necessary to give borough protests "organizational teeth."

The borough "mobilized bias" on the North Slope by holding meetings and hearings, inviting to these gatherings officials of the state fish and game board, ADFG, and state legislators. Borough leaders lobbied at the state legislature, Congress, and in the case of whaling, at meetings of the IWC. Borough leadership then was responsible for the creation of unified public opinion on the North Slope regarding the subsistence use of the two species and the presentation of opinion to higher governments.

The borough's position with respect to the caribou crisis was that the species should be managed locally. A new organization—the borough fish and game commission with representatives from each of the borough's villages—was created to produce region-wide game use plans. Supporting the work of the commission was a new borough department, the Environmental Protection Office, which monitored state agencies and began to collect data on caribou to prove the borough's contention that the species was not declining.[17]

With respect to the management of whales, the borough revived a traditional group—the association of whaling captains which in times past had informally agreed upon the procedures of the hunt and distribution of the annual take. The borough assisted the formation of an Association of Eskimo Whaling Captains (AEWC), supporting it with borough funds and aiding it in gaining funds directly from the state legislature. The mayor's office paid close attention to the development of both organizations and, through a deliberate policy of forming tactical alliances with environmental organizations, it extended the organizational network focussing on protection of the two species.

In 1979 the North Slope Borough asserted its authority to manage caribou and, with the AEWC, whales, contending that subsistence users should be permitted to take species consistent with need and compatible with local use.[18] Although the borough's authority regarding caribou management remains unclear, the federal agency with primary responsibility over whaling in American waters, the National Oceanographic and Atmospheric Administration (NOAA), has entrusted the AEWC with responsibilities for self-monitoring.[19] Thus, the borough now stands as a buffer between Native subsistence users and state and federal agencies that regulate species populations.

Regulation of Resource Development on the North Slope

An issue of concern in the formation of the North Slope Borough was exploration and development of oil and gas properties in territory that traditionally has been undisturbed by machines and industrial activity. A third major consequence of borough government on the North Slope has been regional government participation in the statewide planning process concerning resource development activities taking place in the Arctic.

The borough had limited opportunity to influence resource development activity that predated its incorporation. Oil company activity at Prudhoe Bay, the construction of the trans-Alaska pipeline, exploration on the National Petroleum Reserve—all were uninfluenced by borough protests, for basic decisions already had been made. However, the borough has had some measure of influence over onshore and offshore development activity since that time, particularly in the areas of Outer Continental Shelf (OCS) leasing, coastal zone planning, and transportation corridor planning.[20]

Although the details of borough activity in each case differ substantially, the borough's approach to resource management issues shows several common characteristics: mobilization of opinion against resource development plans that threaten the ecology of the North Slope and appear likely to disrupt the Native lifestyle; development of organizations and alliances with external agencies and higher levels of governments to protect Inupiat interests; and further regional integration into the web of intergovernmental organizations and relations influencing events on the North Slope.

The case of OCS development shows the most significant results of borough attempts to mobilize opinion regionally. The plan to lease lands in the Beaufort Sea for oil and gas exploration touched the consciousness of few North Slope residents when first discussed in the mid-1970s; and it was not then an issue. However, through the campaign of Mayor Eben Hopson against OCS development, leaders and eventually some non-leaders became concerned about the potential dangers of planned development activities.[21] By the time formal hearings were held on Beaufort Sea OCS leasing in 1978-79, leaders of organizations had developed a united stance, and villagers in the areas most likely to suffer direct effects (Kaktovik and Nuiqsut) had participated in hearings and put their views on record. Spurred by Alaska Legal Services lawyers, the villages entered suits in federal court to delay development.[22]

In order to protect the OCS region from oil and gas exploration and development, the borough mayor added staff to the mayor's office, to evaluate potential impacts and protest development. And the mayor and his chief aides established contacts with leaders of other Inupiat communities in Canada and Greenland, holding the first meeting of the circumpolar Inupiat, in Barrow in 1977. An important resolution of this conference was the call for a moratorium on the exploration for oil in the arctic OCS.[23]

Another example of the formation of a borough organizational capability in the area of resource management issues is the borough's development of a coastal zone management (CZM) plan in 1979-80. The borough assumed a role as participant in the Alaska Coastal Policy Council (state level); and the borough planning department and planning commission devoted resources and energy to the development of a comprehensive plan for the mid-Beaufort Sea region. Although the borough ultimately withdrew its plan when it appeared unlikely that the state council would accept the amount of local option for which the plan provided, the borough won a victory by gaining acceptance of its premise that state planning should be responsive to local interests.[24]

Both OCS and CZM planning show the degree to which borough, state, and federal leaders and agencies have become part of an interlocking network of governmental organizations on the North Slope. A third case, the borough's development of a plan for the North Slope Haul Road—illustrates this point clearly. Although the borough objected to any public use of the Haul Road, it became involved with the state's Department of Transportation and Public Facilities and the Department of Natural Resources, which would be responsible for the road's maintenance when opened to the public use. The borough also formed links with the federal Bureau of Land Management (BLM), which simultaneously was developing a utility corridor plan. Borough leaders were not successful in restricting use of the Haul Road (opened to the public by an act of the 1980 state legislature); nevertheless, through coordination and cooperation with state and federal agencies, the borough won some attention for its views about dangers to fish and game habitats and to the Inupiat livelihood of an opening of the road.

In the three issue areas of income and services, subsistence protection, and regulation of resource development, the North Slope Borough has brought about significant improvements for residents. It has given them employment opportunities not previously available, aided them in the presentation of their views to the institutions and agencies that have authority to make decisions on subsistence and resource development, and it has effectively influenced higher governments on their behalf.

In its planning and advocacy role, the borough is indeed a model for other regions of rural Alaska; however, the resources available to the borough make the situation of North Slope Natives unique. Over two-thirds of borough operating budget revenue and all of its capital budget requirements are met through taxation of the vast wealth of oil and gas company properties at Prudhoe Bay. But this source of revenue is not secure. For example, the borough is retiring bonds that finance the CIP on a schedule matching the prime oil production years of Prudhoe Bay. The maturity schedule is designed to pay off all debts by 1993—which is between five to ten years before the end of the expected economic life of the presently known oil and gas reserves at Prudhoe Bay. Most of these costs will be paid off before Native lands are subject to federal corporation taxes in the 1990s. However, unless new oil and gas resources are exploited by the late 1990s, the sunk costs of general government and social welfare programs will comprise an increasing part of a shrinking borough budget. These long-term costs will thus have the effect of continuing the borough's participation in and dependence on an unstable non-renewable resource economy—without the cushion the state has in its permanent fund or development of renewable resources. A further obstacle to the borough's future financial stability is the rising power of urban areas in the state legislature, particularly after reapportionment in 1981. Although the borough is a leading example of government assistance in rural development, its lessons apply directly to no other region in rural Alaska.

QUASI-GOVERNMENT ASSISTED DEVELOPMENT IN RURAL ALASKA

"Quasi-governments" are associations or organizations that serve a public purpose by providing for the needs of communities, but that are limited in significant ways by their lack of legal and constitutional efficacy—that is, they cannot take actions binding on all individuals they serve without legislative authorization of a higher governmental authority. In rural Alaska outside the North Slope Borough and the organized first and second class municipalities, quasi-governments are the only governments that residents have.

Today there are a variety of institutions at the local and regional levels in rural Alaska which enhance the power of rural Alaskans. Those which, in our view, have had the greatest impact on development are the Regional Education Attendance Areas (REAAs), formed in the unorganized borough in 1976; the regional Native non-profit corporations, which have gained control of many federal Indian programs and state development resources since the early 1970s; and the ANCSA regional and village profit-making corporations. We will discuss briefly the REAAs and non-profit corporations.

REAAs and Regional Development

Before 1975, schools in the unorganized borough financed and operated under state law were administered under the centralized, state-operated school system (SOS). This central administrative system provided for the recruitment of teachers and administrators, development of curricula, and construction and maintenance of school facilities in all villages and towns that were neither organized municipalities nor part of a borough.

Although there had been several attempts to decentralize control of the SOS to the regional and local community level, the issue of local control gained popularity only during the land claims movement of the 1960s. Then the passage of ANCSA, by setting up regional and village Native corporations with cash and with wealth in land, created an organizational impetus for decentralized educational services. Native and educational leaders pressured the state legislature in 1975 to decentralize the state SOS system, and in June 1976, twenty-one Regional Education Attendance Areas were created.[26]

The new districts were developed within the boundaries of Native regional corporations. In each REAA, voters could elect a board of from five to eleven members. In addition, initially every community with a school was to have a community school committee (the powers and functions of which have changed substantially in recent years).[27] Unlike organized borough and first-class city district school boards in the state, however, the authority of the REAA boards is not plenary (they have only those powers delegated from the legislature). They may not establish new schools, nor may they supplement revenues for education supplied under the state's foundation program. But REAAs were given de facto control over school budgets and personnel. They have broad curricular powers, including the power to adopt regulations governing the organization of schools, to develop a philosophy of education, and to define school goals. REAA boards may incur debts and contract independently; they hire teachers and staff, set salaries, and engage in purchasing and in disbursing funds.

The major impact of REAAs in rural Alaska has been in the development of regional educational service centers that operate programs which in general are more adapted to local cultures than those of the SOS. Although the REAA system is criticized by urban Alaskans, it has had the effect of enhancing local control of the operation of school programs in many parts of rural Alaska, and it has focused attention anew on the most vital resource in rural Alaska, the human one. Most rural residents are eager to use the REAAs, and there seems to have been a considerably greater degree of involvement in school programs by local people than previously.

REAAs have also been the administrative organizations through which new school construction in rural Alaska has proceeded and, most importantly, in which small rural high school programs have been developed. Before 1976, students from small towns and villages had to leave their communities to attend secondary schools--boarding schools in regional centers, Mt. Edgecumbe in Sitka, and even schools outside the state. In 1976, Alaska Legal Services sued the state (Tobeluk v. Lind) asking it to build high schools in small villages so that high school students would not need to leave their homes to continue their education. The state settled out of court, and the Tobeluk consent decree called for new school programs and the construction of schools in ninety-five small villages.

Through the combined effects of the Tobeluk decree and the formation of REAAs, educational services have now become available throughout all parts of rural Alaska. The development of new school programs and the construction of regional administrative headquarters has also had important local economic side-effects. Although few Natives have been hired as teachers and administrators in new school programs, a significant number of individuals in local communities throughout the state have been hired as teachers' aides in schools. Also a $113 million construction program under the Tobeluk decree alone has created jobs for scores of Native laborers. Purchasing and maintenance contracts have been let to local firms, including village corporations. REAAs have thus brought about a significant improvement in local economic activity that is apart from their role in localizing educational programs.

Obviously, REAAs have had a less significant impact in the second issue area of subsistence protection. But the decentralization of educational programs in some areas has stimulated locally responsive educational programs—the development of courses in Native culture and community history, of skills courses related to subsistence. And some of the REAA boards have adopted daily schedules and school calendars that are adapted to the local subsistence cycle.

The enabling legislation for REAAs gave them a function related to resource management:

> Under the provisions of [an act establishing a mechanism for regions of the Unorganized Borough to establish coastal zone management service areas], any Regional Educational Attendance Area, upon determination by the local electorate, may establish itself as a coastal zone management planning district.[28]

To the present, no REAA has played a significant role in this area, but the potentiality for action remains. Significantly, REAAs, their shortcomings as institutions of local control notwithstanding, have received attention as forerunners of borough governments. The movement to form the Yukon Flats borough was in fact stimulated by the REAA superintendent.[29]

Non-profit Corporations and Regional Development

Each of the twelve regional Native corporations in Alaska was once a multi-purpose land claims association, active in mobilizing Native participation in the land claims movement. After the passage of ANCSA in 1971, the land claims associations remained as non-profit associations with general social service objectives. In some Native regions of rural Alaska, non-profit associations have made strides in regional development, primarily as a conduit for public (both federal and state) funds which are administered regionally.

These objectives of non-profit associations have been facilitated by major changes in the structure of funding available for development activities. In 1976, under terms of the Indian Self-Determination and Education Assistance Act (Public Law 93-638), the centralized BIA programs were decentralized. Essentially, this act provided the legal mechanism for contracting the functions of BIA, including their planning and implementation, to Native American groups—leaving only the monitoring of contract compliance in the hands of the BIA. While non-profit regional Native associations are not the only groups that may contract for BIA funds (traditional councils, village and regional profit-making corporations, and corporations chartered under the Indian Reorganization Act of 1936 are eligible as well), in Alaska non-profit corporations have been the most aggressive applicants to the Secretary of the Interior (regarding BIA programs) for health, education, and social service funds or to the Secretary of Health and Human Services.

In cooperation with Native regional corporations, the non-profit corporations have contracted with the federal Housing and Urban Development Department for housing construction funds, and have managed housing units once constructed. Increasingly, the non-profit corporations have succeeded in gaining state funding for general economic development, health, and social service programs.

Some non-profit corporations have played important roles in stimulating regional economic development. For example, Kawerak, Inc., the non-profit organization in the Bering Straits Native region, has developed a reindeer herding industry. Tanana Chiefs Conference, the non-profit association representing forty-one interior Alaska villages, has engaged in transportation and social service delivery planning for the region. Most regional non-profit corporations have local government assistance sections that aid traditional councils draw up legal procedures, and apply for grants. They have also provided guidance to those villages which seek to incorporate as municipalities under state law. Several non-profit corporations have active subsistence sections which aid residents defend subsistence use and present Native views regarding land use management.

The most recent attempt at borough government organization in rural Alaska, the formation of a borough in the Bethel area of western Alaska, is sponsored by the Association of Village Council Presidents (AVCP), that region's non-profit association.

EMERGING PATTERNS IN RURAL ALASKA DEVELOPMENT

In 1981 most of the areas of rural Alaska left unorganized by the legislature still lack formal governmental powers. We now describe the pressures for change of this condition, the recognized obstacles to change, and the plans currently being considered to develop rural Alaska politically.

Pressures for Change

A decade of experience following the passage of ANCSA has brought little change in the relative position of rural areas of the state (exclusive of the North Slope) vis-á-vis urban areas. Notwithstanding increasing amounts of private capital flowing into these regions, the Native village and regional corporations have not engineered a "take-off" stage of economic growth and development. Thus, one motive behind the desire to develop regional governments in the region, though more implicit than explicit, is an interest in regional economic development that would be funded by state petroleum revenues.

A second pressure for change comes from urban areas of the state. With the development of the North Slope Borough in 1972 and the formation of REAAs in 1976, urban populations living in organized boroughs and cities complained anew that it was unfair that they be taxed while rural areas were untaxed, being provided with "free" governmental services.[30] In the late 1970s, several bills were introduced in the state legislature to create a uniform statewide property tax. The accelerating oil wealth of Alaska in the last few years and the elimination of the state income tax has decreased this pressure, but it has not removed the underlying concern over local tax inequity.

A third concern and pressure for change is the interest of state officials in developing administratively rational and efficient means for the delivery and monitoring of services in rural areas of the state. From the perspective of state officials, especially planners, it is troublesome and inefficient for there to be overlapping jurisdictions for services that must be administered comprehensively and equally statewide. They see unnecessary duplication in the placing of employees in regional offices, and they find little local capability to follow through on the implementation of programs. Also, there are no authoritative, constitutionally-sanctioned structures and officials for them to deal with. Clearly, from their perspective, having administrative units and officials at the regional level that could manage all state functions would be in the general interest of the state.

The fourth and perhaps most important concern from the perspective of those living in unorganized rural Alaska is their current inability to sponsor programs that authentically reflect local needs and values. However alien the borough or municipal government concept may be in rural Alaska, to many leaders of these regions it represents an advance over structures of limited power and dubious legality.

Obstacles to Change

This brief and by no means complete list of pressures for change suggests that there is general support for the organization of regional government units in rural Alaska. Such is not the case, and the current attitude is best described as one of ambivalence. Since the formation of the North Slope Borough in 1972, no other rural region of the state has become incorporated for municipal or regionwide governmental services.

Why hasn't the idea of regional government spread? Because rural regions lack an adequate tax base to finance what have come to be very expensive governmental programs. The financial requirements of a new regional government, while not staggering, are several times greater than can be afforded by Native regions today. And no new large resource has developed in any region outside the North Slope that would encourage the growth of such institutions.

A second reason, mentioned by several of those attending workshops and symposia on local government organization sponsored in rural areas of the state in recent years, is the lack of familiarity with the concept of regional government, and some question about its appropriateness.[31] Just as Natives in the late 1960s during the land claims movement questioned the meaning and appropriateness of the corporation concept, so Natives of the 1970s and 1980s have not found it easy to accept the full legal and conceptual implications of regional governmental organization.

Third, there are questions about the need for regional government in unorganized areas of the state. The creation of school districts at the regional level has removed the major incentive for organization of regional governments. These schools are now cost-free for rural students, but the expenses of planning and zoning, and of the overall bureaucratic structure which most see as likely to develop have discouraged some early proponents of borough government. Those most opposed include Caucasians who live in rural Alaska because, among other reasons, governmental control is weak and there are no taxes. And fourth, leaders and officials in the other established quasi-governments—regional corporations and non-profit organizations—oppose the formation of new organizations that would compete with them for public resources and status.

Until recently, these arguments against change in the pattern of organization of governmental services in rural Alaska outweighed pressures for change.

Proposals for Organization of Rural Alaska Government

Essentially, proposals to organize governments in rural Alaska have focussed on three sets of questions:

- What is the appropriate territorial unit?

- What are the essential government powers?

- Who should pay the bill?

To the present, none of these issues has been resolved.

An early plan to organize governmental services drew neat lines on the map of rural Alaska, creating regions of comparable size that included populations with a resource base sufficient for community development.[32] This ideal-typic map of government service regions has not received support from rural leaders or the statewide administration. A state-sponsored proposal to create six planning regions has received no support outside the state government.[33]

The most popular plans have drawn jurisdictional lines around existing and relatively powerful units. One suggestion was the creation of regional governments coterminous with the boundaries of regional profit-making corporations. The chief problem with such a plan was that some of the regional corporations, for example Doyon in interior Alaska, were too vast, and others too small. A second suggestion has been that several unorganized boroughs be formed. A third suggestion has been the "streamlined borough" concept or the REAA-borough model. This would add governmental functions to REAAs, permitting the merger of smaller REAAs and the carving up of those covering large territories. This compromise has received the most attention, as noted in the regional government study of 1979-80.[34]

A subsidiary question has been whether small villages currently without state chartered governments should be organized. Two bills have been introduced in the 1981 session of the state legislature that would have the effect of making a legal, constitutional entity of any traditional village or IRA council.[35]

Concern over the appropriate powers of regional and local governments has focussed on the strength of the governmental institution (its enforcement capability) and the scope of services it should provide. There has been little support for the creation of multi-purpose regional governments like the North Slope Borough (those of the first class which may adopt a series of services on an areawide basis). There has been greater and continuing interest in the creation of very limited-purpose boroughs, with the power of education, limited taxing powers, and some planning and zoning powers. While for a time the idea of "advisory" boroughs was considered, this idea has not gained much support.

Finally, although the financing issue has not been settled, several formulas have been discussed seriously. One suggestion is that a modified form of state revenue sharing be adopted that would distribute money for governmental services on a per capita basis. A second proposal is the application of the public foundation concept to the financing of Alaska's health and social services programs, as well as to educational services. There is no agreement yet on the areas which should properly be funded in such a formula, however, or over how the rate would be devised. But there seems to be agreement that the best access of rural Alaska to oil revenues is via formal government structures.

What emerges from the brief review of attempts to organize local governmental services statewide is the sense that there is not substantial support for any alternative to the status quo. The prospect, then, for radical change in the manner of service delivery to rural Alaska is not bright.

NOTES

1. George W. Rogers, ed., Change in Alaska. College, Alaska: University of Alaska Press, 1970; and David T. Kresge, Thomas A. Morehouse, and George W. Rogers, Issues in Alaska Development, Institute of Social and Economic Research. Seattle: University of Washington Press, 1977.
2. See, for example, Alaska Department of Commerce and Economic Development, Annual Reports, 1977-1980.
3. The debate over subsistence in the 1981 legislature, in which an urban Anchorage legislator opposed a rural Bethel area Native leader who supported the subsistence preference given to Natives, is a good illustration of this process.
4. An example is the 1980 suit in federal court of the Inupiat villages of Kaktovik and Nuiqsut, which objected to the federal sale of leases in the Beaufort Sea OCS because of danger to the habitat of bowhead whales.
5. For a sophisticated series of petroleum development scenarios, see Kresge et al., pp. 155-179.
6. Larry Naylor and Lawrence Gooding, "Alaska Native Hire on the Trans-Alaska Oil Pipeline Project," Alaska Review of Social and Economic Conditions, Vol. 15, No. 1, February 1978.
7. Mary Clay Berry's study, The Alaska Pipeline: The Politics of Oil and Native Land Claims. Bloomington, Ind: University of Indiana Press, 1975, surveys the relationship between oil and gas development and the Native claims movement. For a

history of the Native land claims movement itself, see Robert Arnold, <u>Alaska Native Land Claims</u>. Anchorage, Alaska: Alaska Native Foundation, 1976; Gerald A. McBeath and Thomas A. Morehouse, <u>Dynamics of Alaska Native Self-Government</u>. Lanham, Maryland: University Press of America, 1980, surveys this period from the perspective of North Slope Natives.

8.   See the article by Dean Olson and Bradford Tuck in this volume.

9.   Thomas A. Morehouse and Victor Fischer, <u>Borough Government in Alaska</u>. Fairbanks, Alaska: Institute of Social, Economic and Government Research, 1971.

10.   For a history of the borough formation process, see McBeath and More-house, <u>Dynamics of Alaska Native Self-Government</u>, pp. 75-82.

11.   Gerald A. McBeath, <u>North Slope Borough Government and Policymaking</u>. Fairbanks, Alaska: Institute of Social and Economic Research, 1981, p. 70.

12.   The North Slope population survey, conducted by the University of Alaska's Institute of Social and Economic Research under the direction of John Kruse, October-December 1977.

13.   Judith Kleinfeld, John Kruse, and Robert Travis. <u>Different Paths of Inupiat Men and Women in the Wage Economy: The North Slope Experience</u>. MAP Monograph No. 2, Fairbanks, Alaska: Institute of Social and Economic Research, 1981.

14.   McBeath, <u>North Slope Borough Government and Policymaking</u>, p. 61.

15.   Margaret Lantis, "The Current Nativistic Movement in Alaska," Paper presented at the Symposium on Circumpolar Problems, Nordic Council for Anthropological Research, Stockholm: 1969.

16.   McBeath, <u>North Slope Borough Government and Policymaking</u>, p. 61.

17.   Ibid., p. 60.

18.   Ibid., p. 79.

19.   Fairbanks <u>Daily News-Miner</u>, April 30, 1981.

20.   For an exhaustive discussion of resource development cases on the North Slope, see Thomas A. Morehouse and Linda Leask, <u>Governance in the Beaufort Sea Region: Petroleum Development and the North Slope Borough</u>. Springfield, Virginia: National Technical Information Service, 1978.

21.   McBeath and Morehouse, <u>Dynamics of Alaska Native Self-Government</u>, p. 96.

22.   McBeath, <u>North Slope Borough Government and Policymaking</u>, p. 59.

23.   The catalyst for both the borough's opposition to OCS development and its organization of the Inuit circumpolar conference, was the Dome petroleum water blowout in the Canadian Beaufort Sea of 1976. See, McBeath and Morehouse, <u>Dynamics of Alaska Native Self-Government</u>, p. 94.

24.   McBeath, <u>North Slope Borough Government and Policymaking</u>, p. 57.

25.   Ibid., p. 54.

26.   Frank Darnell, "Education Among the Native People of Alaska," <u>Polar Record</u>, Vol. 19, No. 122, p. 441.

27.   See Mark Roye, "Victim of Desire: The Myth of Local Control," <u>Tundra Drums</u>, April 23 and April 30, 1981.

28.   Patrick K. Poland, "SB 35 and Regional Government," in Kathryn A. Hecht and Ronald K. Inouye, <u>New School Districts in Rural Alaska: A Report on the REAAs After One Year</u>. Fairbanks, Alaska: Center for Northern Educational Research, 1978, p. 138.

29.   Personal interview with administrator, Yukon Flats School District, October 17, 1980.

30.   An early study of the tax equity issue is that by Richard W. Garnett, "Equalization of Local Government Revenues in Alaska," Fairbanks, Alaska: Institute of Social, Economic and Government Research, Occasional Paper No. 9, January 1973.

31. State of Alaska, Alaska State Legislature, Joint Senate and House Community and Regional Affairs Committee, "Local Government Study—1979: Final Report."

32. Victor Fischer and Thomas A. Morehouse, Issues of Regional Government in Alaska. Fairbanks, Alaska: Institute of Social, Economic, and Government Research, 1974.

33. State of Alaska, Division of Policy Development and Planning, "Alaska State Planning Regions and Substate Districts," December 1976.

34. State of Alaska, "Local Government Study—1979."

35. Alaska State Senate Bill No. 341, "An Act relating to Native village governments," and Alaska State Senate Bill No. 350, "An Act establishing Regional Service Authorities."

Part Three:
Changing Values in the
Rural Development Process

11
The Human Resources Approach to Native Rural Development: A Special Case

Michael Gaffney

The indigenous Alaska Native community is now approaching the close of its first decade of self-directed development under the provisions of the 1971 Alaska Native Claims Settlement Act (ANCSA). For the majority of those Native people who live in remote, sparsely populated areas of the state, "development" means the building of new social and economic institutions which requires adaptation to culturally different cognitive styles and forms of human relationships. According to a specific formulation of the "development" concept, this article attempts to:

1. describe the issues, processes, and conditions of Native institution-building, and

2. delineate, as a special case, the efforts of one Alaska Native group, the Inupiat Eskimo of the Northwest Arctic, to manage the impacts of severe social change through a regional strategy of "human resource" development.

Before introducing the human resources approach to development, it is essential to recognize that the central feature of the special case is a regionwide strategy for the systematic and integrated development of the rural economy and rural education. Moreover, within the special case region of the Northwest Arctic Native Association (NANA), the three major institutions that plan and manage these processes are new organizations controlled <u>de jure</u> by the NANA people.

The first of these organizations, and the one which gives this development case its most distinctive qualities, is the NANA corporation, one of the twelve Native regional profit corporations established by ANCSA. NANA Corporation exercises the leading role in the rural development strategy by using its share of the land and cash settlement of ANCSA to systematically build a regional employment structure. The second organization, Mauneluk Inc., is the non-profit regional Native organization responsible for providing human services in such areas as health, subsistence economics, vocational training, and adult education. It is also Mauneluk's responsibility to carry out community surveys and inter-agency coordination upon which the overall regional strategy is based. The third organization that is part of the strategy, the Northwest Arctic School

Originally prepared for the Center for Cross-Cultural Studies, University of Alaska, Fairbanks.

District, operates the region's formal school system according to Alaska State regulations, under the immediate supervision of a locally elected Inupiat Regional School Board. It is the role of the school district to organize the factors of formal education in ways that are consistent with the cultural life of the community and with their projected employment requirements.

To explain the context in which NANA's approach has developed, we will discuss: (1) relevant development strategies, (2) major conditions influencing Alaska Native development, (3) NANA as a case of rural development, and (4) some nonformal educational consequences of the NANA corporate approach.

DEVELOPMENT STRATEGIES: A CONCEPTUAL STATEMENT

The issues and conditions which frame the NANA regional strategy suggest certain parallels with those found in many Third World political economies. Foremost among these parallels is that, early on, the NANA regional leadership had to formulate a basic philosophical position involving fundamental questions of ethics and morality as well as of techniques and technology. At the very heart of choosing an overall development approach under conditions of rapid social change are the a priori questions: what kind of society do we wish to build? and what human costs are we willing to bear in its construction?[1] The institutional goals, management styles, and participation encouraged by regional leadership are dependent on critical assumptions about what kinds of development and change are most desirable for NANA communities.

The parallel continues in that, like Alaska Native leadership generally, the NANA regional leadership faced a choice between two development approaches. The first is that of economic development which maximizes corporate income. This position holds that: (1) an increased rate of "economic growth," through capitalization of human and material resources, is the key to development; (2) as capital formation proceeds through growth of aggregate economic indices such as GNP, per capita income or, in reference to the NANA region, corporate earnings and assets, the entire community will benefit through a "trickle-down" effect; (3) the model against which one measures progress in economic growth is mass urban-industrial society; and (4) if some segment of the developing community is resistant to assimilation, then this "cultural deficiency" must be overcome before there can be a "take-off" to sustained economic growth.[2]

Realizing that this approach would probably aggravate rather than relieve the dislocations caused by social change in the region, the NANA leadership opted for an alternative approach. It is the use of the alternative approach, a "human resources" approach, which identifies NANA as a special case of development.

The concept of human resource development originated with the work of the late Frederick Harbison. He suggested that the development of human and not material resources, should be the dominant strategy. Human resources are the "energies, skills, talent, and knowledge of people which are, or which can or should be, applied to the production of goods or the rendering of useful services." Harbison further commented:

> Human resources—not capital, nor income, nor natural resources— constitute the ultimate basis for the wealth of nations. Capital and natural resources are passive factors of production; human beings are the active agents who accumulate capital, exploit natural resources, build social, political, and economic organizations, and carry forward...development.[3]

Elaborating on Harbison's thesis, this paper proposes that development should progress on a number of dimensions of human resources that are equal in importance to capital formation: stable and productive employment opportunities, health and nutrition services, equitable justice and security systems, access to education that enhances power and self-esteem, and ecologically sound resource use.[4]

This approach receives support from a more recently established school of thought which argues for "another development." Proponents of this school present data showing that Third World nations built on the traditional growth model have achieved little success in reducing disparities of economic and political power, either between these nations and the technologically advanced societies or, domestically, between elites and masses. The data reveal no noticeable reduction in Third World economic dependence on foreign trade, capital and technology—a dependence which fosters a technologically inappropriate and elitist-oriented economic base. Strikingly, the evidence appears to suggest that in fact these negative development conditions have worsened under growth model strategies.[5] Moreover, continued economic dependency also forces greater dependence on the cultural products of the technologically advanced countries. The initial impetus of this cultural dependency was the experience of colonialism; it is currently reflected in Western-inspired economic consumption patterns, educational aspirations, and in popular culture creations by mass media.[6] The "import substitution" that does take place is directed at satisfying the appetites of elites and not at the development of a productive, self-sufficient economic base benefiting the entire society.

As indigenous, culturally different minority groups living in sparsely populated areas of an industralized society, Alaska Native people must contend with unique conditions imposed by the environment and history and by the immediate political economies of Alaska and the United States. Nevertheless, whether it is applied to sovereign Third World nations or to Native corporate efforts in rural Alaska, the human resources approach embodies the development goal of building enduring economic-occupational structures which promote self-sufficiency in the face of pressures toward greater external dependency relationships; for it is technologically appropriate to existing ecological constraints and consonant with evolving cultural forms in the community. Effective exercise of its regional leadership role in the attainment of this goal requires the NANA corporation to attend to imperatives dictating the use of their land and money resources for corporate income-maximization. Yet, very significantly, the NANA corporation's use of the multi-dimensional human resources approach to managed social change has not prohibited reasonable levels of profits in the conventional corporate sense.

ALASKA NATIVE RURAL DEVELOPMENT: SCOPE AND CONTEXT

To appreciate the issues and conditions surrounding economic and educational development activities in the NANA region requires familiarity with important aspects of the Alaska Native development context. I shall start by defining the term "rural" and elaborating "Alaska Native" as a political-legal concept. Then I will describe the prescriptions and imperatives of ANCSA within the evolution of the Alaskan political economy.

Rural Alaska is where approximately 77 percent of the state's Native citizens live, in villages consisting of 25 to 3,000 residents, the greatest number of whom support themselves mainly by mixing subsistence hunting and fishing activities with cash income employment. Moreover, with few exceptions, Native people are the majority population in rural Alaska. As a consequence, they are able to exercise political power consonant with their numbers for purposes of self-determined local development and, as a statewide rural voting bloc, for purposes of greater statewide political leverage in the legislature. In this article, therefore, "rural Alaska" and "Native Alaska" are viewed as synonymous and used interchangeably.

The significance of the term Alaska Native lies in its development as a political-legal concept, and not as a sociological or anthropological concept. Culturally or linguistically, there is no such person as an Alaska Native. There are, however, approximately 60,000 living descendents of the original peoples of Alaska who may be considered to form three ethnic groups: Eskimo, Aleut, and Indian. Yet even these ethnic divisions do not accurately capture the diversity of cultural-linguistic traditions or the varieties of subsistence resource uses practiced within these categorical groups. The different Native culture areas and geographical locations are summarized in Map 11.1. Although the concept Alaska Native glosses the variety of indigenous persons, its popular usage by Natives and non-Natives alike signifies more than mere verbal shorthand. What the concept functionally connotes is the existence of major commonalities in Native political realities and interests which, vis-à-vis the larger non-Native society, transcend cultural and linguistic diversity.

While the term Alaska Native was historically forged as a culturally myopic legal concept, threats to the land rights of all Native groups during the 1950s and 1960s resulted in vigorous efforts by Native activists to politicize the concept. This politicization process served to establish a common political identity for Alaska Natives, which transcended cultural differences and which provided the symbolic and idealogical basis for the statewide political mobilization of Native communities over the issue of Native land claims in the 1960s.[7] After a decade of political organizing and maneuvering at both state and national levels, the Native land claims movement achieved what is perhaps the most comprehensive legal settlement of aboriginal claims to land and its resources yet witnessed—the Alaska Native Claims Settlement Act (ANCSA) of December 18, 1971. It is not unwarranted to suggest that only the national independence gained by Third World peoples goes farther toward the potential achievement of indigenous political, economic, and cultural self-determination.

As with much historically significant legislation in the United States, ANCSA is the product of a complex series of political negotiations worked out among special interest groups: the Alaska Native community represented by the Alaska Federation of Natives, varieties of national viewpoints represented in the U.S. Congress, interest of the state of Alaska, and the specific interest of the multi-national petroleum industry in the legal disposition of Alaska's lands.[8] It is therefore not surprising that the result was a document containing much vague and complex language which, to this day, continues to generate political and legal conflict, both among the different Native corporate organizations established by the Act and between these organizations and the federal and state governments.

The key provisions of ANCSA conveyed to Alaska Natives 40 million acres of land to be selected by them from larger tracts of land withdrawn by the Secretary of the Interior from areas not previously owned by the federal government, the state, or private interests. In addition, just under 1 billion dollars was designated to be paid into the "Alaska Native Fund" according to a specified timeline. Responsibility for payment into the Fund has been almost equally divided between the federal government and the state, with the latter making its payment from a 2 percent royalty levied on exploitable mineral resources, mainly petroleum, produced in Alaska. In return, of course, Alaska

MAP 11.1

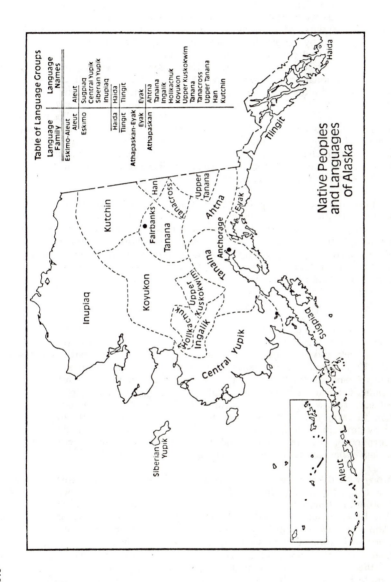

Native Peoples and Languages of Alaska

Table of Language Groups

Language Family		Language Names
Eskimo-Aleut	Aleut	Aleut
	Eskimo	Sugpiaq
		Central Yupik
		Siberian Yupik
		Inupiaq
Haida	Haida	Haida
Tlingit	Tlingit	Tlingit
Athapaskan-Eyak	Eyak	Eyak
	Athapaskan	Ahtna
		Tanaina
		Ingalik
		Holikachuk
		Koyukon
		Upper Kuskokwim
		Tanana
		Tanacross
		Upper Tanana
		Han
		Kutchin

Natives gave up legal right to further pursuit of land claims based on the aboriginal use and occupancy concept.

To implement the Settlement Act, i.e., to receive and distribute both the money and the land among legally entitled Native claimants, twelve Native regional profit-making corporations were established. The geographical boundaries of these corporations approximate those of pre-ANCSA Native associations politically organized to serve areas populated by people sharing similar cultural styles and languages. Within an area served by a regional corporation, there are a number of Native villages which also incorporated as profit corporations. The village corporations, working in collaboration with the parent regional corporations, may select 22 million of the allotted 40 million acres, to which they are granted surface rights, the regional corporation retaining sub-surface rights. Of the remaining 18 million acres, 16 million were to be selected by six regional corporations according to a "land lost" formula, whereby allocations were based on the area claimed, rather than on the population of the claimed area, with the balance designated for special categories. During the five years following enactment, regional corporations had to distribute no less than 10 percent of all funds to shareholders and no less than 45 percent of all funds to village corporations in the respective regions, with the latter amount increasing to 50 percent thereafter.

Regional and village corporations are governed by state regulatory laws of incorporation and operation, which impose controls on the issuance of stock, payment of dividends, financial accountability, the rights and privileges of stockholders, and procedures for the election of members to the board of directors. Additional controls are imposed by the Act itself. After initial distribution to shareholders and village corporations, the regional corporations may use the remainder to engage in all production and investment profit-making activities usually associated with corporate functioning. However, regional corporations can require village corporations to submit plans for approval before they can use ANCSA monies for such activities.

On the other hand, Native corporations are obviously unlike other corporate enterprises, because they have received initial capital and land assets through federal legislation. They also are different in that stock cannot be voluntarily purchased or alienated. Upon enrollment in a Native corporation, the member stockholder receives 100 shares of common stock, the rights to which cannot be sold or transferred, except through inheritance to another Native, until 20 years after the enactment date. This provision cuts two ways. First, it affords the Native corporations twenty years of protection to carry out Native self-directed economic development without fear of takeover by powerful outside interests. However, it also locks shareholders to the fate of the corporation over this time period; that is, unlike conventional corporate shareholders, Native shareholders cannot "vote with their feet" until 1991.[9]

Along with the purpose of accomplishing a just settlement of Native land claims, ANCSA also has the tacit intention of providing Native communities with the instruments (corporate structures) and resources (money and land) for the exercise of power within the larger society. Indeed, as the largest land holders in Alaska outside of the federal and state governments, and as the possessors of extensive liquid assets for the exploitation of investment opportunities, Native corporations currently wield considerable power within the Alaska political economy, both in rural and urban areas. Certainly, from the perspective of the traditional economic growth model, this situation appears quite reasonable. However, the perspective of the human resources approach, with its emphasis on the equitable distribution of "quality of life" benefits based on the principles of self-determination and self-sufficiency, cautions us to look closely at the way in which Native development has taken place. For a closer view, we will examine the NANA region.

THE SPECIAL CASE OF NANA DEVELOPMENT

The implications of NANA as a special case of Alaska Native rural development amid a climate of rapid social change may be recast into two propositions. First, the NANA corporation has resisted the press of the larger political economies for conventional corporate growth and adopted significant elements of the human resources approach to development. Secondly, in pursuit of a comprehensive regional development strategy, people of the NANA region and their leadership have forged links between the production and investment functions of the Native profit corporation, on the one hand, and the manifest human resources-oriented functions of the Native non-profit association and of the regional school district on the other.

In setting forth these two propositions, the intention is to single out from the varieties of Alaska Native development efforts the NANA case as most illustrative of the human resources approach at this time. Certainly what is not intended is a final and complete statement on the nature of Alaska Native development. Nor are these propositions intended to imply an "either/or" premise to undertaking Native development. The very diversity of conditions under which each of the different Native corporate regions must operate axiomatically means there will be a diversity of development approaches. As shall be noted, in fair part the "specialness" of the NANA case may be accounted for by certain special conditions not present in other Native corporate regions. Description of the special case proceeds with a brief physical and social profile of the NANA region, discussion of the salient features of the NANA corporation's human resources approach to development, the purposes and structural characteristics of the regional development strategy, and a summary of issues facing NANA development.

The NANA Region

The Northwest Arctic region of Alaska is the ethno-linguistic homeland of approximately 4,500 Inupiat Eskimo who live in eleven villages, the populations of which range from 2,500 in Kotzebue, the region's trading center, to 60 at the inland river village of Kobuk. The NANA corporate boundaries established under ANCSA include all eleven villages, and comprise an area of 36,000 square miles (see Map 11.2). No road or rail system connects this sparsely populated region with other parts of Alaska, and there is no road or rail system connecting the villages with each other. The region's arctic climate has just three ice-free months a year, light precipitation, and winter temperatures averaging below 0° F along the coast and -20° F inland from the sea.

The traditional economic basis of existence among NANA people is hunting, fishing, and gathering. Today this subsistence life style is augmented substantially by a cash economy consisting mainly of seasonal wage employment and government assistance payments.[10] Surface natural resources most significant to the subsistence economy are caribou and fish, with moose, seals, whales, and small land animals playing subordinate roles. In recent years commercial salmon fishing in Kotzebue Sound has become a major part of the region's cash economy. Subsurface, non-renewable resources having greatest potential for commercial exploitation are copper, lead, zinc, gem quality jade, and silver. Coal deposits and the surface resource of timber offer some promise as regional, energy-producing enterprises, with timber also having possibilities as a regional source of construction material.

MAP 11.2

THE NANA REGION

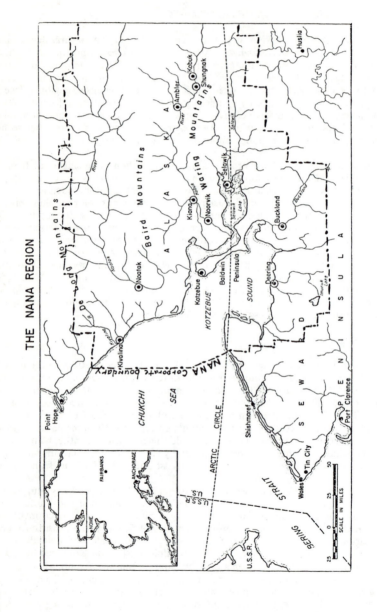

The NANA Regional Profit Corporation

As its share of the cash and land provisions of ANCSA, it is estimated that the NANA corporation will receive approximately $59.5 million and title to 1.9 million acres of both surface and subsurface estates, with rights to an additional 365,000 acres of subsurface estate. At the end of 1980, NANA had received approximately $42 million of its allotted ANCSA cash settlement, with the balance to be received by the end of 1982.[11] When fee simple title to all selected lands is actually conveyed, the NANA corporation and its villages will own the great bulk of the coastline and significant segments of the river systems within their corporate region.

While NANA people must share land ownership with the federal and state governments within their corporate boundaries, their selection of coastal and riverine lands allows control of access, and thus assurance of involvement in future developments on those federal and state lands in the area. Also, the withdrawal of federal lands for additions to national parks, forests, monuments, wildlife refuges, and wild and scenic river systems adds a measure of environmental protection for the region's traditional life style, if the regulations governing these lands allow for continued subsistence use.

The NANA corporation's efforts to manage the impacts of social change through the human resources approach are reflected principally in three orientations: a primary goal of subsistence protection; localization of production and investment functions to promote regional economic self-sufficiency; and a quasi-governmental "constituency" approach to management.

The basic philosophy of the NANA corporate approach is expressed in both the language and original priorities established by its board of directors. Foremost are the tandem goals of "instilling pride and confidence in the shareholders and Natives of the NANA region," and to "preserve and protect the resources essential for continued subsistence living." The emphasis of specific objectives listed under these goals is on sustaining the connection between cultural heritage and land use, fostering local employment opportunities, and developing forms of shareholder participation which encourage solidarity and involvement. An additional objective is that, "Capital must be preserved and developed for the future benefit of shareholders," with the qualifier that, "investment of capital resources should consider increased employment and career development."[12] In the 1979 NANA Annual Report, Robert Newlin, Chairman of the Board of Directors, reaffirmed the essence of the original goals:

> . . . our greatest challenges and our greatest needs, now and for the future, are the protection of our subsistence rights and the preservation of our cultural heritage. The continued use of our natural resources is necessary to our economic and physical well being and to the survival of our culture. Without adequate subsistence rights, we would be dependent on government programs to meet our physical needs. But, government programs cannot meet our cultural needs. Our traditions are centered on subsistence as a way of life; and it is essential that laws and regulations be passed that protect our subsistence life style.[13]

If the written goals and objectives neatly fall within the human resource development framework, the question then becomes: Are the principles they espouse translated into actual production and investment functions? Analysis of NANA corporate activity according to the remaining human resource development orientations suggests an affirmative answer.

Fundamental to the human resources approach is the development of continuing employment opportunities which promote self-sufficiency and which are consonant with ecological constraints and evolving cultural life. In line with this precept, NANA consistently has maintained a balance between profit-making statewide operations and less solvent regional operations—this is, between profitable delocalization of capital resources and non-profitable, but human resource-oriented, localization of capital resources. Data illustrating this balance as of 1979 are contained in Tables 11.1 and 11.2. In addition to the balance between statewide and regional operations, these data are instructive from several other points of the human resource development perspective.

Notably, NANA made an overall profit in 1979 of $635,932, an increase of $151,705 over the previous year. Clearly, then, revenues from the statewide operations are buying time for the regional operations to financially sort themselves out, given the uncertainties characteristic of any developing rural economy. Not only has NANA been able to sustain a localization of capital resources effort and still remain one of the few Native regional corporations showing any consistent profit, but also it continues to take sharp losses in those regional enterprises which it thinks eventually have a chance to decrease the region's dependency on external economic forces and government assistance payments.

Aside from fuel projects, construction enterprises, and tourist-oriented facilities (corporate activities which directly contribute to regional employment opportunities by localizing capital and being labor intensive), perhaps the best example of NANA's concern for long-term self-sufficiency at the expense of short-term profits is its persistent effort in reindeer herding. One of the very first regional operations NANA engaged in was the development of reindeer herding for commercial purposes. From the onset, this enterprise has been both financially and managerially frustrating. Nevertheless, potentially, this activity may significantly decrease the region's dependency on costly external sources of protein. Successful reindeer herding also can mean an alternate internal source of protein to supplement subsistence hunting, particularly in lean years when there is little caribou harvesting. Moreover, NANA, together with Mauneluk Association, recently has taken over the financially troubled Kotzebue Sound Fishermen's Cooperative. The objective is to provide a stable capital base and management system which will make the summer salmon harvest more profitable for local fishermen and allow for development of other kinds of commercial fishing in the region.

The second unique feature of NANA's human resources approach has been the conscious attempt of the leadership to view the corporation as performing predominantly quasi-governmental functions in the region. The essential premise for NANA's localization of capital resources is that regional development is not synonymous with corporate growth; corporate members are to be treated as regional "constituents" in the public service sense as opposed to stockholders in the corporate sense. In the initial formulation of the NANA regional development strategy, John Schaeffer, NANA president, publicly stated that, "three organizations fill in where regional government usually works—NANA, Mauneluk, and the Northwest Arctic School District."[14] Indeed, when added together as a total developing structure, the quasi-governmental functions of the NANA corporation, the human and social service functions of Mauneluk, and the formal education functions of the regional school district conform to the multiplicity of functions regularly associated with legally established regional government, e.g., a borough, county, or parish.

TABLE 11.1
NANA STATEWIDE OPERATIONS

	Revenue	Expenses	Divisional Profit (Loss)
NANA Construction	$12,454,520	$11,749,636	$ 704,884
NANA Environmental Systems	5,837,937	5,711,029	126,908
NANA Oilfield Services	4,207,453	3,716,808	490,645
Purcell Services	3,188,429	2,666,861	521,568
Arctic Utilities	834,815	422,377	412,438
NDC/Commercial Catering	551,496	537,187	14,309
Great Northern Express	80,684	73,487	7,197
NANA Jade Marketing	6,209	15,250	(9,041)
NANA Joint Ventures	185,634	- - -	185,634
	$27,347,177	$24,892,635	$2,454,542

TABLE 11.2
NANA REGIONAL OPERATIONS

	Revenue	Expenses	Divisional Profit (Loss)
Fuel Projects	$ 298,815	$ 300,326	$ (1,511)
Building and Maintenance	20,092	75,801	(55,709)
Drift Inn Apartments	80,480	126,800	(46,320)
Jade Mountain Products	56,421	52,786	3,635
Kiana Hotel	2,218	20,169	(17,951)
Kivalina Housing	2,700	10,308	(7,608)
Nul-Luk-Vik Hotel	1,256,239	1,622,310	(366,071)
Tupik Building Supply	730,703	848,431	(117,728)
Museum of the Arctic	148,914	214,703	(65,789)
Qungniq	10,451	249,839	(239,388)
	$2,607,033	$3,521,473	$(914,440)

Source: NANA Annual Report, 1979.

NANA's "constituency" approach to rural development is further reflected in the continual performance of an "advocacy function," which speaks to both economic and non-economic conditions of the regional community, and to the very nature of its management style. The need for an advocacy role arises mainly from the social effects which state and national political economies have on rural Native life. State and national land use and resource development policies in and around the NANA region, including the Outer Continental Shelf (OCS), have a significant impact on a subsistence-based rural life. Consequently, the NANA shareholder constituency expects its corporate leadership, along with its elected representatives in the formal political domain, to forcefully act in whatever ways will favorably shape social realities in the NANA region. The very first sentence of the NANA President's annual message to shareholders in 1974 is ". . . protecting the natural resources of our region from those who would build roads or regulate resource use to our detriment has occupied many hours of our time."[15]

One prime example of NANA advocacy is the considerable attention it gave in recent years to the Native lobbying effort on the Alaska lands legislation in the U.S. Congress. Assisting the Alaska Federation of Natives on this legislation at the national level became a corporate responsibility involving the expenditure of leader's time and energy. At stake were critical amendments to the original "termination of protection" provisions of ANCSA and legal prescriptions for Native subsistence use of federal lands in Alaska. Final passage of this legislation in a form reflecting statewide Native interests was due in some measure to NANA's unconventional view of itself, and to its capacity to translate this view into broader human resource development dimensions.

The NANA Regional Strategy

The premises of development which form the essence of the NANA regional strategy have been expressed by John Shively, Vice President for Operations of the NANA Development Corporation. He suggests that ". . . the question of development in Alaska needs to be attacked from two perspectives: (1) the relationship between federal, state, and local policy as it relates to development, and (2) the relationship between economic development in Alaska and human resource development and education."[16] Working from these premises, the NANA regional strategy may be defined as the process which systematically organizes the quasi-governmental functions of the region's dominant Native-directed institutions into a single, coordinated effort of social change management. According to the NANA formulation, then, effective management of social change requires regionwide institutional solidarity for the purposes of (1) providing a power base united in its representation of local development policy vis-a-vis the larger political economy (i.e., self-determination), and (2) providing clear direction to interconnected social, economic, and education development processes.

Much of the impetus for institutional solidarity as a mechanism for self-determination comes from continued conflict between Native interests and the land use and resource development policies of the larger political economy. As discussed earlier, the presence of lands owned by non-Natives in and around the NANA corporate region requires constant attention from the NANA leadership. However, another significant impetus derives directly from the historic impacts of many government social and economic development policies on the NANA community. In numerous cases, government-sponsored programs have, at best, achieved no significant results and, at worst, have had the unintended effects of increasing people's dependency upon costly external economic resources—a condition which, paralleling many Third World situations, has strengthened rather than lessened the dependency-poverty syndrome in the NANA region.

The example most often cited by NANA leadership of the dependency-poverty syndrome at work in their region is the government housing program. John Shively shows how the syndrome resulted in a dramatic shift in NANA corporate development policy which, in turn, has considerable implications for the future of the subsistence life style in the NANA region:

NANA's highest land priority has been protection of the subsistence economy. The native culture is tied to the land and the ability to live off it. Because of this NANA shareholders, for the past several years, have rejected corporate participation in mining ventures. This year that position was completely reversed. There was an overwhelming vote, eighty to ninety percent, that declared the people wanted NANA to look at mining. There is no question that mining will not assist the people in retaining a subsistence life style. How can this change be explained? The new policy voted by the native shareholders goes back to a government policy that the rural residents of the area should have new houses. Government personnel declared that people had poor housing; we should do something about it. What they neglected to tie to this observation was that the people have poor housing because they are poor. You don't make them richer because you give them a house with payments and stoves, refrigerators, and oil furnaces which result in higher utility bills. You make them poorer. People see the houses as something desirable, but with increased energy costs they cannot afford to live in them without a job. Thus, mining becomes very important. It probably is the only major development that can take place that will allow people to work in the region they are from.[17]

In order to determine what development policies might be pursued as part of the NANA regional strategy, a comprehensive planning process was undertaken in 1978 and 1979. Mauneluk Association, in cooperation with the Alaska Public Forum, took the issue of development policy to all eleven villages of the NANA region. The purpose of this planning strategy was to identify and develop regional goals and objectives through comprehensive involvement of the constituency. The process consisted of a program of survey research followed by a series of community workshops in all villages. The survey research gathered base-line information on people's attitudes and activities in the areas of subsistence, employment, transportation, housing, and education. Follow-up community workshops were designed to report the survey results to the communities and to initiate village discussions on priorities for regional development policy and cost benefit analyses of such policy priorities.[18]

Within the region the responsibility for coordinating the planning process and administering much of its activities rested with the second institutional driver of the regional development strategy—Mauneluk Association, the regional Native non-profit corporation. In addition to its administrative role in the regional planning strategy, Mauneluk's quasi-governmental functions are manifested in the realm of human resource development. Under federal statutes governing American Indian affairs, Alaska Native regional non-profit organizations are recognized as the functional equivalents of legally constituted lower-48 "tribal organizations," and thus eligible for a variety of federal Indian funds. Moreover, in accord with the 1978 Indian Self-Determination and Educational Assistance Act, Alaska Native non-profit organizations are also eligible to apply for the direct operation of existing federal Indian programs and services historically under the control of such federal agencies as the Indian Health Service and the Bureau of Indian Affairs. As a result of this special legal status and its regionwide Native service domain, Mauneluk currently receives each year millions of dollars in government funds to operate programs in the areas of education, health, social services, and community planning and development. The range and depth of Mauneluk's activities are displayed in Figure 11.1.

The results of Mauneluk's planning survey show a repeated emphasis on "the desire of individuals, families, and villages to pursue both subsistence and cash economy activities." The report further notes that while many of the goals revealed by the study "would apply to most people anywhere in the world—there was one that wouldn't—that is the desire and the need the NANA people express about continuing their traditional subsistence activities." For 90 percent of the people, subsistence is the main source of meat, and 70 percent use subsistence foods "for more than half of all their meals." The data reaffirm the critical notion that subsistence "is far more than pure economic necessity—it is the basis of Inupiat cultural heritage and tradition." Furthermore, the study finds that NANA constituents perceive jobs as "increasingly important to pay for basic goods and services. . . [but] . . . to meet these needs, planning for government programs and development projects must be presented in a manner that allows clear identification of choices and ample time for adequate public involvement."[19]

Finally, in keeping with the concept of self-determination through regionwide institutional solidarity, the report states:

> The NANA people have taken this first step toward creating a regional planning strategy. Government agencies and private entities that seek to develop programs and projects in the region should note that residents continually stressed local control over local developments. When new facilities and services are planned, community support and ability to pay for operation and maintenance costs are critical to success. . . . Taken together, these reports can provide valuable guidance for NANA residents as well as [for] those who will effect change from the outside.[20]

It is significant that funding and support services for this planning strategy resulted from a federal-state-local consortium effort involving the U.S. Department of Housing and Urban Affairs, the Alaska Public Forum, Alaska Department of Community and Regional Affairs, Alaska Department of Transportation and Public Facilities, and, locally, the City of Kotzebue, Mauneluk Association, and the NANA Regional Corporation.

The third institutional force in the regional development strategy is the Northwest Arctic School District (NWASD). In 1975, the Alaska state legislature, in response to public sentiment and emerging Native political power in support of greater local control of education, divided one large State Operated School System (SOS) for the "unorganized borough" of rural Alaska into twenty-one Regional Educational Attendance Areas (REAAs), thereby ending seventy years of centrally controlled territorial and state administration of Native education. As one of the REAAs, the NWASD is governed by a regionally elected school board that employs a superintendent as chief administrator, determines fiscal procedures, and exercises control over the employment of all school district personnel.

In important respects, REAAs have autonomy comparable to that of American school districts generally. But as a recent study has pointed out, they are "extraordinary units of government," not only because of the unique physical and cultural conditions under which they operate, but also because they are neither cities nor boroughs and, consequently, there is no provision for their existence "in either the Alaskan constitution or in statutes defining local and intermediate government." Upon specifying the legal constraints to REAA authority which contribute to their "anomalous

FIGURE 11.1

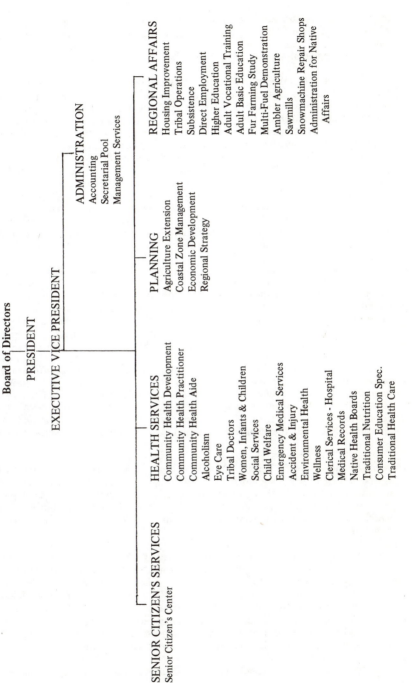

MAUNELUK ASSOCIATION

Board of Directors

PRESIDENT

EXECUTIVE VICE PRESIDENT

ADMINISTRATION
Accounting
Secretarial Pool
Management Services

SENIOR CITIZEN'S SERVICES
Senior Citizen's Center

HEALTH SERVICES
Community Health Development
Community Health Practitioner
Community Health Aide
Alcoholism
Eye Care
Tribal Doctors
Women, Infants & Children
Social Services
Child Welfare
Emergency Medical Services
Accident & Injury
Environmental Health
Wellness
Clerical Services - Hospital
Medical Records
Native Health Boards
Traditional Nutrition
Consumer Education Spec.
Traditional Health Care

PLANNING
Agriculture Extension
Coastal Zone Management
Economic Development
Regional Strategy

REGIONAL AFFAIRS
Housing Improvement
Tribal Operations
Subsistence
Direct Employment
Higher Education
Adult Vocational Training
Adult Basic Education
Fur Farming Study
Multi-Fuel Demonstration
Ambler Agriculture
Sawmills
Snowmachine Repair Shops
Administration for Native
Affairs

nature" and "questionable legal foundation," the study concludes that real control of Native education by Native people remains problematic "because REAAs have less authority than ordinary school districts they may be said to be agencies empowered more to manage than control."[21]

Almost simultaneously with the establishment of the REAAs was another legal event which further changed the nature of Native education in rural Alaska. Although primary school programs and facilities operated by federal and state agencies have long been a standard fixture in rural Native communities, secondary education has not. For the past thirty years, secondary school Native youth have attended school in boarding institutions or at municipal secondary schools in Alaska's urban centers through boarding home programs. In 1976, suit was brought against the State of Alaska (Tobeluk v. Lind) on behalf of a secondary school student from a Central Yupik village in Southwest Alaska. The suit charged that the lack of secondary school programs in the home communities of rural Native students deprived them of equal educational opportunity. Moreover, since the predominantly non-Native communities of Alaska were provided state-funded secondary programs, the issue of racial discrimination was strongly implied. The result was an out-of-court settlement in the form of a consent decree requiring state-funded and maintained secondary programs in approximately 100 Native villages.

In two major ways, then, the NWASD is a structure which has radically changed the nature of formal educational services to the NANA region. Notwithstanding the lingering question about the extent of its authority as an REAA, it is now the institution directly responsible for education in the region. Just six years into the learning process of being a local educational authority, it has also been charged with the implementation of another recent and radical departure from the past: small high school programs for nine of its ten outlying villages. Currently NWASD serves 716 primary school students (grades 1-8) and 703 secondary school students. Its regionwide professional staff of principals and teachers numbers approximately 150; and its central office in Kotzebue consists of superintendency functions along with programs in special education, bilingual/bicultural curriculum development, community education, and media services. It is within this framework that NWASD carries out its role in the NANA regional development strategy: the organization of the factors of formal education in ways that are consistent with the evolving cultural life and employment opportunities of the region.

In more specific terms, NWASD is charged with developing a regional school system which provides students with a sound basic education to serve as a foundation for whatever life style they ultimately choose. Very significantly a major goal arising from the regional planning survey was to "maintain freedom of choice in life style—whether subsistence, cash economy, or both."[22] The survey data strongly reflect this goal:

> NANA residents strongly supported local job training in the employment section. But they show an even higher commitment to the teaching of the basics—math, English, writing, reading, history, etc., when asked "What high school courses would you like your children to study?" More than half the respondents chose that response as compared to fourteen percent for trades, eleven percent for cultural, six percent for domestic/human services, eight percent for office work, and five percent for professional. Seventy-five percent answered that they would attend adult education classes if offered in their community.[23]

Although they are a culturally different minority group living in a remote, sparsely populated area, it appears that NANA constituents want NWASD to offer a strong academic program, but one that is responsive to the cultural and economic opportunity structure of the region. Certainly they perceive a need for a strong cultural heritage component to NANA education, which is reflected in the substantial bilingual/bicultural curriculum development carried out by the school district. But "cultural relevance" is not viewed as an either/or proposition; nor is development—including educational development—perceived according to a linear theory of social change positing traditional culture as the start and urban-industrial culture as the finish with no possibilities in between. What the NANA regional development strategy seems to suggest is a "cross-cultural" approach to education.

One illustration of NWASD's cross-cultural approach to education is its proposal for the establishment of an Institute Arctica which is described as "a cross-cultural leadership development program for rural Alaska youth." What NWASD seeks is a ten-month residential school for selected NANA secondary students that would be outside the typical routines and functions of the formal education system. The leadership program would operate as a self-contained institution with emphases on Inupiat heritage, including language development and subsistence skills; cross-cultural issues in the areas of politics, economics, community organization and communications; and applied leadership skill development for cross-cultural settings. What is informative about this concept is its recognition that (1) the increasingly pluralistic conditions of Native life are placing inordinate demands on Native leadership, because of the simultaneous requirements of being makers and brokers of culture as well as being technically proficient institutional organizers; and (2) by its very nature the formal school system does not easily lend itself to accomplishing extraordinary cross-cultural objectives, particularly when that system's basic rules are beyond NWASD's control and when 95 percent of the district's administrators and teachers are non-Native.

The issue of NANA leadership is not only one of quality but also of quantity—of the numbers of appropriately trained Native people ready to assume high- and middle-level positions within the three dominant regional institutions. Not only are 95 percent of NANA's professional educators non-Native, but also significant numbers of the staff of the NANA Corporation and Mauneluk Association are also non-Native. Indeed, development of a postsecondary trained cadre of Native manpower in a variety of fields is a vital issue of self-determination within the total Alaska Native community.

Another element of the cross-cultural approach is the school district's attempt to expand the scope of educational possibilities, hence different life style opportunities, to NANA people within the region. The formal school system must necessarily concentrate on basic education at the primary and secondary levels, and the organization of other forms of educational opportunity, both academic and vocational, has become one of its quasi-governmental roles.

This expanded role of the school district is shaped directly by the regional strategy in three respects. First, expanding educational opportunity conforms with the expressed goal of maintaining the freedom of choice in life style that has been reported by the planning surveys. Secondly, as the formally prescribed regional educational institution, it logically follows that NWASD should be responsible for the provision of specific training geared to the current and anticipated employment opportunities within the region. As a consequence, a multi-million dollar technical institute is now under construction in Kotzebue which will fall under the administrative domain of NWASD. Thirdly, in accord with the principle of self-determination, it should be the basic unit for the exercise of local control over the entire system of educational services to the region. This last aspect has generated considerable controversy. Taking advantage of an arcane statute governing the original establishment of community colleges by memorandum of agreement between a particular school district and the University of Alaska, NWASD recently sought to take over the state university's fledgling community college in Kotzebue. NWASD argued that the community college's efforts to serve community needs had been unsuccessful and, in fact, the nature of a statewide University mitigated against meeting unique, locally determined rural needs. The other side argued issues of accreditation and the maintenance of quality education. To the present, the institutions on both sides of the controversy have been unable to negotiate a resolution and the college is temporarily closed while the question of control remains open.

In addition to the three dominant institutional managers of the regional development strategy, there is one other critical element. Intimately involved in the entire process is the region's political representation in the state legislature. Using the leverage offered by the "Bush Caucus" and the seniority of its senator, the NANA region has been at the forefront of political action on behalf of the Native community. From the passage of the 1975 REAA legislation to other more recent legislative appropriations to NWASD to manage the Kotzebue community college (which were eventually vetoed by the Governor), the concern for self-determination and local control has been well defended in the larger political domain. However, it bears repeating that the reapportionment of the state legislature following the 1980 census is likely to result in a serious diminishment of this political leverage.

ISSUES IN NANA REGIONAL DEVELOPMENT

Perhaps what is most significant and "special" about the NANA regional development strategy is the basic fact of its existence. The coming together of three emerging but dominant bureaucratic structures, each of which prima facie is chartered to attend to quite different orders of phenomena, into one concerted development strategy— particularly a human resource development strategy—is a rare accomplishment, not only within the Alaska Native community but within the world of development generally. However, what the future holds for NANA's regional human resource development strategy may rest on resolution of two fundamental issues rooted in the dynamics of severe social change.

The first issue has to do with the future of a subsistence-based life style in the face of a regional development policy encouraging mining activities. It will be recalled that the dependency-poverty syndrome has forced a turnabout in NANA policy, from protection against mining to development of the mining industry as the basis for increased employment opportunities. The extractive nature of hard rock mining can portend harsh consequences for the environment and for the social organization of the people who provide its labor supply (if, in fact, the enterprise is labor intensive). This seems definitely the case in those systems where the labor supply is viewed simply as another resource to be extracted. To minimize these conditions will require the NANA community's control over the mining industry, a requirement the NANA leadership certainly has under analysis.

The basis of NANA's power is its corporate ownership of the most likely access routes to and from potential mining sites as well as its potential ownership of some sites. NANA can exercise this power by seeking strong measures of environmental protection and provisions for unique kinds of labor force work schedules which allow adequate time for village subsistence and family life. In short, given the increasing pressures of daily life, and the attractiveness of mining as a stable, within-region employment source,

NANA's movement to a full-fledged mixed economy has been already determined. Now the important issue is the extent to which the NANA regional development strategy can manage further social change through management of its new mixed economy.

The second fundamental issue facing the NANA region is the apparent massive alienation of adolescents and young adults. Despite the eloquence of the regional strategy in rhetoric and structure, the NANA region has one of the highest rates of attempted and accomplished suicides among youth in the Alaska Native community. Closely connected to this social fact is alcohol and drug abuse. More than any other segment of the population, the adolescent and young adult groups appear to be having the greatest difficulty developing a "sense-making function" for dealing with the new social, cultural, and economic pluralism of Native society. Not only does this malaise have tragic consequences in individual and family terms, but the loss of human resource potential to Native institution-building is also of tragic proportion. The results of this apparent alienation can be seen by everybody, and most persons have a theory or notion as to its generic causes. What is much more elusive is a collective solution to a collective problem, i.e., beyond conventional one-on-one treatment, are there strategies available which will inspire changes in the ethos or spirit of a human collectivity such as Native youth? The manifestly human resource-oriented institutions of the NANA region, Mauneluk, and the Northwest Arctic School District, obviously have great concern for this condition as witnessed by their varied programs. But if it may be presumed that this form of social pathology is subject to resolution by big institutions (indeed it may not be), than the question becomes: Can or should any organizational strategy, including the NANA strategy, seek to control the myriad human conditions and social variables thought to be contributing to the pathology? Values as well as pragmatics are very much a part of any discussion or action on this issue.

THE NANA CORPORATE APPROACH: SOME NON-FORMAL EDUCATIONAL CONSEQUENCES

In the discussion outlining the special case features of the NANA regional profit corporation, attention was paid to the quasi-governmental role of the corporation and its "constituency" approach as opposed to a conventional stockholder model to relations with the corporate membership. This constituency approach is reflected in the effort the NANA corporate staff expends on fulfilling an advocacy function on behalf of the constituency in economic and non-economic arenas. This section of the paper is devoted to another part of the NANA operational mode reflecting the constituency approach: the unique structure and functioning of its management style. This aspect of the NANA corporate approach is being singled out here in order to present some thoughts on possible non-formal educational consequences inherent in this management style.

Olsen and Tuck have analyzed ANCSA Native regional corporation management styles according to an open versus closed participatory decision-making model.[24] They find the NANA management style to be the exemplar of the open decision-making type. By this they mean that both the events (i.e., board meetings) and the executive officers of the decision-making process are made more directly accessible to the corporate membership than is the case with other corporations. They observe that in NANA "the pace of development in critical policy areas is controlled by the elders who have direct access to the president and chief executive officer."[25]

Constituency participation in decision-making processes directly affecting their realities is a basic tenet of the human resources approach to development. However, the NANA approach takes this tenet one step further in that the very process of its management style is participatory and encourages "active" rather than "passive" constituency involvement. Structurally, this is accomplished through the unconventional composition of its board of directors. Each village in the region is represented by two members on the board. Additionally, there are at-large members. The result is proportional representation simultaneously of constituent and corporate interests. Interestingly, although NANA is one of the smaller Native regions in terms of shareholder enrollment (4, 900), its twenty-three member board is the largest corporate decision-making body. Furthermore, all board meetings are open to the general membership.

Functionally, active participation of the NANA constituency is promoted in two ways. First, annual shareholder meetings are rotated among the villages of the region. While Kotzebue, the regional center, has logistical advantages as a meeting place, NANA leadership has determined that administrative convenience must give way to the kinds of active constituent involvement which community settings encourage. Secondly, major policy decisions are viewed as a shareholder prerogative, not a board prerogative. For example, the issue of mining as NANA policy was decided by a vote of the shareholders before the fact, and not simply by a vote of the board.

There is, therefore, much more to the open participant style of NANA corporate management than the passive participant aspect of accessibility. Also, the NANA style includes more than forms of passive participation such as principal decision-makers keeping their "finger on the pulse of the community"—a process which can be self-deceiving. The active participation achieved by NANA is based on bringing the decison-making apparatus to the community—by literally forcing it to work in the domain of the community. Critical to this process is active constituent involvement in the first order of decision-making, that is, in the actual framing of the decision-making context itself. Clear examples of this framing process are the planning component of the regional strategy and the issue-specific mode of participation established to deal with the mining issue.

Put another way, the NANA management style may be characterized as an "empowering process," and in this connection it may be seen to have latent, non-formal educational consequences. Operating from the perspective offered by the "another development" school, Kindervatter suggests that non-formal education be viewed as an "empowering process" in and of itself. She defines the concept, empowering, as: "People gaining an understanding of and control over social, economic, and/or political forces in order to improve their standing in society."[26] She states that non-formal education (NFE) is ordinarily thought of in terms of divisions proposed by Coombs, all of which are to be distinguished from the bureaucratically regulated and grade-sequenced formal education system (schooling). Coombs' divisions include "adult education," "continuing education," "farmer or worker training," "accelerated training," "on-the-job training," or "extension services."[27] For Kindervatter, NFE as an empowering process "includes such divisions but with a new focus":

> Rather than promoting only the acquisition of information and skills, NFE as an empowering process emphasizes the utilization of these capabilities for collaborative problem solving . . . NFE as an empowering process is oriented toward influencing socio-economic structures and relationships through group action-taking.[28]

To summarize the relation between the perspectives of "another development" and the role of NFE as a development entity, she stresses:

the need for NFE to enable people to develop skills and capabilities which increase their control over decisions, resources, and structures affecting their lives. . . . In particular, power must be shared more equitably so that all have the opportunity to affect development policy (at least at the local level) and to gain development benefits.[29]

For purposes of the special case presented here, the notion of NFE is stretched beyond the bounds of the divisions outlined by Coombs to include any process, manifest or latent, which has the effect of "empowering" a group of people, as this concept is defined by Kindervatter. The manifest purpose of NANA's open decision-making style is active constituent involvement in the corporation's affairs; the latent or "spinoff" function of this style is the development of modes of participation which, by the very nature of the communications networks and problem-solving processes they encourage, serve to empower the NANA constituency.

This paper can offer no "scientific proof" that in fact the NANA management style is having all the prescribed empowering consequences. But what the relationship between this management style and latent NFE empowering does suggest is a hypothesis: compared to the constituencies of other Native corporate regions, the NANA constituency should measure higher in each of the criteria listed below. Based on the work of the Interamerica Foundation, Kindervatter offers the following as reconstituted, measurable indices of the empowering process:

1. Access: greater opportunities to obtain resources;

2. Leverage: increase in collective bargaining strength;

3. Choices: ability and opportunity to choose amongst options;

4. Status: improved self-image, esteem, and positive sense of cultural identity;

5. Critical Reflection Capability: using experience to accurately assess the potential merits of competing problem-solving options;

6. Legitimation: people's demands considered by officials as just and reasonable;

7. Discipline: self-imposed standards for working productively with others; and

8. Creative Perceptions: a more positive and innovative view of one's relationship to his/her milieu.[30]

Significantly, almost all of these indices have been touched upon, in one form or another, within the broader discussion of NANA as a special case of development. Although certainly not hard evidence, it is also significant that in the larger Alaska Native community, NANA is pointed to as the region displaying the least amount of internecine conflict. Evidence for this observation is the continuity of NANA corporate leadership and staff over the first decade of ANCSA, and the relative ease with which NANA took advantage of the 1976 amendments of ANCSA to accomplish a merger with all of its village corporations excepting the corporation for the town of Kotzebue. This merger, which has pooled the region's resources, both human and material, into more appropriate economies of scale, could not have been accomplished if village people had perceived themselves as giving up power and development benefits as a result. It is further significant that NANA has been one of the few regions to achieve such a merger even though the rationale, albeit an economic rationale, applies as well to most other Native corporate regions. Because of limited resources and technical skills the future of many small village corporations is seriously in doubt. Some villages have merged with other villages or formed a consortium for the contracting of management functions, but there has been no merger with a parent regional corporation as far reaching as that achieved by NANA.

CONCLUSION: SPECIAL CONDITIONS OF THE SPECIAL CASE

From a specific development perspective, this paper has attempted a description of the issues and conditions of Alaska Native rural development and social change, with special attention to one case considered to illustrate this perspective empirically. The anchoring perspective has been the human resources approach to development, which has definable properties that distinguish it from the conventional corporate growth model. The essential feature of the human resources approach is that it places ahead of material resources the development of human resources and the quality-of-life conditions which nurture this development. This essential feature includes development of employment opportunities which promotes self-sufficiency through such policies as: (1) localization of capital resources; (2) import substitution enterprises; (3) labor-intensive economics; (4) uses of technology within ecological constraints; and (5) goal formulation consistent with the evolving cultural life of the community. Also included is the notion that simultaneously with economic growth there must occur development of: education, health services, political participation, and equitable justice and security systems. These are real life social processes and social facts which are intimately interconnected.

From among the twelve different Native corporate regions established by ANCSA, the Northwest Arctic Inupiat region (NANA) has been singled out for analysis as a special case of Native rural development. NANA is a special case because the structures and functions of its development efforts best reflect translation of the human resources approach to current existing strategies. Without doubt, the author of this paper finds NANA's concept of development eloquent, and the methodologies of its implementation to date an extraordinary achievement. However, it must be reiterated that the intent of this special case analysis is not to represent NANA as the right path to Alaska Native development. Such a declaration would be quite specious because, not only is it too early in the history of post-ANCSA Native life for these kinds of interpretive judgments, but also there exist in the NANA region at least four special conditions, any combination of which are not present in many other Native regions and, hence, confound comparison and generalization.

The first of these special conditions is that the NANA region is culturally homogeneous. In precise cultural terms, the region may be divided into five sub-groupings according to differences of dialect, location, and subsistence resource use. But a history built upon a network of social alliances and trading relationships among the eleven villages, together with a common linguistic tradition, has forged an identifiable regional cultural identity and common political interests.

A second condition is the compact configuration of the area embraced by the NANA corporate boundary. It is true that the size of the NANA region compares roughly to that of the state of Illinois. Relative to sizes and shapes of some other Native regions, however, the logistics of communication and transportation in the NANA region are reasonably manageable.

A third significant condition is the fact that the geographic and constituency domains of the three dominant Native-directed institutions in the NANA region are coterminous. Consequently, the coordination and singleness of effort required by the regional development strategy is not confused by either a multiplicity of institutional charters within the region or an overlapping of jurisdictions beyond the corporate boundary.

The fourth special condition is that the corporate membership is firmly village-based. By this is meant that the majority of the voting membership resides within the region and either participates directly in a traditional village-based subsistence life or has strong, immediate ties to this life. As a result, NANA is subject to much less of the urban versus rural, and to the regional perspective versus village perspective conflicts generated by ANCSA implementation provisions.

It remains to be seen if these are necessary and/or sufficient conditions within which to carry out a NANA-styled human resources approach to Native development in Alaska.

NOTES

1. Peter Berger et al., The Homeless Mind: Modernization and Consciousness. New York: Vintage Books, 1973.

2. Walter Rostow, The Stages of Economic Growth: A Non-Communist Manifesto. New York: Cambridge University Press, 1960; and Alex Inkeles and David H. Smith, Becoming Modern: Individual Change in Six Developing Countries. Cambridge, Mass.: Harvard University Press, 1974.

3. Frederick Harbison, Human Resources as the Wealth of Nations. New York: Oxford University Press, 1973.

4. Michael Gaffney, "Economic and Educational Development in Rural Alaska: A Human Resources Approach." In Barnhardt, R. (ed.), Cross-Cultural Issues in Alaskan Education. University of Alaska, Fairbanks, Alaska: Center for Northern Educational Research, 1977.

5. Charles Wilber (ed.), The Politics of Development and Underdevelopment. New York: Random House, 1973; and Marc Nerfin, Another Development: Approaches and Strategies. Uppsala, Sweden: Dag Hammarskjold Foundation, 1977.

6. Martin Carnoy, Education as Cultural Imperialism. New York: David McKay Co., 1974; and Ali Mazrui, "The African University as a Multi-National Corporation: Problems of Penetration and Dependency." Harvard Education Review, Vol. 1, May 1975.

7. Gerald McBeath and Thomas Morehouse, The Dynamics of Alaska Native Self-Government. Lanham, Md.: University Press of America, 1980, pp. 39-53.

8. Mary Clay Berry, The Alaska Pipeline: The Politics of Oil and Native Land Claims. Bloomington, Ind.: Indiana University Press, 1975.

9. Importantly, both dimensions of the 1991 date recently have been amended by the U.S. Congress. The law now reads that after 1991: (a) Native corporations, if the majority of the shareholders agree, have "first option" to buy Native stock, and any stock which actually becomes alienated to non-Natives is not votable; and (b) undeveloped Native lands shall be subject to taxation, not twenty years from December 18, 1971, but from the time of the actual conveyance of land to the corporations by the federal government and, if desired, these lands may be tax sheltered through the concept of a "land bank." (Significantly, as of the end of 1980, only some 16 million of the 40 million acres actually have been legally conveyed.)

156

10.   The data source for this discussion is Mauneluk Association, <u>The NANA Region: Its Resources and Development Potential</u>. Kotzebue, Alaska: 1974.

11.   NANA Corporation, <u>NANA Regional Corporation Annual Report</u>. Kotzebue, Alaska: NANA Corporation, 1979.

12.   John Schaeffer, "NANA Goals and Investment Strategy." Kotzebue, Alaska: Memorandum to the NANA Board of Directors, October 20, 1980.

13.   NANA Corporation, 1979 Annual Report.

14.   Mauneluk Association, The NANA Region.

15.   Ibid.

16.   Frank Darnell, Proceedings Report of an International Seminar on "Education and Local Development in Rural Communities." Sponsored by: National Institute of Education, Education Research and Innovation Project, Organization for Economic Cooperation and Development; Center for Cross-Cultural Studies, University of Alaska, Fairbanks, Alaska: April 1980, pp. 31-32.

17.   Ibid., p. 33.

18.   Mauneluk Association, The NANA Region.

19.   Alaska Public Forum and Mauneluk Association, <u>NANA Regional Strategy, 1979 Report</u>. Juneau, Alaska and Kotzebue, Alaska: 1979.

20.   Ibid., p. 4.

21.   Frank Darnell, "Education Among the Native People of Alaska." <u>Polar Record</u>, Vol. 19, No. 122, 1979, pp. 443-444.

22.   Alaska Public Forum and Mauneluk Association, <u>NANA Regional Strategy</u>, p. 7.

23.   Ibid., p. 11.

24.   Dean Olsen and Bradford Tuck, "The Economic Consequences of ANCSA Implementation." In Commission Study No. 44, Federal-State Land Use Planning Commission for Alaska. Anchorage, Alaska: 1979.

25.   Ibid., p. 46.

26.   Suzanne Kindervatter, <u>Nonformal Education as an Empowering Process</u>. Amherst, Mass.: University of Massachusetts, Center for International Education, 1979.

27.   Ibid., p. 282.

28.   Ibid., pp. 12-13.

29.   Ibid., pp. 61-62.

30.   Ibid., p. 63.

12
The Native Claims Settlement Act and Self-Determination Values in Alaska's Development Process

David Maas

The provisions of the Alaska Native Claims Settlement Act (ANCSA) have been reviewed extensively; however, less attention has been paid the effectiveness of these provisions in achieving the purposes of the legislation.[1] The purpose of this study is first to offer a framework for evaluating the political consequences of ANCSA, and, secondly, to suggest tentatively what effects one might expect given the history of Indian-white relations, the political characteristics of the United States, and the nature of government and society in Alaska.

Ideally, legislation is best evaluated on the basis of what it tries to accomplish. While one could easily argue that ANCSA incorporates numerous environmental, economic, and political objectives, indisputably the Act, along with related efforts, is meant to promote Native self-sufficiency, or what is more commonly termed self-determination. ANCSA then can be viewed as another congressional effort to decentralize power and responsibility, an effort which began with the 1954 federal Housing Act mandating citizen participation, through the anti-poverty legislation of the 1960s, to model cities, neighborhood reorganization, electoral reform, and community-controlled education. However, ANCSA offers a unique opportunity to study the development of decentralization, its strategy and effects, and the efficacy of direct political involvement. This is so first because of the strong constitutional position of Native Americans, second because of statutory support for self-determination, and third because of the nature of the settlement itself.

The analysis that follows will first review, historically and philosophically, decentralized government in the United States. The second section will offer comments and observations on the effects of the Act based on what we have learned about decentralization.

DECENTRALIZATION IN THE UNITED STATES: A FRAMEWORK FOR ANALYSIS

A perennial question in American political history is whether governmental power enhances or inhibits individual freedom.[2] The debate over the ratification of the United States Constitution revolved around this question. Those who wrote the Constitution

Originally presented at the 31st Alaska Science Conference, Anchorage, Alaska, September 17-19, 1980.

argued that individual liberty was best insured through a national government—one guided by those who were most informed, most successful and therefore the most perspicacious and capable. The writers of the Federalist papers and supporters of ratification

> ... marked the first concerted effort on the part of the business and professional class, together with prosperous landowners to arrogate to themselves direction of the nation's affairs. Having already solidified their economic position, the Federalist merchants, lawyers, speculators, bankers and landowners undertook to put into practice the maxim that those who owned the country ought to run it.[3]

For the Federalists the failure of Congress to govern under the Articles of Confederation and the excesses of the French Revolution only seemed to confirm their critical view of man's weaknesses. While the Framers of the Constitution rallied against the Congress of the confederation and its failure to find a dependable source of revenue and to uphold the new nation's international influence, their fundamental criticism was directed to the power of the states and the existence of an imperium in imperio. As Alexander Hamilton argued:

> The great and radical vice in the construction of the existing Confederation is in the principle of legislation for states or governments, in their corporate or collective capacities, and as contradistinguished from the individuals of whom they consist.[4]

There existed no independent basis for national authority, because the power of the central government rested on the individual states, not on national citizenship. National government lacked the capacity to legislate or to coerce, and policies could not be considered publicly, because the states, which ultimately decided whether to accept or reject federal recommendations, would judge each act according to the "conformity of the thing... to their immediate interests or aims; and the momentary conveniences or inconveniences that would attend its adoption."[5] Therefore the Federalists maintained that individual freedom and interest would be better served by a central government—one of independent influence and power.

The Federalists offered a consistent philosophy of national power. Their initial premise was based on the Lockean equation that property equals liberty, and for one to be free, his rights of ownership must be secure. Since it was the propensity of mass democracy and, by extension, (locally-controlled or decentralized) government to invade these rights, liberty was threatened without the union of national authority. Thus, private property was the edifice upon which a strong prosperous unified nation would rest. The Federalists' ideal polity consisted of "a nation [in] which property was beyond the reach of envy, contracts were sacred, the financial obligations of government were strictly honored and the people were immune to the wiles of demagogues."[6]

Antifederalists, in opposition to the national constitution of the Federalists, provided a reasoned defense of state and local authority. Their underlying criticism of the Constitution dealt with the issue of size. They were convinced that republician government required a small area, one in which citizens could best express and intelligently understand their own interests. As Montesquieu argued:

> In a large republic the common good is sacrificed to a thousand considerations; it is subordinated to various exceptions; it depends on accident. In a small

republic, the public good is more strongly felt, better known, and closer to each citizen; abuses are less extensive and consequently less protected.[7]

The act of political association creates a collective will concerned with the common interest. A "common interest" requires a self-sufficient area built on unity, legislative equality, and more important, understanding. Therefore Montesquieu further argued that the constitution of a state should be based on an informed and intelligent public, an arrangement maximized in an immediate small political arena.[8]

> The idea of an uncompounded republic, on an average one thousand miles in length and eight hundred in breadth, and containing six million of white inhabitants all reduced to the same standard of morals, of habits, and of laws, is in itself an absurdity, and contrary to the whole experience of mankind.[9]

Patrick Henry added his concern by asking why people would feel loyalty, or patriotism to a government so distant. He concluded that they would not and therefore only military force could control a large heterogeneous population.

The Antifederalists also had a profound distrust of power and those who exercised it. This suspicion led to a denunciation of the proposed constitution and its provision for a strong national government (particularly the elastic and supremacy clauses and the Constitution's failure to guard against usurpation and tyranny).

> Scruples would be impertinent, arguments would be in vain, checks would be useless, if we were certain our rulers would be good men; but the virtuous government is not instituted; its object is to restrain and punish vice; and all free constitutions are formed with two views—to deter the governed from crime and the governors from tyranny.[10]

Many Antifederalists later became leaders and active supporters of Madison and Jefferson's Republican Party in 1792.[11] However, unlike the Antifederalists, Republicans supported the Constitution and the division of power between the federal and state governments. Republicanism was primarily a defense of local rights and initiative, a position that received most of its support from the work of Thomas Jefferson. Jefferson argued that the linchpin in a republican system of government should be the ward, a local organization designed to control intimate leadership, educate and activate the citizenry, and guide surrounding experience and wisdom. As Jefferson explained in a letter to Joseph Cabell:

> No, my friend, the way to have good and safe government is not to trust it all to one; but to divide it among the many, distributing to every one exactly the functions he is competent to [perform].....Let the National government be entrusted with the defense of the nation, and its foreign and federal relations; the state governments with the civil rights, laws, police administration of what concerns the state generally; the counties with the local concerns of the counties; and each ward direct the interests within itself. It is by dividing and subdividing these republics from the great National one down thru all its subordinates, until it ends in the administration of every man's farm and affairs by himself; by placing under every one what his own eye may superintend, that all will be done for the best.[12]

Given the range of purported differences between Federalists and Republicans it has been appealing, at least within American historiography, to interpret the American past in light of this division. Historians, particularly after the Civil War, felt the development of the U.S. centered on the conflict between national sovereignty and state and local rights. William G. Sumner, Henry C. Lodge, and a few post-war Republicans extolled the virtues of a strong national government while Jacksonian democrats like Martin Van Buren credited Jefferson with vindicating the public spirit.[13] In the twentieth century Hamilton continued to receive support from major groups, particularly the Progressives and the New Nationalists, who were attracted to his ideas of a managed economy.

The more common response to the conflict between national power and local rights was found in two major intellectual works: Claude G. Bower's Jefferson and Hamilton: The Struggle for Democracy and Vernon Parrington's two volume Main Currents in American Thought. Bower viewed the Jefferson/Hamilton struggle as a classic war between democracy and aristocracy,[14] while Parrington felt their philosophic positions offered distinct answers to the major question in post-revolutionary America: "the urgent problem of the form and control of the new political state to be erected; whether it should be the coercive sovereign of the whole, or should share its sovereignty with the several states."[15]

Contemporary scholarship continues to speak in similar dualities: between localism and nationalism, union and disunion, and central planning versus sectional planning. While this controversy may reveal the historian's penchant for using the past to justify the present, and add support to Montaigne's claim that "truth is not indubitably revealed but claimed by conflicting parties," it also serves as a convenient distinction for the interpretation of American political thought.

What emerges from the seventeenth and eighteenth centuries is a reasonably complete picture of the philosophy of decentralized government. First is a strong tradition of local government, a tradition nurtured by a British government that allowed local opposition to appeal the decisions of colonial executives. As one historian explains:

> On any one issue local opposition, frustrated by the actions of a determined executive, could go over the governor's head; turn his flank; get around behind him, by appealing directly to the higher authorities in England, authorities to which the opposition maintained often more permanent and reliable channels of communication than the governors.[16]

The Articles of Confederation represented a vindication of local initiative and a philosophical defense of the Declaration of Independence. Historically, the Articles have been judged a failure; but this judgment is made by supporters of the 1789 Constitution, not by the advocates of decentralized power. The Articles supported two important ideas: state's rights and the desirability of small political units of government. As the Articles make clear:

> Each State retains its sovereignty, freedom and independence, and every power, jurisdiction and right which is not by this confederation expressly delegated to the U.S. in Congress assembled.

And to insure against legislative unrepresentativeness, the Articles provided that "no person shall be capable of being a delegate for more than three years in any term of six years."[17]

> Town meetings are to liberty what primary schools are to science; they bring it within the people's reach, they teach men how to use and how to enjoy it. A nation may establish a free government, but without municipal institutions it cannot have the spirit of liberty.[18]

Thus, through self-determination and association people learn to adapt to a common purpose, develop a sense of public virtue and prevent the growth of both national despotism and uniformity.

Madison treated similar ideas in Federalist terms: factionalism and local interests were to check national power and collective tyranny. "Extend the sphere and you take in a greater variety of parties and interests; you make it less probable that a majority of the whole will have a common motive to invade the rights of other citizens."[19] Madison's support of diversity and division would also extend to the American theory of federalism, in which power would be divided between a national government, which would deal with matters of general public policy, and states which would be more concerned with parochial objectives. Thus, federalism would inhibit concerted action against the central government because of the plethora of state interests.

A third aspect of American decentralism is an inordinate fear of the state. Although the English felt liberty was best preserved through a constitutional mix between the Crown, the Commons, and the House of Lords, Americans defined liberty in terms of the absence of power, and sought to limit its effects. National government was at best to be a referee and restrained by state power. To this sentiment Hamilton reported that individual freedom required general citizenship (not just a state or particular relationship), a "strict and indissoluble Union," and a "consolidated system," in which the states would be subordinate. However, it was James Madison who more clearly represented the Framer's view of the jurisdiction of government: one which is enumerated "and leaves to the several states a residuary and inviolable sovereignty over all other objects."[20]

Finally, arguments for local control are closely linked to the American interest in private property. This interest in property explains the paradoxical fact that the primary defense of decentralized liberty came from the South, an area developed through the institution of chattel slavery. Slaves represented a substantial investment, and Southerners felt threatened by the mercantilism of Hamilton. As one historian comments:

> Jefferson and his followers had seen the unhappy effects of British governmental interference in American affairs and they regarded Hamilton's system of state economic activity. . . as merely a continuation at home of English economic ideas. Hamilton had set the government to helping the capitalist at the expense of the agrarians. The Jeffersonian response was not to call for a government that would help the agrarians at the expense of the capitalist, but simply for one that would let things alone.[21]

This historical and philosophical review suggests numerous expectations as to what the effects of decentralization should be. Local initiative and control is justified in terms of individual rights, (the property ownership each has in his own liberty), the importance of private influence, defense of individual liberty, and distrust of national government. Offered as propositions, these aspects of decentralization would include:

Proposition I

Decentralization will lead to more responsible and responsive government, because the people involved will better understand their own conditions, interests and needs. Thus government decisions will be more informed and applicable to the conditions in which most people live and logically more effective. One then avoids the "mobilization of bias" associated with political pluralism and the distance and irresponsibility of more centralized bureaucratic rule.[23]

Proposition II

Based on John Dewey's idea that man can only gain knowledge of the world by acting in it, decentralization results in more civic activity and the development of community organizations that will allow for local discussion, politics and protection. Correlatively, such efforts will lead to increased participation and, mutatis mutandis, a more democratic system and a more democratic citizen. Despotism may encourage moral and political passivity, but participation develops a sense of efficacy and individual control over one's life. Intellectual and moral excellence are the result of effort and activity, not resignation and dependence. If people develop an ability to struggle to understand the political process, and to develop a sense of power, they insure their independence and avoid the necessity of relying on others and the possibility of exclusiveness. By participating directly, particularly at the local level, one not only learns the meaning of democracy, but learns to express and organize the unique interests of his own community.

Proposition III

Decentralization also serves an educational function in that it encourages an informed citizenry, the recognition of a wider society and a feeling of shared interest, respect, tolerance and understanding—the foundations of a meaningful self-government. Thus decentralization not only offers a defense against others, but also a guard against unbridled individualism, a condition that could only lead to competition, selfishness, and a disregard for the commonweal—which are poor conditions for the growth of a democratic spirit. Through associational activity one learns to adapt to a common purpose.

Proposition IV

Because decentralization promotes a "public-regarding ethos," it also leads to a more equitable allocation of economic resources, for individuals are forced to consider policies agreeable to others and not just ones that are personally advantageous. If all participate, then the costs of benefits will be shared by all. Participation leads to economic equity for the same reasons that it leads to political equity. The individual develops a concern for the economic welfare of all, realizing that to achieve the common interest it is essential that private efforts be coordinated and on occasion, subordinated to efforts concerning others.

One would also expect economic efficiency to increase because leaders would know best where to invest resources, an argument that parallels the idea that those closest to the community are most aware of its potential, it wants, and its abilities. Economic production might increase as well, because given the opportunity to make independent decisions and actually affect the whole community one will work with more enthusiasm and initiative.[24]

Supporters of decentralization argue then that the reorganization of power can offer considerable advantages both to the community in terms of economic, political and individual development, and to the central authorities because their decisions will be more informed, and perhaps more acceptable. What remains is to assess the empirical validity of these propositions, an assessment that will be based on an analysis of the Alaska Native Claims Settlement Act.

THE ALASKA NATIVE CLAIMS SETTLEMENT ACT: SOME PRELIMINARY OBSERVATIONS

At first glance, the political and economic position of the Alaska Native is impressive. He has achieved a considerable monetary settlement. He owns (or soon will as land is conveyed by the Bureau of Land Management) more land than the entire Native American community, and he is supported by an impressive smorgasbord of government services and programs guided by a philosophy of self-determination supported by Congress. There is the Indian Education Act (1972), the Indian Self-Determination and Education Assistance Act, the Indian Health Improvement Act, and federal support for subsistence activities in the Marine Mammal Protection Act, the Endangered Species Act, and the Walrus Protection Act, all of which protect Native cultural activities and support Native American self-determination. The courts have acknowledged the necessity of Native involvement in decisions which affect them, and there exist numerous Native organizations, including village and regional profit corporations and non-profit regional corporations which contract for national, state and BIA programs. There are also Indian Reorganization Act (IRA) federal corporations, and two important statewide organizations (the Alaska Federation of Natives and the Alaska Native Foundation) which provide support for research and a continuous lobbying effort.

There are, however, a number of important questions that are raised by the nature of the settlement, questions that should serve as a basis for evaluation and study.

1. What are the degree and amount of power and opportunity that have been delegated by ANCSA? In response, one could imagine a continuum, the divisions of which rest on the opportunities a community has to influence the decision-making proce process.

CONTINUUM OF INFLUENCE

Administrative Decentralization   low community
                                                                          influence
Voting on government programs

Consultation regarding community programs

Advisory role in program administration

Delegation of power to community agencies

Administrative control of programs

Community Control

Community election of program officials

Authority to make and fund budgets   high community
    for programs   influence

Activities such as voting or providing information require minimal effort and therefore involve little influence. However, participation in the development of programs or formulation of a budget involve important decisions about services and the distribution of resources. Distinctions between government decentralization and the transfer of power to communities (community control) are important, because they reveal the differences between delegation and control. For example, Alaska regional non-profit corporations are the result of federal efforts to decentralize services and administrative duties. Although they may have some latitude in the selection of services, non-profit corporations are also required to meet organizational and policy criteria established by the federal government. Under such an arrangement authority is delegated from the top down; objectives and performance guidelines are set by the central agency and, ultimately, success is based on conformity to the needs of the higher organizations, not the interests of those being served. In contrast an "independent" community's authority is derived from below, i.e., the electorate, objectives are locally inspired, success is based on local opinion, and the selection of staff and the definition of needs are the products of the local political and administrative process. Thus, to properly assess the degree of political authority of Alaska Natives, one would have to consider the powers and capabilities of their various organizations, such as ANCSA corporations, regional non-profit corporations, city and borough councils, individually and collectively. One would also have to understand the role of the Secretary of the Interior, the actions of the BIA and the non-profit corporations in the contractual control over health and educational services, and the relationships that exist between local units of government and their more central sponsors, e.g., Congress and the state legislature.

2. To what extent does the goal of economic development conflict with that of Native self-determination? Congress is committed to the economic development of the Native community, and at the same time is supportive of the idea of self-determination. Conceivably, the quest for both may be mutually exclusive. Native dependence on unknown markets, problems of leadership and organization, a tendency toward political centralization, the division between traditional and modern leaders, and the uneven impact of change—are all attendant effects of economic growth. Collectively they also are a challenge to the independence and formation of consensus in a community. The modernization of rural Alaska raises a sequence of dilemmas.

a. Social and economic change results in a society that is at once more sharply differentiated, complex, fragmented, and externally oriented.

b. Because society is more fragmented it requires a government that is able to reconcile numerous and often opposed interests.

c. However, increased political control (or self-determination) is problematical given the influence of outside interests, rapid change, federal domination, community factionalism and conflict, jurisdictional confusion, and the scarcity of indigenous skill and capability.

3. What is really meant by the term self-determination when applied to communities in a nation? This is perhaps the most difficult question because it requires an explanation of what Native Americans mean by self-determination. Does it imply absolute cultural freedom and community autonomy, or does it imply local authority within certain constitutional and congressional guidelines?

Self-determination may be defined as the right of a people "to constitute an independent state and determine its own government for itself."[25] As defined, it is not clear what the limits of self-government for Alaska's Native people are. Does self-government mean the right to a regional profit or non-profit corporation? a village corporation? an IRA or traditional council? a second class city council or, at least in one case, a home rule borough? This is a perplexing problem in Alaska because of the absence of tribal government recognized by consensus; nor is there agreement as to which government is best equipped to deal with existing problems.

Paradoxically, self-determination may not even mean independence. Historically, smaller powers depend on larger ones for their protection and prosperity. Thus Natives are confronted with a legal tradition that offers independence, as seen in, Worcester, Cherokee Nation v. Georgia, U.S. v. Kagama, etc., and an economic future which seriously challenges the possibility of independence.

4.   To what extent does decentralization require full and active participation of all? Many applaud ANCSA and related congressional legislation because of their support for decentralization and, by extension, democracy and participation. According to the 1971 Act, "the settlement should be accomplished rapidly, with certainty, in conformity with the real economic and social needs of Natives, . . . with maximum participation by Natives in decisions affecting their rights and property."[26] However, the movement to achieve a settlement was not popularly inspired; instead it was led by a select small group of skillful leaders with tenuous ties to tradition or local villages. What then are the effects of an Act for which there was little general demand and even less general understanding?

The decentralization of government responsibilities may have the untoward effect of discouraging participation and encouraging local pockets of resistance, reinforced by kinship and ethnic loyalty. The fragmentation of policy may create a situation which reinforces existing privilege and helps the interests of a few at the expense of most. Thus decentralization may result in the reinforcement of power and privilege, not its dispersion.

In a fragmented private world the word political may lose its meaning and democracy may be inconceivable. As one author argues:

Political responsibility has meaning only in terms of a general constituency, and no multiplication of fragmentrary constituencies will provide a substitute. Similarly, to contend that individual participation can be satisfied in a political way within the confines of non-political groups is to deprive citizenship of its meaning and to render political loyalty impossible. When used in a political sense, citizenship and loyalty have meaning only in reference to a general order.[27]

Have ANCSA and related decentralization efforts produced a more active citizenry, a citizenry that is more interested and tolerant? Recent studies indicate that there has been no significant increase in Native political participation. However, a satisfactory answer to this question would require an understanding of who makes decisions about Native affairs in Alaska, and who expresses interest in political and organizational involvement, a study that begs for completion.

5.   Has ANCSA made government programs more responsive to the needs of Alaska Natives? Our final question deals with the effect of decentralization and participation on the responsiveness of government and logically the distribution of resources. If people influence public policy, then we would expect government to meet their demands and thereby promote a degree of social and economic equality. Evaluation of

such effects would first be based on demonstrable changes in agency-client relationships, program services (expenditure and direction) and economic development. To understand the effects of ANCSA in this area, we require further study of the attitudes and feelings of the Alaska Natives.

SUMMARY

It is not enough to talk about the legal prerogatives of Native Americans, the level of government activity, or the importance of subsistence and land to a distinctive way of life; what is also needed is an evaluation of what specific changes have occurred. While offering no conclusions, this paper has raised a number of observations and questions that might serve as prolegomena to future research and to a constructive political analysis of recent public and private efforts to assist the Alaska Native.

NOTES

1. In conducting research on the political effects of the Alaska Native Claims Settlement Act (ANCSA) one is initially impressed with the wealth of written material. There are the legislative records of the Congressional Committees on Interior and Insular Affairs, and of the Conference Committee, the journalistic reviews of the struggle to reach a settlement and of events since 1971, numerous legal analyses of the Act and, finally, the records and reports of the Native organizations themselves. Yet one is also confronted with the dearth of work which evaluates the results of the Act. The only expections remain the 2(c) Report and 1979 summary published by the Federal-State Land Use Planning Commission for Alaska, the baseline studies for the Alaska OCS studies program, and a few financial and legal articles of more limited scope.

2. This duality has guided many important portrayals of American political culture including Herbert Croly's The Promise of American Politics and Vernon Parrington's Main Currents in American Thought.

3. John C. Miller, The Federalist Era. 1789-1801. New York: Harper and Brothers, 1960, p. 109.

4. A. Hamilton, J. Jay, J. Madison, The Federalist Papers, ed. by C. Rossiter. New York: New American Library, 1969, p. 108.

5. Ibid., p. 111.

6. J.C. Miller, "Hamilton: Democracy & Monarchy." In Jacob E. Cooke (ed.) Alexander Hamilton: A Profile. New York: Hill & Wang, 1962, p. 162.

7. Baron de Montesquieu, L'Esprit des lois. Volume I. Book VIII. Paris, 1961, p. 131.

8. For the development of Montesquieu's reasoning see J.J. Rousseau, The Social Contract. Book II.

9. The Agrippa Letters in Paul Leicester Ford's Essays on the Constitution of the United States. Brooklyn: Historical Printing Co., 1882, p. 65. Quoted in C. Kenyon (ed.) The Anti-Federalist. Indianapolis, Ind.: Bobbs-Merril Publishing Co., 1966, p. XXXIX.

10. Jonathan Elliot, The Debates in the Several State Conventions as Recommended by the General Convention at Philadelphia in 1787. Five Volumes. Philadelphia, Penn.: J.B. Lippincott. Second Edition, 1896, quoted in C. Kenyon's The Anti-Federalist, pp. IXIII to IXIV.

11. However there are exceptions. Patrick Henry and Richard Lee later supported the national economic policies of Hamilton; and Rhode Island, opposed to the Constitution in 1787 became a Federalist ally in the 19th century.

12. Letter to Joseph Cabell (Monticello, February 2, 1816) quoted in Adrienne

Koch, The Philosophy of Thomas Jefferson. Gloucester, Mass.: Peter Smith, 1957, p. 163.

13.   See Willaim Graham Sumner's Alexander Hamilton. New York:1890 and H.C. Lodge's Alexander Hamilton, Boston: 1899.

14.   Claude G. Bower, Jefferson and Hamilton: The Struggle for Democracy. Boston: Houghton Mifflin, 1925.

15.   Vernon Parrington, Main Currents in American Thought. New York: Harcourt Brace & Co., 1927. Volume I. The Colonial Mind, p. 267.

16.   Bernard Bailyn, The Origins of American Politics. New York: Vintage Books, 1967, p. 91.

17.   Articles of Confederation. See also Merril Jensen, The Articles of Confederation. Madison, WI: University of Wisconsin Press, 1962.

18.   Alexis de Tocqueville, Democracy in America. ed. by J.P. Mayer & M. Lerner. New York: Harper & Row, 1966, Volume I.

19.   James Madison, "# 10." In The Federalist Papers, p. 81.

20.   James Madison, "# 39." In the Federalist Papers, p. 245.

21.   Richard Hofstader, The American Political Tradition. New York: Vintage Books, 1948, p. 48. It was John Taylor who gave a more complete intellectual apology of the agriculture order. He saw the benefits of Hamilton's policies accruing only to a few moneyed interests who lived off the work of the many; a development that was logically inconsistent with the representative democracy—a government which, by definition, represents the interests of the majority, that is, the American farmer.

22.   Virginia Magazine of History & Biography (XLVI), 1938, quoted in Miller's, The Federalist Era.

23.   J.S. Miller, Collected Works. J. Rubon ed. Toronto, Canada: University of Toronto Press, 1965, p. 792. Quoted in Carole Puteman, Participation & Democratic Theory. Cambridge, Mass: Cambridge University Press, 1970, p. 25.

24.   G.D.H. Cole develops a similar argument in Self-Government in Industry. London: G. Bell's Sons, 1919. And Chaos & Order in Industry. London: Meth en, 1920.

25.   Samuel P. Huntington, Political Order in Changing Societies. New Haven, Conn.: Yale University Press, 1968, p. 9.

26.   United States, Public Law 92-203, 92nd Congress, H.R. 10367, Alaska Native Claims Act, Sec. 2(b), December 18, 1971.

27.   Sheldon Wolin, Politics and Vision. Boston, Mass.: Little Brown and Co., 1960, p. 433.   •

13
Subsistence in Alaska: A Look at the Issue over Time

William Schneider

Subsistence: the very word conjures up an array of meanings and connotations that defy the best efforts at definition and understanding. We speak freely of subsistence activities, subsistence values, subsistence resources, subsistence issues and subsisters, but when we are pressed to explain what each of these includes, we fall hopelessly into disagreement. Most attempts at definition begin with the activities. We say that subsistence is hunting, fishing and gathering, but many people would also add trapping and a few would add reindeer herding. For some cultural groups, subsistence activities are incorporated into a world view basic to each member's identity. However, what about newcomers who are trying to establish such an identity or those who were raised in a subsistence tradition and are now reaching out in different directions? When does subsistence become a way of life? When does it cease to be a way of life?

Attempts to define subsistence characteristically fail to account for the historical record which reflects the important survival values of flexibility, innovation, and change. Survival in a subsistence economy depends upon a blend of traditionally proven patterns and an opportunistic eye for improving chances in the hunt. This has always been the case even though the modern Euro-American concept of subsistence emphasizes the traditional patterns and fails to appreciate the adaptive dimensions.

Recent approaches to describing subsistence[1] attempt to account for various adaptations by emphasizing commonly occurring variables and the range of patterns within each. For instance, the level of technology employed in subsistence is a commonly recognized variable, characterized at one extreme by mechanized transport like airplanes and at the other extreme by the absence of mechanized transport. Other variables such as tradition of use, dependency on the resources, and average time spent at subsistence during the year might be added, creating a configuration of variables, each characterized by gradations along a continuim. When applied over time, this approach graphically describes variations and changes in individual and collective patterns. Unfortunately, there is no agreement on the variables to be included.

Defining or describing subsistence is an issue for researchers and managers, but not for most of the people who are living on the land. For them, the issues are: 1) access to resources, 2) competition for scarce resources, 3) acquiring and maintaining the means with which to participate in subsistence, and 4) maintaining a way of life that is important to them.

THE NATURE OF THE SUBSISTENCE ISSUE

We will discuss these four dimensions of the subsistence issue from the perspective of those who live on the land, and then consider briefly changes in the rural-urban pattern of subsistence. First, subsistence is based upon the availability of fish and game in sufficient numbers to meet people's needs. Shortages of certain fish and game resources occur from time to time, and the managing agencies often respond by limiting the harvest. For example, the Alaska Department of Fish and Game manages game resources on a sustained yield basis. By issuing permits, setting seasons, bag limits and means of hunting, it controls the number of resources taken. When a particular resource is depleted (often a point of contention), restrictions are imposed, and some people will get less than they want—or none at all. They then may make subsistence an issue, claiming that the species is important to their livelihood, or that others are being given preferential access to resources which they believe belong to everyone.

Under the state subsistence law,[2] in times of resource scarcity, preferential use is given to subsistence users: to those persons who demonstrate customary and direct dependence on the resource, local residency, and lack of available alternative resources. Sports hunters, urban based hunters, and fishermen are worried that they may be restricted at these times. These fears are justified, for shortages are most likely to occur near large populations centers. Moreover, most urban hunters have not customarily or directly depended on subsistence resources, and alternative resources are more readily available to them than to rural hunters. Some urban hunters may qualify for preferential treatment in times of resource shortages, but they will be a minority. Tensions between users are further strained by regulations in certain areas where sports hunting has been banned and hunting is limited to local residents. This has created rifts between users and has forced big game guides to change areas, activities, and sources of income.

Second, rural Alaskans feel imposed upon by urban hunters and fishermen who drive, boat, or fly to areas rural residents depend upon for fish and game. The combination of air, road, and river access enables an urban hunter to haul large quantitites of meat; airplanes alone permit nearly unlimited access to hunting areas and can be used for spotting game over many miles. The problem of "outside" hunters with mechanized transport becomes particularly acute when the local hunters have been unsuccessful and are in immediate need.

Third, the means of acquiring resources have changed. Cash has become an increasingly important part of subsistence, and no one is living completely off the land nor is anyone totally self-reliant. Cash has played an integral part in subsistence for many years, but dependence on cash for fuel and equipment makes it necessary to generate large sums in order simply to get out on the land.[3] Some subsistence users realize the growing dilemmas and talk about using dogs instead of snowmachines. Although few people find it feasible to give up outboard motors, some are using closer fishing sites or are limiting the number of trips to check nets in order to save gasoline.

Reports of high income levels by trappers in a particular year lead some observers to conclude that they are no longer subsisting—or that trapping is not a subsistence activity. However, others point to the long history of trapping in Alaska and to its integration with other subsistence activities.[4]

At the village level, the increased need for cash has recently become an issue. The issue is prompted in part by greater exposure to urban hunters who rely on high technology to travel to hunting and fishing areas, and by the realization of some rural users that it is simply costing them more to live. Urban hunters point to dependency of rural Alaskans on store-bought goods and claim that for this reason economics should not be a factor in deciding who can hunt and fish. Cash, therefore, has become an issue, but the conclusions that are reached differ according to the interest group.

Fourth, subsistence for many is part of a total way of life that has cultural, social, and economic meanings. For many individuals and cultural groups, subsistence is an integral part of their identity and world view. Without subsistence, they would have to redefine their lives, their concepts of achievement, and their very concepts of homeland.

The identification with particular areas, and the learning of values over time through participating in common activities result in a flexible but coherent and meaningful way of life. This is why Alaska's Native groups have such an important stake in the future of subsistence. Without it, many would have to develop substitutes for the value of living together out on the land, a value that has its roots in generations of shared experiences in hunting. Their way of life is at stake each time a decision is made on subsistence.

The adaptation of some non-Natives to certain Native cultural patterns has occurred for generations; but it receives little attention, because few non-Natives stay on the land in any one area. A small but very significant number of non-Natives live in rural Alaska all their lives. Some live in villages and travel out to subsistence areas; others have little if any contact with villages and as a result are not well understood by researchers or agency officials. Living in remote locations, they are removed from the communication networks necessary for involvement in political associations and advocacy groups that would represent their interests. They have consciously chosen to live a particular way, in large part because they have rejected what they would term the "rat race." Subsistence is an issue for them, because they know what they have given up to live on the land, and they appreciate what they have gained.

Subsistence issues are often couched in terms of rural-urban differences, which obscures the complex changes that are occurring. Until a few years ago, except for school teachers, missionaries, and traders, all who lived in rural Alaska villages engaged in and depended upon some form of subsistence. Most villagers did not have ready access to store-bought goods, and imported fuels played a small part in their lives. Subsistence was a way of life and a physical necessity. To varying degrees and with the exception of fuel, this picture still holds. However, in regional centers such as Bethel, Kotzebue, and Barrow, wage labor opportunities are now more prevalent; and there is a growing non-Native work force that is brought in to do technical work. These workers differ from previous "newcomers" in that they are paid for a wide range of skills. Their jobs, such as those of accountants, construction foremen, plumbers, and planners are new in rural Alaska. The subsistence way of life is not critical to their lives and their interest in hunting and fishing varies by individual. New job opportunities have developed for Natives too, particularly in the regional centers. Unlike the non-Natives, many of them are still committed to subsistence activities and to eating wild game. The rural villages, in contrast to the regional centers, have few job opportunities, and everyone participates in some form of subsistence—if only, to mention an extreme case, by eating the products of another's hunt.

Subsistence patterns of urban residents are complicated and, at best, poorly understood. Some Natives live in the city for only part of the year in order to earn money, to attend school, to receive medical assistance, or to visit with relatives, returning to rural areas for seasonal activities or for extended visits. Their roots are in rural villages. Some elders move to the city in winter where living is easier, but return to the village for summer activities. The extent of this movement is not known.

A second group of urban subsistence users is based permanently in the city and returns to villages only to take part in activities such as summer fishing or fall hunting. To varying degrees they depend upon their success in these activities. A third group of urban subsistence users is new to the region and the state. There is no historical record of these patterns, but the increased growth of urban centers has certainly had an important impact on the number of people seeking subsistence options.

Midway between rural and subsistence users are populations in the larger communities along the road systems. With the growth of highways, once rural or semi-rural communities like Nenana, Talkeetna, Delta and Glennallen have increased in size. Yet some residents of these communities have long-standing traditions of subsistence use.

DEVELOPMENT OF THE SUBSISTENCE ISSUE

Confrontation Over Land and Water

The subsistence issue is integrally tied to the history of competing claims for land and resources. Competing land uses affect the habitats of fish and game, which, in turn, affect adversely the chances for successful subsistence activities.

Just prior to the turn of the century, the salmon rich streams of Alaska drew the attention of large commercial fishing interests who came in increasing numbers to develop the fisheries for commercial purposes. One of the earliest conflicts was caused by the blocking of streams. This enabled companies to harvest large numbers of fish, but the action created severe hardship for the Native fishermen who lived upstream and who depended upon salmon runs for their food. In 1895, Karluk River on Kodiak Island was blocked by commercial fishermen. This action was reported by an agent of the United States Treasury Department who described the adverse effects on Native subsistence fishermen.[5]

The blocking of fish streams and other encroachments of outsiders on Native subsistence in southeast Alaska were the subject of discussion in a meeting at the Juneau Public School House, on December 14, 1898. Territorial Governor John Brady invited Native leaders from Southeast to come and voice their grievances. They told how their salmon streams had been blocked, how gold mining operations on Douglas Island interfered with traditionally used fishing areas, and how the land where they hunted and trapped had been taken. One speaker described these areas succintly as "places where we used to make food."[6]

The Klondike Gold Rush and the growth of canneries had brought many people to southeast Alaska, but there were no means of regulating these newcomers and the indigenous population suffered. The governor was sympathetic to the Natives and aware of the need for regulation, but the means of enforcement were simply not present. For instance, there was a fish inspector but as the Governor had noted in the Annual Reports, this inspector had no boat in which to make inspections.[7]

The dialogue between the Native leaders and Governor Brady is instructive, because it reflects the ways that subsistence issues were viewed as the time. After the Indian chiefs concluded their remarks, the Governor addressed them saying that their rights were protected under the law of 1884 (the Organic Act). However, he went on to state that they were "entertaining wrong notions of how much land they own."[8] He presented two options for the protection of their property rights. Indians could settle down, fence their land, improve it, and build houses. If these conditions were met, then officials would be bound to protect Native rights.[9] Alternatively, Indians could establish a reservation on an island. These options were drawn from a Western legal framework of land law that was irrelevant to Native land use patterns. The options were inconsistent with Native subsistence patterns, but the Governor believed they were generous and perhaps more importantly, that under the strained conditions of the times they provided the only chance for Natives to maintain property rights. The meeting failed to resolve conflicts between commercial and subsistence interests. The gathering was a prelude to many others where subsistence users were forced to justify their way of life against the onslaught of competing interests better understood and accommodated under Western law.

Conflicts over land claims were the reason for the first Tanana Chiefs Conference in 1945, a gathering in which Athabascan leaders from the Fairbanks area met with former Judge James Wickersham, then Alaska's Delegate to Congress.[10] Well meaning officials realized that the planned railroad to Fairbanks would bring in newcomers and that the Native concerns over encroachment on their lands should be addressed. The Native leaders, for their part, voiced concern that their hunting and fishing over large areas would be restricted. The judge listened to their testimony and suggested that they apply for homesteads or ask for a reservation. What is left of the record (a transcript from Wickersham's file titled "Proceedings of a Council"[11]), shows similarities in outline to the Juneau School House meeting in southeast Alaska. The chiefs and the judge expressed very different viewpoints. The judge suggested what he thought was the best legal means of protecting land. The Indians declined to accept a compromise which would change their way of life and restrict them to small parcels. Chief Ivan of Crossjacket (Coskaket) stated:

> We don't want to go on a reservation, but wish to stay perfectly free just as we are now, and go about just the same as now, and believe that a reservation will not be a benefit to us.[12]

Changes in Native subsistence patterns were also influenced by other types of pressure. The development of schools and missions in villages attracted families who had been living in isolated seasonal camps. To make a livelihood, however, the men were obliged to return to traditional areas to hunt, to trap, or to herd reindeer.[13] These dual tensions—to consolidate into villages and to subsist on the land—drove a deep wedge into the family social structure and made it more and more difficult for children to learn the necessary skills needed for successful subsistence life.[14] For the first time, the lessons necessary for young subsistence hunters were seriously interrupted, an interruption which continues to the present. This development made it necessary for rural Alaskans to learn two ways of life, formal schooling in order to deal with the encroaching western presence and the lessons of survival out on the land. No longer would traditional skills be sufficient.

Competing land uses received attention anew during the 1960s, when the political climate of the country was experiencing growing ethnic and racial unrest. This was a particularly important time for the development of Native political leaders, many of whom had gained valuable experience with western ways in the military during World War II.[15] The battles fought and won during the 1960s supplied the needed momentum for addressing the unsolved questions of Native land claims. A number of key factors came together: 1) support from sympathetic national groups, like the Association of

American Indian Affairs,[16] 2) the emergence of state government, and 3) the discovery of rich oil deposits which attracted national attention. During this period (1960-71), the Native leadership was able to achieve land claims settlements which would alter the course of their lives and would provide new power for influencing land and resource questions. Highlights of these events will be described with specific reference to the growing political dimensions of the subsistence question.[17]

The Political Dimension to Subsistence

In the early 1960s, the Atomic Energy Commission announced plans to detonate an atomic device at Cape Thompson, to create a deep water port. Project Chariot, as the project was called, focused national attention on subsistence values, this time in northwest Alaska. The planned atomic blast was also the catalyst for the development of new political organization and leadership on the North Slope.[18] Howard Rock, an Eskimo from Point Hope, but with many years of experience outside the state, became particularly concerned about the threats which this project posed.[19] With encouragement and backing he later became the editor and driving force behind Tundra Times, a newspaper developed to provide a forum for statewide communication of Native concerns.[20] Project Chariot stimulated subsistence research in the Cape Thompson area,[21] and provided information to outsiders concerning the environment and Native life. The project was eventually cancelled for this and other reasons, and the defeat of the project signalled a victory for subsistence users in northwest Alaska in that it demonstrated that their way of life could be considered in national planning efforts.

Subsistence use patterns were directly challenged in Barrow during the spring of 1960 when two hunters were arrested for taking waterfowl out of season.[22] Community members responded by presenting themselves to the federal game official for arrest, each with waterfowl in hand. The charges were eventually dropped,[23] again showing the power of local political organization and demonstrating that subsistence users were even willing to risk arrest to protect spring waterfowl hunting practices.

Plans in the early 1960s to build a dam across the Yukon River at Rampart to provide hydro-electric power again focused attention on subsistence and community values, this time in the Interior. The dam would flood the entire Yukon Flats, one of the richest waterfowl breeding areas in North America, eliminate seven villages and directly affect the subsistence resources of still others.[24] This proposal was abandoned, but it raised the issue of how large scale projects could affect villages. The proponents of the dam pointed out the positive values of inexpensive energy; the opponents pointed out the effects of displacing villagers from their homeland and life ways. At the time the villagers on the Yukon Flats formed their own association, Gwitchya Gwitchin Ginkhye (3Gs), to provide political leadership on issues affecting the villages.[25]

The court battle of the Tlingit-Haida shows another facet in the development of political support for subsistence. In a decision by the Court of Claims in 1959, reiterated in 1968, the Tlingit-Haida were promised compensation for lands which had been taken by the United States Government.[26] One of the court's conclusions was that the government had failed to protect the rights of the Indians.[27] This demonstrated a radical shift from the attitudes of Governor Brady and Judge Wickersham who proclaimed that Native land rights could only be protected if the Natives followed the western patterns of settled village life,[28] and the decision signalled a victory for Native subsistence. It indicated that the judiciary could be receptive to forms of land use and occupancy outside of the customary Euro-American patterns.

The Tlingit-Haida decision was the precursor to the movement for a land claims settlement for all Alaska Natives. The question of when to push for settlement was answered when national attention turned to the rich oil reserves discovered at Prudhoe Bay on the North Slope in 1968. Political pressure to settle the land claims so that oil development could occur, and the combined efforts of Native leaders and the state government culminated in the Alaska Native Claims Settlement Act (ANCSA) of 1971.[29] While the act did not directly address subsistence,[30] it was agreed that Native subsistence needs would be considered by the Secretary of the Interior and the State of Alaska.[31]

Finally, there were laws that recognized subsistence as a value to be protected, opening the way for continued evaluation of subsistence against other values of the lands and waters. But ANCSA was more than a Native land settlement; the act cast the die for new land classifications across the state. Where once the map of Alaska had few management boundaries, now it is a mosaic of federal-state classifications, each representing particular management concerns. The act signals the beginning of a new era in which hunters and fishermen whose use patterns cut across boundaries will have to work closely with managers of the respective areas to insure that their way of life is considered by the area management.

ANCSA set the stage for legal recognition of subsistence, accomplished by the state legislature in 1978 and by Congress in Title 8 of the Alaska National Interest Lands Conservation Act of 1980. However, these laws have not resolved questions concerning subsistence use and its protection. We turn briefly to some recent cases of the issue.

The hotly contested Beaufort Sea Joint State-Federal Lease Sale of 1979 has raised serious questions about the effects of off shore drilling on certain subsistence resources, such as whaling and the importance of whales to the Inupiat of the North Slope. This issue was also raised by an external stimulus, in this case the International Whaling Commission (IWC). The Commission in responding to perceived declines in the bowhead whale population, and the pressures of certain environmental groups, attempted to ban and then strigently limit Eskimo whaling. Thus, while the United States and the state of Alaska were planning to lease areas for oil drilling in the Beaufort Sea outer continental shelf, the IWC was attempting to protect the bowheads from subsistence hunters. The Inupiat were caught in the middle. Their efforts were devoted to fending off plans for off shore oil development which they felt could be disastrous for the whale population upon which they depend, while, with equal energy, they were trying to convince the IWC that their take of whales would not further endanger the species. The appointment of a member of the Alaska Eskimo Whaling Commission (AEWC) to the IWC signalled a major political achievement. David Case points out:

> This may be the first time that representatives of America's aboriginal people participated on behalf of the United States in international negotiations directly affecting aboriginal rights.[32]

A major stride toward local subsistence management was taken in May 1981. The federal government entered into a cooperative agreement with the AEWC giving it the authority to manage the whale hunt for two years.[33]

While whaling focused international attention on Alaska Native subsistence, developments occurring within state government brought to light conflicts between subsistence and other land uses. Responding to the demands of Alaskans for private land, the state of Alaska began a large scale land disposal program in 1979-80. State lands are distributed to citizens of the state through a lottery system. Some of these lands are used, however, by Native and non-Native subsistence hunters and trappers. Inadequate or non-existent information on these use patterns has created conflicts between subsisters, who find their traplines and hunting areas divided into rural parcels, and Open-to-Entry participants who are trying to establish themselves. With adequate documentation before the selection, some of the conflicts could have been avoided.[34]

At the time of this writing (May 1981), the state of Alaska is considering a move to repeal the state subsistence law. If the state abdicates responsibilities for subsistence, then the federal government will assume responsibility, as provided for in the 1980 national interest lands legislation, but only on federal lands. The fate of people who use state lands for subsistence remains a critical question. Furthermore, if the law is repealed then the state government's Subsistence Section and its research staff may no longer be functional, again bringing to a halt the description of subsistence uses and values.[35]

This introduces another issue, that of descriptive documentation. Strikingly absent from the history of subsistence is the development of a cumulative descriptive record of land and resource uses. The research record is marked by substantial achievements, but the subject suffers from sporadic and inconsistent attention. This on-again, off-again approach has thwarted the attempts of researchers to develop a cumulative and comparative perspective. Instead, the record is marked by products designed to address "crisis level" situations which call for immediate information. Examples of this are the National Park Service studies conducted during the early 1970s[36] and the resource value studies mandated under the Naval Petroleum Reserve Production Act.[37]

Each new plan for development of the state's resources calls for a consideration of resources which may be affected, and researchers are finding that they must understand completely the activities and implications of each type of development. They are also finding that, unlike other types of resources, subsistence defies the cold hard prioritization that is often called for by planners.

THE FUTURE OF SUBSISTENCE: MORE CHALLENGES AND FEWER OPTIONS

Within the past two years, subsistence users have acquired two powerful but controversial legal tools for the protection of their way of life. These are the state subsistence law and Title 8 of the national interest lands legislation. Despite these tools, or in part because of them subsistence hunters and fishermen are forced to spend more and more of their time justifying and defending their activities. This point was nicely illustrated by Rosita Worl when she noted that the modern subsistence hunter has to know about d-2, OCS, and NPR-A, as well as possess the traditional skills of the hunt.[38] Hardly far fetched is the image that can be conjured up of the modern hunter heading out to subsist with a mini-computer mounted to the seat of his snowmachine. When game is spotted, he punches in his location, the date, and species desired. He receives a response as to where he can shoot. The printout might also indicate the latest interpretation of how subsistence values are being weighed against other values—those of wildlife, recreational interests, and sport hunters. Where once in the not so distant past subsistence values were the only land use values (despite significant periods of interruption by commercial and development interests in some rural areas) now they are but one of many values—each competing for management consideration. While some would consider the legal recognition of subsistence values a victory for subsistence users, there will be greater pressure on individuals to work with managers in justifying their claims.

At best, we are entering a paperwork maze of permits and tight control of subsistence options. For instance, users will have to be very careful to note the entire history of their use patterns so that managers do not take a narrow perspective on the extent of land and water used. If they take too narrow a view then they will cut off options for people to respond to changes in animal migration patterns and resource levels. However, if they take too broad a view, then other users will claim that their decisions have little relevance to actual present practices. The realitites of this conflict were made evident to the writer in some recent work in the Upper Kuskokwim where hunters described hunting patterns reaching as far as the Alaska Range—patterns dating from the time when the elders were young adults. While they still view these patterns as part of their options, they have not actually used some of the areas in many years.

Subsistence has always depended upon the development of accumulated experience of lifetimes and on drawing upon that experience under specific conditions. In describing the North Slope Inupiat, Richard Nelson expressed the point in this way:

> In order to understand Inupiat associations with the land, therefore, we must extend our perspective to include several thousand years of intensive use and occupancy. Thus we encompass the individual collective lifetimes of association with each significant place, and we begin to understand the depth of inter-relationships between people and the land. Indeed, we witness here the growth of a culture and its ideas not on a landscape but from a landscape.[39]

We can expect subsistence hunters who share in these deeply rooted traditions to continue to view their activities historically, but their success in educating managers to this perspective is dubious. There will be less and less room to maneuver.

There is a misleading assumption that subsistence hunters can use any land. In reality, however, there are very complicated patterns of land use already in existence and locally established mechanisms for insuring rights to use. For instance, in some areas traplines and fish camps are passed on through the family; in other places traplines are sold. Trapping, fishing, and hunting partnerships help individuals respond to new opportunities and to survive hardships. These partnerships like other kinds of associations are based upon mutually agreed conditions, which insure flexibility in the land use system. Such mechanisms will certainly undergo changes with new management schemes, but the changes at the local level will evolve over time and will be based upon the way traditional mechanisms of control are shaped by the constraints and opportunities created by management. To the extent that land managers acquaint themselves with local dynamics they will be effective in maintaining policies which bridge locally acceptable means of reconciling conflicts and the legal realities of state and federal laws.

Newcomers who are trying to establish a subsistence life style face the difficult tasks of learning existing and historical patterns, learning what the laws say they can do, and finding areas where they can establish themselves. Their tasks are particularly difficult, because they do not have local ties and lack relatives who can teach them how to live on the land. We can expect that fewer and fewer newcomers will be able to realize their dreams of living on the land.

We have seen the issue of subsistence evolve through stages of competing land uses, a growing political consciousness and the development of a base in national and state legislation. As we look to the future, it is clear that land managers will play a critical role in establishing opportunities and constraints. It is also clear that subsistence users will have to play a more active role in describing their activities and values. An important role can also be played by researchers in helping to bridge the gap between

178

management concerns and subsistence values, but they will only be effective if they are given the time and resources to develop cumulative information from all sectors of the population.

NOTES

1.   See for instance, Stell Newman, "The National Park Service and Subsistence," a position paper developed in preparation for national interest lands legislation. See also the Alaska Department of Fish and Game, "Subsistence: A Position Paper." November 24, 1980, p. 1-17.

2.   Alaska State Statute, Ch. 151/sla 1978- SCS CSHB 960 am S.

3.   Ray Bane, "Subsistence—Running out of Gas?" Unpublished, "n.d.", p. 1-4.

4.   William Schneider, "Trapping Furbearers in Alaska: A Legacy and Perhaps a Destiny," Alaska in Perspective, vol. III, no. 1. Anchorage: Alaska Historical Commission, 1980.

5.   Robert Arnold, Alaska Native Land Claims. Anchorage: Alaska Native Foundation, 1978, p. 75-76.

6.   Ted C. Hinckley, "The Canoe Rocks—We Do Not Know What Will Become of Us," The Western Historical Quarterly, vol. 1, no. 3, 1970, p. 274.

7.   Ibid., p. 286.

8.   Ibid., p. 285-286.

9.   Ibid., p. 286.

10.   Arnold, Alaska Native Land Claims, p. 81-82. See also Stanton H. Patty, "A Conference with the Tanana Chiefs. . .a memorable gathering at Fairbanks in the summer of 1915," The Alaska Journal, vol. 1, no. 2, 1971, pp. 2-18.

11.   Patty, p. 2-18.

12.   Patty, p. 7.

13.   Ernest S. Burch, Eskimo Kinsmen: Changing Family Relationships in Northwest Alaska. The American Ethnological Society, monograph 59. St. Paul, Minn.: West Publ. Co., 1975, p. 31.

14.   Gary Holthaus and Raymond Collins, "Education in the North: Its Effects on Athabascan Culture," Northian. Saskatoon: University of Saskatchewan, May-June 1972, pp. 21-24.

15.   Margaret Lantis, "The Current Nativistic Movement in Alaska," Circumpolar Problems: Habitat, Economy, and Social Relations in the Arctic. Gosta Berg, ed. Oxford: Pergamon Press, 1973, p. 115.

16.   Arnold, Alaska Native Land Claims, p. 100.

17.   For a more detailed discussion of this period, see Lantis, "The Current Nativistic Movement in Alaska,"pp. 99-118.

18.   Arnold, Alaska Native Land Claims, p. 94-95.

19.   Ibid., p. 95. See also "A Last Interview with Howard Rock" in Tundra Times, October 5, 1977.

20.   Lantis, "The Current Nativistic Movement in Alaska," p. 106.

21.   Don Foote, a geographer working under the auspices of this project initiated one of the first studies to describe subsistence patterns and use areas (see Don Foote, The Eskimo Hunter at Point Hope, Alaska: September 1959 to May 1960, report submitted to the U.S. Atomic Energy Commission. Further references are available from the Don Foote Collection, University Archives, University of Alaska. The results of a wide range of scientific research in the Cape Thompson area are reported in Environment of the Cape Thompson Region, Alaska, Norman J. Wilimovsky and John N. Wolfe, editors.

22. Lantis, "The Current Nativistic Movement in Alaska," p. 101.

23. Arnold, Alaska Native Land Claims, p. 95.

24. Ibid., p. 102-103, and Lantis, "The Current Nativistic Movement in Alaska," p. 106.

25. See correspondence from Executive Director of Association of American Indian Affairs, Inc. to Executive Committee and Alaska Policy Committee, regarding Alaska-Rampart Dam, April 22, 1964, in Don Foote Collection, folder: Alaska, Rampart Dam, box 1. University Archives, University of Alaska, Fairbanks.

26. See The Tlingit and Haida Indians of Alaska and Harry Douglas et al., Intervenors v. The United States [no. 47900. Decided January 19, 1968]. The United States Court of Claims, January 1, 1968-February 29, 1968. vol. CLXXXII. Washington, D.C.: U.S. Government Printing Office, 1968.

27. Arnold, Alaska Native Land Claims, p. 92.

28. See Walter Goldschmidt and Theodore Haas, "Possessory Rights of the Natives of Southeastern Alaska: A Report to the Commissioner of Indian Affairs," 1946. This study delineated Native rights to sites and subsistence activity areas and added academic credence to the Native claims.

29. Mary Clay Berry, The Alaska Pipeline: The Politics of Oil and Native Land Claims. Bloomington: Indiana University Press, 1975.

30. Subsistence patterns were addressed by the Federal Field Committee for Development Planning in Alaska. Their study, Alaska Natives and the Land, Washington, D.C.: U.S. Government Printing Office, October 1968, performed a valuable function by providing information to policy makers in Washington, D.C. Unfortunately, in the Overview, the authors tied subsistence to the then popular question of poverty, creating an emphasis which tended to overshadow the positive social and cultural values of subsistence. Noticeably lacking from the study is consideration of non-Native subsistence. This is understandable but unfortunate because it gave the impression that only Natives are involved with subsistence.

31. David S. Case, The Special Relationship of Alaska Natives to the Federal Government: An Historical and Legal Analysis. Anchorage: Alaska Native Foundation, 1978, p. 104.

32. Ibid., p. 106.

33. "Whalers, U.S. reach Agreement," in Tundra Times, vol. XVIII, no. 13, April 1, 1981.

34. The residents of Lake Minchumina, a predominantly non-Native community have taken an important step by documenting their subsistence needs for the State (see letter from Minchumina Homeowners' Association to Howard C. Guinn, Land Management Officer, North Central District Office of Forest, Land, and Water Management, State Department of Natural Resources, Fairbanks, August 17, 1979). Another response to land disposal programs was initiated by the Talkeetna Historical Society. It sponsored Robert Durr to interview people in the Talkeetna area and to describe their attitudes about the land and the state policy of land disposals. See Robert Durr, "The Open-to-Entry Land Experiment," in Minus 31 and the Wind Blowing: 9 Reflections about Living on Land. Anchorage: Alaska Pacific University Press, 1980, p. 71-79.

35. Federal agencies are preparing to manage the National Interest Lands, but to date there are few indications that they are going to concentrate on studying subsistence.

36. Two of the studies represent some of the first scientific attempts to understand non-Native subsistence. See Richard Bishop, "Subsistence Resource Use in the Proposed North Addition to Mt. McKinley National Park," and Richard Caulfield, "Subsistence Use in and Around the Proposed Yukon-Charley National Rivers."

37. The Naval Petroleum Reserves Production Act of 1976 called for a description of resources within the Naval Petroleum Reserve (NPR-A) on the North Slope of

180

Alaska and an analysis of potential impacts of petroleum development. See North Slope Borough Contract Staff, National Petroleum Reserve in Alaska, Field Study 1, Native Livelihood and Dependence: A Study of Land Use Values through Time. Anchorage, Alaska: Bureau of Land Management 105(c) Land Use Study, 1979.
    38.   Rosita Worl, "Values of Subsistence to North Slope Inupiat Culture," in Native Livelihood and Dependence: A Study of Land Use Values through Time, p. 17.
    39.   Richard Nelson, "Cultural Values of the Land," in Native Livelihood and Dependence: A Study of Land Use Values through Time, p. 28.

I would like to express appreciation to the following people for reviewing and commenting on an earlier draft of this paper: Ray Bane, Marsha Bennett, Gary Holthaus, Randall Jones, Jack Kruse, Sverre Pedersen, Charles Smythe, Rob Walkinshaw, and Cynthia Wentworth. I, of course, assume all responsibility for the interpretations, conclusions, and any inaccuracies which may have been made.

14
Reconsidering Rural Development Strategies

Bradford Tuck

Economic development has been a major point of focus in the public policy sphere for many decades. A variety of national and international organizations have come into existence to deal specifically with the economic problems of countries variously referred to as underdeveloped, less developed, or "Third World nations." Various national, regional, and local institutions have emerged within the "developed" nations to deal with lagging or declining regional economies, all with the avowed purpose of promoting economic development. Our own topic is another manifestation of the concern with economic systems that are somehow not developed.

While most people (and particularly the "have nots") probably favor economic development it is important to dwell for a moment on what economic development represents to these people. In other words, what images come to mind when we think of economic development? Certainly, an abundance and variety of goods and services for consumption is part of the picture. Along with this goes high and rising per capita income, reasonably well distributed. More generally, the image probably includes at least some elements of modern and widely available health care and education, efficient transportation and other infrastructure. A variety of social amentities and general political and economic stability and freedom serve to round out the picture.

For the economist the image may be more specific. To the preceding list might be added large scale production, with high marginal and average productivity of factors of production, and a high level of specialization and exchange (and interdependence between economic units within the system). Also included would be substantial and sustained rates of capital accumulation and technological innovation.

It is also worth asking what images are absent when "thinking" economic development. The absence of high, permanent rates of unemployment or underemployment is one dimension. The absence of wide spread poverty, disease, illiteracy, and famine would also come to mind.

If we modify economic development with the adjective "rural" does this change the image? Certain elements will probably differ. In place of urban industrial settings one might substitute agriculture, forest products, fisheries, or mining, but the other

---

Originally presented at the American Association for the Advancement of Science— Alaska Section 1980 Conference, Anchorage, Alaska, September 17-19, 1980.

dimensions remain largely the same. High levels of factor productivity, capital accumulation, specialization and exchange, production, income, and infrastructure, etc., remain part of the picture.

How does all of this compare with the image we get when we narrow our focus to rural economic development in Alaska? Certainly, a reasonable level and distribution of per capita real income, synonymous with consumption of a large variety of goods and services is one element. Employment stability and security is another. Adequate, affordable housing, modern educational facilities, convenient and efficient transportation (for goods and people) and other elements of up-to-date infrastructure are also part of the image. To this would probably be added a "healthy" environment, not only in terms of health care, but in regards to clean air, clean water, waste disposal, etc. In addition to these physical elements, freedom of choice in terms of where to work, what to do, and where to live, as well as economic, political, and cultural autonomy would also be on the list. Since we are discussing all of rural Alaska it is certainly implied that these conditions will prevail throughout the area, and not just in isolated localities.

The elimination of various characteristics of undeveloped or underdeveloped economies would also be of concern. Poverty, unemployment (of an involuntary nature), economic hardship, disease and illiteracy are all features that presumably we would like to see reduced. A reduction of the economic costs that these conditions imply, both in terms of foregone production and with respect to economic burdens carried by other elements of the state and national economy may also be in the back of some people's minds.

While individuals may disagree about what constitutes "adequate," "acceptable," "comfortable," or "modern," etc., there is perhaps general agreement within broad parameters as to what is included in our image of a developed rural Alaska. If we can at least use this as a working model, then there are several issues and questions that can be addressed in discussing strategies for development.

The first point that needs to be made is that our image of economic development reflects only one aspect of the phenomenon, namely the end result. Alternatively, our picture is really one of goals of economic development. What is conspicuously absent is any description of the process of economic development, and it is the absence of a functioning process that is at the root of the whole problem.

Prior to the question of process, however, should come the analysis of our goals. On this point there are three crucial questions. First, are the goals sufficient? If we achieve these goals will the end result, in terms of economic society and economic well-being, accurately reflect what we set out to accomplish? This is not something I can answer, but it is a concern that must be addressed by those who initiate policies aimed at achieving economic development.

A second dimension of the sufficiency questions is whether or not the goals are adequately defined. In other words, do the goals provide a substantive frame of reference against which policy alternatives can be judged, evaluated, and implemented, and against which the success or lack of success can be measured? This is an obvious question but one that is frequently ignored.

The next important question concerns the consistency of the goals. Are the goals consistent or does the achievement of one preclude the achievement of another? Even if one does not preclude another, are the tradeoffs so large as to significantly reduce the increasing level of specialization and exchange and the associated degree of interdependence between economic units within the system.

When the form of this process is regional, as it is in the case of rural Alaska, there are important additional dimensions to consider. In particular, the region is not an autonomous area within which growth occurs, but rather is a subunit within a broader aggregate system. This means that the region must establish its own niche in the broader system, becoming a "specialized" part of the whole. In fact, specialization and exchange are more important for the region than for the whole. There is simply no way that the region (especially rural Alaska) can produce the diversity of goods and services that are implicit in the concept of economic development set out above.

In short, the region must not only produce some goods and services for its own consumption and investment, but it must also produce for "export" and exchange with the rest of the world. Not to do so means that the region is restricted to consuming only what can be produced within the region.

The basis for this inter-regional (and international) specialization and exchange is rooted in the notion of comparative advantage. In essence, regions produce those goods and services that they can produce most efficiently and trade their surpluses for what others produce more efficiently. Thus, central to the question of the feasibility of economic development for rural Alaska is whether or not some form of comparative advantage can be identified and exploited.

If we look to the economic history of the region, the prospects are not good. It is clearly the absence of any sustainable comparative advantage that in large part accounts for the absence of economic development of an ongoing nature in rural Alaska today. What has occurred instead has been episodic periods of natural resource based extraction and exploitation. While such activity has led to some capital accumulation and temporary economic growth, the effects have generally been short-lived and certainly have not resulted in a sustained process of diversified economic growth.

There are some exceptions to this, of course. The timber industry of southeast Alaska has established at least a tenuous hold and has led to some regional growth. Several communities have long histories based upon exploitation of fisheries resources, although their growth potential is limited. Petroleum resource development has resulted in some rural development, although this growth tends to be indirectly rather than directly causally related. But by and large, economic growth, particularly that based on comparative advantage, simply has not occurred in rural Alaska.

In view of the supposed abundance of natural resource wealth throughout rural Alaska, it is important to ask why sustained economic development has not occurred. Over the long history of Alaska many explanations of this have been forthcoming. Many have laid the blame at the feet of over-regulation, under-regulation, or other interference or lack of cooperation on the part of one or another level of government. At various times the controlling influence of various corporate monopolies has been blamed. These were at least some of the justifications for the move for statehood.

While there may be some truth to these assertions, there is a more basic explanation. The fundamental, underlying economic conditions necessary for development of the natural resource endowment of Alaska simply did not exist. While Alaska may have had the resources, it did not have a comparative advantage in resource exploitation.

combined gains? In general I think that there is some consistency in the goals presented above. While there are tradeoffs between development and the quality of the natural environment, it is not necessary that the two be incompatible. There is another dimension to the goals, however, that does represent a serious contradiction.

It is clear that many of the traditions, customs, beliefs, and practices of the Native cultures are rooted in the economic organization of early Native societies. I am referring specifically to what economists have labeled the "subsistence economy." By definition, a subsistence economy is one in which production is primarily oriented towards consumption to the present or near term future. Allocation of resources and the decisions regarding what to produce, how to produce, and how to distribute what has been produced are made on the basis of long established traditions.

Furthermore, the capital stock which supports this production is limited and in a technical sense primitive, although it certainly does the job for which it is intended. Another characteristic of the capital stock is that it tends to be of relatively short durability, or subject to a high rate of depreciation. As a result "investment" consists primarily of replacement investment, rather than net investment. In short, a constantly growing capital stock, one of the primary elements in the process of economic development and growth, is lacking.

This type of subsistence economy was in place in Alaska for centuries before contact with the non indigenous peoples occurred. While the full dimensions of the subsistence economy have steadily eroded ever since, there is ample indication that many of the economic values and practices that were central to a subsistence economy are important in Native decision making today. But by the very nature of economic development (as defined above) there is a contradiction and conflict with traditional subsistence values and practices.

Even if such a process of development could occur without the basic conflict (and it cannot), other aspects of development will cause difficulties in any event. Specifically, development of a scale and diversity implied in our discussion would require a workforce that would quickly exhaust the existing labor supply. In other words substantial population migration would occur and lead to heightened inter-cultural contact, changing land use patterns and, most likely, conflict. In short, maintenance of traditional lifestyles (and many of the associated values) and sustained economic development of the type portrayed above simply are not compatible.

Let us now look at the third question regarding goals. Are the goals realistic, and can they be achieved? To answer this it is first necessary to consider why it is that regions grow. At the risk of oversimplification, economic growth is made possible because of a continually increasing level of the stock of factors of production—labor, capital, and natural resources. Factors of production, combined in some aggregate production function, yield a flow of goods and services available for consumption and investment.

When the flow is adequate, and society so chooses, investment is sufficient to increase the size of the capital stock, and lead to the potential for successive increments in total production in future rounds of production. Natural population increase leads to growth in the stock of labor as well, although without growth of capital per capita production may not increase. Less visable, but perhaps most essential to the process, is the general growth of knowledge, and technology that results in qualitative growth of the factors of production. Accompanying this growth, and part of it, is a continually

If we look to the future, instead of the past, does the picture change? To respond, we must consider to what extent these fundamental economic conditions have changed. It is true that major legislation over the past two decades (in particular the Statehood Act and the Alaska Native Claims Settlement Act) and the Alaska Lands Conservation Act of 1980 significantly affect land and resource ownership and management parameters. Both the Statehood Act and ANCSA have at various times been held out as "catalysts" for development, but the results to date have not been significant. Neither are the possible negative consequences of legislation on Alaska's national interest lands going to be the catastrophe that some would suggest. In short, I do not think that any of these pieces of legislation significantly alter the economic parameters within which economic development must occur.

The underlying problem has been and remains the economic costs of resource development in relation to the potential for economic benefits and profits. Alaska is a "price taker" in terms of its resource exports (with the possible exception of fisheries), and therefore dependent on prices in a competitive market structure. Thus an assessment of future resource development depends largely on what happens to world prices and costs of production in Alaska. But in terms of Alaska's comparative advantage, the cost side is more important than world prices.

Time and space do not permit a detailed review of Alaska's natural resource development potential here, but some of the general dimensions can be suggested. It is clear that expanded exploration and development of petroleum resources will continue over the foreseeable future. Much of this effort, however, will be concentrated in the nearshore and offshore (OCS) areas of the state, and this is significant both in terms of the location of activity and in terms of the economic benefits to the state.

Some expansion of the timber industry may also occur, largely in southeast Alaska and in scattered coastal areas of southcentral Alaska. However, the forest resources of interior Alaska do not appear to offer the basis for any form of sustained yield management or development at this time. This is not to say that some utilization of the timber resources will not occur, but rather that utilization as a basis of sustained economic growth does not appear feasible.

Some expansion of the fisheries industry may also occur. However, in the absence of massive subsidization this expansion will be based primarily on greater exploration of the traditionally harvested species and not in the bottomfish species.

Development of hardrock mineral resources is a much touted source of economic growth in some circles, but the economic realities seem to tell a different story. Whether the problems are economic or otherwise, it is unlikely that hardrock mineral development will ever be more than a locally significant element in rural development. Twenty to forty years from now we may see two or three major mines in production, but their economic significance will be site specific and of minor overall economic importance. Similar comments are appropriate with respect to the coal resources of Alaska.

Whether or not these projections are accurate, there are several implications of a resource based development strategy that should be considered. First, the nature of resource development implied by Alaska's geography and economic costs is large scale development. This means large projects, large infrastructure support, and probably large scale population impacts. If the projects are of a "Prudhoe Bay" type, however, the regional or local rural impacts may be slight. While there may be some positive aspects to this, it does not lead to significant rural development either.

Another implication of resource development is that, under alternative conditions, the impacts at the local level may be extremely large. This is particularly true in the case of petroleum development or hardrock mineral development, but it is also implicit in any other large scale resource development such as expansion of the bottom-fish industry.

Third, because resource development will necessarily be large scale development in Alaska, the number of projects will be quite limited and clearly site- or area-specific. This is not the type of development that will lead to widespread diversification of growth throughout rural Alaska.

In short, there are serious problems in terms of the feasibility of our economic development goals. The potential for resource development appears to be limited to one or two resources at best, and such development would occur on a highly localized basis. It would not result in a diversified process of rural development throughout rural Alaska. Furthermore, resource development occurs where the resources are located, not necessarily where people are located, and so development probably requires relocation and migration from existing communities. At a minimum this implies major tradeoffs in the achievement of at least some of the development goals.

In summary, our discussion has looked at implicit goals of traditionally defined economic development in the context of development strategies for rural Alaska. It has been suggested that serious conflicts exist within the goals themselves, particularly between the implications of development, per se, and the retention of traditional cultural values and economic practices. A second, and equally serious problem is that existing and prospective economic parameters, within which development must occur, will not support the type of economic growth implied by the goals. A regional comparative advantage based on natural resource development simply is not a workable basis for broadscale development. Finally, economic development, even if it did occur on such a basis, would probably lead to structural changes in rural society of such a magnitude that the results would be incompatible to the indigenous people of the region.

In short, the traditional goals of economic development for rural Alaska are probably unachieveable, and even if attainable are probably not what the majority of rural Alaskans are looking for in the first place. This clearly suggests that the real starting place for developing strategies for rural Alaskan development is in a redefinition of development appropriate to the goals and aspirations of rural Alaskans, not in the image of traditional economic policy makers.

15
Alternative Perspectives
on Alaska's Rural Development

Gary Anders

Alaska, the last frontier, has captivated the attention of some of the most ambitious minds in recent times. If the patterns of development evidenced historically can condition the potential development of the state, then it is safe to argue that dependent development will continue to occur here until there are no more relatively cheap resources left to exploit. In this article, we shall attempt to provide an alternative perspective on the potential development of rural Alaska.

A central argument of this article is that the type of economic development inherent in Alaska's growth is that which polarizes regions into areas of development and underdevelopment. We will describe the way that inherent economic processes divert scarce resources from hinterlands within the state to areas (particularly Anchorage and metropolitan centers outside the state) where short-run returns can be maximized. As a result of the concentration of economic activity in one large metropolis and the overspecialization in the production of exports, Alaska's economy is lopsided. Since many benefits of this export-oriented growth are temporary in nature, a more balanced pattern of development emphasizing long-run considerations aside from profit maximization should be considered.[1] Such a balanced development approach must be the product of careful planning and state policies which promote a diversification of the existing economic base of the state.

ECONOMIC THEORY AND ALASKA'S GROWTH

Before considering the public policy issues, it is first necessary to spell out the theoretical context for the arguments for balanced growth by focusing on certain general properties of the dynamic forces which regulate economic growth. The conceptual basis for this approach is predicated upon various theories of development which have been used widely elsewhere.[2] The use of such a theoretical framework seems justified by parallels between Alaska and other regions that have undergone similar developments. Specific application of this theory emphasizes historical conditions which were set in motion during the formal colonial periods and the rise of the state as a prominent supplier of natural resources within the world economy.

The author would like to express his appreciation to Professors Gerald McBeath and Peter Cornwall for their patience and encouragement, to Professor Monica Thomas for her helpful discussions, and to Professor Russ Currier for his comments on an earlier draft.

Development and underdevelopment are linked through constellations of inter-connected economic ties. Although conditions vary with particular historical influences, generally regional integration or the bifurcation of regions into areas of development and underdevelopment has occurred in accord with the region's ability to exercise some leverage in promoting its own growth. Obviously this activity has not worked to the advantage of weaker and more disadvantaged areas which are heavily dependent upon exploiting their share of the total world supply of primary products and agricultural commodities. Assuming an inelastic demand for such output and a growing reliance on foreign exchange to finance imports, variations in world demand and market price have acute effects on those countries' domestic economies.

In this way the economies of larger and more powerful nations—buffered by their large internal markets—come to control market trends for the smaller weaker ones.[3] Long-run consequences of relying upon foreign trade, even under the most favorable of conditions, exacerbate the tendency to switch from efforts to satisfy domestic needs to production for export. As a direct result, many countries which were previously self-sufficient in the production of foodstuffs have become net food importers.[4] Such dependence generates development which is inherently dualistic in nature.[5] Negative side effects of dependent development are reflected in inequalities in the distribution of important economic benefits such as high-paying jobs.

To clarify this point, consider the following illustration of the disruptive effects of unbalanced export-oriented development. In a competitive market, industries must remain profitable by producing a larger output at a smaller price. The larger the overall market, the greater the potential economies of scale and the lower the production costs. For commodity producers, however, expanding output results in a lowering of market price and a decrease of total revenues, since the gains in efficiency tend to concentrate on the demand side in the form of a "consumer surplus." Switching to more techno-logically advanced, capital intensive methods of production increases output temporar-ily, but also displaces laborers and magnifies problems of unemployment. For the export economy, it should be clear then that such a concentration of economic activity increases the likelihood that additional growth does not yield permanent long-term benefits which promote internal growth, but can actually worsen chances for balanced development with an equitable distribution of income. Yet, if the decision were made for a transition from exports to self-initiated development, it is entirely possible that without massive amounts of surplus capital structural rigidities and deficient markets almost would insure catastrophic results. Thus most export-oriented countries caught in such a double bind have opted to band together in an attempt to increase their share of manufactures and nuture a larger economy through industrial diversification.[6]

OPEC countries such as Venezuela, Mexico, and Saudi Arabia, with control over a large share of the world's supply of petroleum, have used a different tactic. By creat-ing a cartel, these countries have used the inelastic or rigid demand for their output to maximum advantage, extracting higher prices and forcing the Western countries into making political concessions. In these instances, economic diversification is now being carried out on a massive scale through heavy government subsidies. It remains to be seen whether or not there has been sufficient preparation for the establishment of self-perpetuating economies in these three countries. One outcome of their efforts that has some bearing on the Alaskan Economy is the fact that higher oil prices, in addition to generating more revenues, have also stimulated research and development for alternative energy sources, thus providing for that time in the near future when the oil boom will come to a halt.[7]

APPLICATION OF DEPENDENCY THEORY TO ALASKA

The notion of dependent development can be used to provide an understanding of Alaska's economic development. This fundamental thesis can, to a large degree, be substantiated by three important points of agreement derived from the literature on this subject. In his recent book, Dependency Approaches to International Political Economy, Vincent Mahler identifies a number of indicators that have been used by various writers to indicate the existence of dependence.[8] Of these, three appear to have great relevance for Alaska.

The first indicator is the historical factors which have conditioned development within a region. Numerous dependency writers have shown that previous colonial economic and political ties have influenced the development of certain parts of the world.[9] Case studies of former colonies that have recently gained their independence note that even after these formal colonial ties are broken, the economic processes that have been set in motion continue to operate at the expense of the developing country.[10] Implicit in this arrangement is the secondary status imposed on a territory, and its role as a supplier of goods and services for the benefit of outside interests. Alaska may on the surface appear to be an exception to this rule, but on closer examination it appears that up until the early 1970s the Alaskan economy was very depressed. Rogers, for example, has written that:

> Looking at the total pattern of contemporary Alaska, the dominant characteristic is the lack of any self-sustaining and basic economic activity at its core. Viewed from the Alaskan level only, military construction has been a vast public works program providing jobs for overlapping periods of time and resulting in the erection of impressive and successively obsolete monuments to the progress of defense technology. It is not self-sustaining, nor does it induce further development beyond the period required for the completion of each project or program of projects. Furthermore, it has generated a large and costly social and political superstructure without fostering the potentials for further basic economic growth necessary for its continued support.[11]

The production of oil has done much to improve this situation, and now the per capita income of the state is reported to be the highest in the United States.[12] Yet, much of the state continues to be undeveloped. In the rural areas especially there is widespread poverty with all the corresponding social and health problems. Despite the production of more than 6.3 billion dollars worth of oil and gas in 1979, major parts of Alaska continue to be economically underdeveloped. See Table 15.1 for a comparison of Alaskan and U.S. energy resources.

Another indicator of the existence of dependency is the significant concentration of exports to a single country. In addition to the tremendous output of oil which was destined for U.S. markets, Alaska's exports have largely been shipped to Japan. Data presented in Table 15.2 show that more than 80 percent of all the exports of fish, timber, and natural gas go to Japan. While there is no apparent danger in strong economic ties to an ally, the fact that such a large portion of the export economy is controlled by a single market gives cause for concern.[13]

In addition to the two previous indicators, the third and perhaps most important consideration deals with the concentration of economic and political power. Myrdal in his many writings has stressed the notion of "spread" and "backwash" effects of development. He has argued that specialization in commodity exports many times

TABLE 15.1
ENERGY RESOURCES IN ALASKA AND THE UNITED STATES

	Alaska	USA	Alaska as a percentage of US
Population (1980 census)*	400,481	226,504,825	.1%
Land Mass (sq. miles)	585,412	3,615,122	16.2%
Coal Resources (Trillion Short Tons)	1.86 - 4.99	4.76 - 7.89	39 - 63%
Hydroelectric Potential (MWH)	176,290,145	675,133,838	26%
Oil, Onshore Undiscovered Recoverable Resources (Billions of Barrels)	6 - 19	37 - 81	16 - 22%
Oil, Offshore Undiscovered Recoverable Resources (Billion of Barrels)	3 - 31	10 - 49	16 - 22%
Oil, Onshore Measured Reserves (Billion of Barrels)	9,944	31.030	32.2%
Oil, Offshore Measured Reserves (Millions of Barrels)	0.150	3.220	4.7%

Source: Alaska Division of Energy and Power Development,
          Alaska's Energy Resources Findings and Analysis,
          October 1977, p. 9.

* Preliminary estimate as of April 1, 1981.

TABLE 15.2
ALASKAN EXPORTS FOR 1979 IN U.S. DOLLARS

	All Exports	Exports to Japan	Percentages
Major Exports Total	825,352,708	703,305,600	85.2%
Forest Products	271,135,894	236,369,589	87.1%
Seafood	357,047,566	344,400,051	96.4%
Natural Gas	122,536,000	122,536,000	100.0%
Other Items	74,633,248	35,140,061	47.0%
Total All Exports	913,047,417	738,445,661	80.8%

Source: Alaska Department of Commerce and Economic Development,
          Alaska Statistical Review, June 1980.

leads to a concentration of economic activity across regional lines. In other words, rather than spreading out the benefits of growth, the growth of certain sectors of the economy can inhibit balanced growth in an area and keep it underdeveloped. Frank has expanded this analysis and in his treatment of Latin American economic development can occur through the rise of metropolis/satellite relations. This structure of dominant-dependent economic relations ties one part of the region to outside controlling interests and leads to a lopsided pattern of development that serves to retard the formation of a strong internal economy.

> The history of Brazil is perhaps the clearest case of both national and regional development of underdevelopment. The expansion of the world economy since the beginning of the sixteenth century successively converted the Northeast, the Minas Gerais interior, the North, and the Center-South (Rio de Janerio, Sao Paulo, and Parana) into export economies and incorporated them into the structure and development of the world capitalist system. Each of these regions experienced what may have appeared as economic development during the period of its respective golden age. But it was a satellite development which was neither self-generating nor self-perpetuating. As the market or the productivity of the first three regions declined, foreign and domestic interest in them waned; and they were left to develop the underdevelopment they live with today. In the fourth region, the coffee economy experienced a similar though not yet quite as serious fate (through the development of a synthetic coffee substitute promises to deal it a mortal blow in the not too distant future). All of this historical evidence contradicts the generally accepted theses that Latin America suffers from a dual society or from the survival of feudal institutions and that these are important obstacles to its economic development.[14]

This phenomenon of uneven development that Frank speaks about is nowhere more obvious than in the existing interregional disparities which exist between rural and urban Alaska. Both the historical and contemporary evidence suggests that to a very high degree trade and commerce is by multinational corporations controlled through a regional metropolis (Anchorage) which serves as a conduit for transferring out a surplus for the benefit of economic interests outside the state.

> From its earliest period of colonial exploitation up to the present, Alaska's basic economy has been dominated by giant national and international business corporations. The New England-based whaling fleets were followed by large-scale New England and San Francisco fishing and fish processing enterprises. Then, after the initial free-for-all periods of gold rush prospecting, the capital required to exploit gold and cooper brought in the giants of the nation's mining industry. During the territorial period the Alaska legislature was strongly influenced and at times controlled by the joint canned salmon and mining lobbies. Because of the role played by smaller subcontractors and suppliers, the construction industry, created during the period of defense buildup, had a more diversified range of enterprises under its umbrella, but again the national prime contractors were economically and politically at the heart of the industry. The post-World War II developments in forest products were for the most part on a scale exceeding the ability of local sources of investment capital to manage and again were accompanied by another influx of national and international (Japanese) business consortia. The corporate nature and scale of contemporary international petroleum industry in Alaska needs no comment.[15]

At this point it will be helpful to define some key terms. For our purposes, the notion of a peripheral area that produces exports of raw materials refers specifically to the non-urban regions of Alaska. A regional metropolitan center is the city within the peripheral region that serves as a headquarters for the agglomeration of interests that control business investment in the region. Regional enclaves within the periphery are the sources of raw materials and are generally found near smaller cities which have been deliberately established to facilitate the flow of wealth out of the periphery. The metropolitan center is the focal growth pole within the developed country that consolidates and redistributes the income generated by investments in peripheral areas.[16]

Using this taxonomy, we may classify Anchorage as a regional metropolitan center that contols the major economic and political dealings within the state. Next come a few subsidiary cities such as Fairbanks, Valdez, Juneau, and Ketchikan, which exist because of their location with respect to major economic activities such as the trans-Alaska oil pipeline, the state government, and the fishing industry. Finally there are a number of regional enclave areas and a corresponding third tier of towns (e.g., Nome, Barrow, and Sitka) which were historically centers for various economic activities that once dominated the state such as gold mining, timber, whaling, and seal hunting. This pattern of structural relations has been summarized by Kresge, Morehouse, and Rogers:

> Geographically, most of the economic and broader prospects we have been describing will be concentrated in Anchorage and its shadow in Fairbanks. Whether petroleum development takes place in the Arctic, the Gulf of Alaska, the Bering Sea, or elsewhere, the principal social and economic impacts will be in Anchorage. Outside this area, however, lies another Alaska with quite different characteristics and possibilities. There is a succession of southern coastal communities stretching from Ketchikan into the Bering Sea whose economic lives are supported by renewable resources of the sea and land. To the west and north are the bush communities which are sometimes outposts of the central economy, but in varying degrees represent semi-subsistence economies.[17]

According to these observations, the recent debates over the move of the state capital to Willow (only thirty miles from Anchorage) would reinforce the centrifugal tendencies inherent in this regional economic structure, thereby further serving to insure the continuation of underdevelopment in the outlying areas of the state.

Conventional theories of economic development take a much different perspective on what has happened in Alaska. Rather than considering the long-term effects of regional differences in the state and their impacts on the quality of life for Alaskans, the conventional (Neoclassical) models deal specifically with equalization effects. According to this view, existing disparities will eventually become negligible as factor prices and rates of profit from different types of investments converge toward some equilibrium level. Since Neoclassical economics is based upon a very narrow notion of comparative advantage, the assumption of mutual benefits of trade and development indicate that the state is best off pursuing a type of development predicated upon a singular specialization in resource production where it has an absolute or relative advantage. Efficiency is thought to mean using capital and labor in such a way as to maximize profits. Given these considerations, the theory holds that when strictly regulated by market forces, production and exchange lead to an optium allocation of scarce economic goods. It is a strongly pro-development view that relies heavily upon technology, but scarcely mentions the negative effects of uncontrollable market forces.

In the conventional economic paradigm, continued growth regardless of the consequences is good as long as it is profitable. No special attention is given to environmental considerations since the true calculations of market prices should reflect accurately the value of the output.[18] Intergenerational effects of development activities over time are discounted using the rational market calculus and an "appropriate rate of interest" which provides the discount measure used to determine what a lump of coal mined in the next decade may be worth today. Furthermore, the Neoclassical view discounts the effects of foreign control by arguing that foreign investment leads to increased technical progress, improved productivity, and capital accumulation which through the "terms of trade" benefit producer and consumer alike. Thus, the Neoclassical or conventional theories of development assume that Alaska's specialization in primary products (e.g., fish, timber, and energy resources) serves as a powerful engine for growth that will eventually link up all the sectors of the economy.

Of course this brief treatment is quite simplified and overlooks a number of important factors such as the enormous political and economic influence that the state and federal governments have on Alaska's economy. Yet, comparative analysis strongly supports the argument of a limited potential for development within the dependency mode. The process of capitalist development which Schumpeter reverently called "creative destruction,"[19] if allowed to follow its course, will inevitably lead to a continuation of boom-bust economic growth and further erode the chances for balanced development with an equitable distribution of benefits. The major consequences of such a continuation of previous economic patterns are too wide ranging to attempt to predict in such a short space. The policy considerations, however, call for analysis, even in a preliminary fashion.

POLICY CONSIDERATIONS

In the conventional usage, development is understood as a process synoymous with economic growth. Many scholars have already criticized this approach by stressing the importance of distinguishing between the two terms economic growth and economic development.[20] The term economic growth refers to a teleological process in which the goal, as conventionally assumed, means the attainment of modern industrial economic relationships. Etymologically, the term economic development refers to an unfolding, with the thing unfolded taken as a given. In the conventional economic literature the intrinsic value of that which is unfolded is assumed a priori; its value is not a matter of dispute.[21] The case of Alaska, however, presents data for an inquiry into the accuracy of this conventional understanding.

Todaro argues that development "is both a physical reality and a state of mind in which society has, through some combination of social, economic, and institutional processes, secured the means for obtaining a better life."[22] With this broader conception of development in mind, it is appropriate to point out that:

> The term "development" may apply not only to economic, but also to political and social aspects of life in a country or region. Again, the term implies the creation of opportunities for "self-determination," for a country or region's political and sociocultural experience to be shaped by internal forces. . . .

> The preoccupation with growth has also overshadowed the question of who would benefit from developing the north. The easy and seemingly persuasive answer was simply that everyone would. So long as there were no apparent losers, the question was not politically sensitive. The fact that the permanent population of the north had a negligible interest in or opportunity to participate

in the political process, also helped to gloss over potential problems. Now the situation has changed and the question of who will benefit dominates discussions of northern development.[23]

This is a thorny issue for which conventional economic theories postulate the market solution.

In a market system, a free flow of resources is crucial for efficiency. Since people constitute a particular economic resource, namely labor, it is vital that migration be allowed to take pace both intra- and inter-regionally. In essence this means that when economic growth occurs in an area, it acquires its own dynamics that create a "self-fulfilling" prophecy of more jobs and higher incomes. Through multiplier effects and the enlargement of linkages with other sectors of the economy, a whole range of new opportunities is created. It also creates a vacuum which is inevitably filled by migrants who move into the region to take advantage of these opportunities.[24]

The latest demographic statistics from the 1980 census indicate that between 1970 and 1980, population growth for the state of Alaska was 32.3 percent. Most of this influx of population was concentrated in six major areas of the state: Fairbanks, the Matanuska-Susitna Borough, the Municipality of Anchorage, the Kenai Peninsula, the Valdez-Cordova Area, and the City of Juneau. (See Table 15.3 for a presentation of the actual distribution.)

As can be seen in the demographic data, Alaska has experienced a massive influx of migrants from outside. A large portion of this increased population during the decade of 1970 to 1980 can be explained by the construction of the trans-Alaska oil pipeline and related activities. Increasing migration into the state is an important public policy consideration especially when the impact of these newcomers and the continuation of pro-growth policies encroach on the lifestyles of older residents of the state. The current debate over the issue of subsistence provides a good example of this point.

Incentives such as higher paying jobs and better career opportunities will increasingly bring migrants to the state. Over time their political clout will become a powerful force shaping public policies towards future growth. If this takes place on a continual basis, there will be increased demands to remove many of the obstacles that stand in the way of widespread modernization, and value conflicts will emerge between those who want to maintain a particular way of life and those seeking change.[25]

The process of development as it is conventionally understood encourages migration and therefore strengthens political alliances that favor maximum growth. In the extreme case this can lead to "overdevelopment" whereby some people feel that progress generates too much urbanization, too much congestion, and too many social problems so that the overall effect is a decrease in the quality of life.

This pattern of growth and change has taken place before, and each time the profile of Alaska has come to reflect the current economic interests of outside profit-makers. Little concern was given to the preservation of the land or different ways of life. George Rogers, the dean of Alaskan economists, has written that:

The course of Alaska development since the midcentury mark has been further influenced by political changes which were the product of conflicts of interest and differential effects of development upon social groups and upon human

TABLE 15.3
ALASKA POPULATION GROWTH BETWEEN 1970 AND 1980

	1970	1980	Percent Change
North Slope Borough	3,451	4,160	20.5
Kobuk Census Area	4,048	4,799	18.6
Southeast Fairbanks Census Area	4,179	5,664	35.5 (6)
Bethel Census Area	8,873	10,671	21.3
Dillingham Census Area	3,827	4,594	20.0
Matanuska-Susitna Borough	6,509	17,938	175.6 (1)
Municipality of Anchorage	126,385	173,992	37.7 (5)
Kenai Peninsula Borough	16,586	25,072	51.2 (3)
Valdez-Cordova Census Area	5,000	8,546	70.9 (2)
Skagway-Yakutat-Angoon Census Area	2,763	3,436	24.4
City-Borough of Juneau	13,556	19,483	43.7 (4)
City-Borough of Sitka	6,073	7,769	27.9
Wrangell-Petersburg Census Area	4,949	6,133	23.9
Total All Census Regions	302,583	400,331	32.3

Source: Alaska Department of Labor,
Alaska's 1980 Population: A Preliminary Look,
January 1981.

development and public welfare. The Statehood movement which culminated in the granting of full Statehood to Alaska in 1959, for example, was the result of conflict between resident and non-resident interests. The process of exploiting Alaska's gold, copper and fisheries resources required heavy capital investment and large markets for disposal of products which could only be provided from outside sources. Economic development followed traditional colonial lines in ignoring local interests and in being specialized and ruthlessly exploitative.[26]

In a frontier, however, a unique situation exists for innovations that are beyond the grasp of established ways of doing things. As a frontier, Alaska has an opportunity to adopt alternative models of development. We have attempted to show that the pattern of structural relations embodied in the dependency relationship will condition the development of Alaska as a resource exporter. Our belief is that such an arrangement, although historically implanted and in operation now, can be broken, and that a new type of development can take its place.

RECOMMENDATIONS

Alaskan cities have, of course, long recognized the need for a more balanced type of economic environment. For instance, the voters of the state approved a constitutional amendment on November 2, 1976 which established a Permanent Fund. According to the amendment,

at least 25 percent of all mineral lease rentals, royalties, royalty sales proceeds, federal mineral revenue sharing payments, and bonuses received by the state shall be placed in the Permanent Fund, the principal of which shall be used only for those income-producing investments specifically designated by law as eligible for Permanent Fund investments.[27]

In 1980 new legislation raised the share to 50 percent of revenues from rentals, royalties, and bonuses; and it established goals, objectives and an organizational structure for management of the Permanent Fund. At the present time, sixteen specific types of investments have been identified as eligible for the Alaska Permanent Fund corporation. These range from obligations of the United State government to notes secured by mortgages of residential real property. See Table 15.4 for a breakdown of investments.

Although the Alaska Permanent Fund generated a high return on its investments during fiscal 1980—averaging 11.3 percent—and despite the fact that the last session of the legislature voted an additional $900 million contribution to the fund, the Alaska Permanent Fund has had a negligible effect on the state's economic development.[28] The intent of the legislature to undertake investments which would strengthen and diversify the Alaskan economy has been undermined by an investment strategy which places heavy emphasis on generating the greatest revenue for the investment portfolio. To date, the Permanent Fund has largely been invested outside the state while numerous opportunities for small scale projects with high income and employment possibilities fall outside the current investment policy. For example, a recent newspaper reported that only 2 percent of the Fund is invested in Alaska and that this has been deposits with Anchorage-area banks and savings and loans.[29]

Of course, other funds exist and will be created that may channel some resources in this direction,[30] but the point is that the mechanisms for fostering decentralized development in the rural areas of the state are not functioning well. Another example which could be cited are the twelve Native Regional Profit Corporations created under

TABLE 15.4
ALASKA PERMANENT FUND*

Statements of Net Assets
As of June 30, 1979 and 1980

	1979	1980
Cash in Savings Account	$ 30,714	$ 39,019
Contributions Receivable from the State General Fund	239,701	34,251
Interest Receivable	2,441,133	9,376,844
Marketable Securities - At Cost:		
U.S. Treasury notes and bonds	72,434,149	303,963,813
Certificates of deposit	5,013,836	111,879,066
Bankers acceptances	28,352,723	23,509,738
U.S. Treasury bills.		20,582,673
Corporate bonds	13,487,625	13,487,625
Federal agency notes and bonds	7,995,625	13,004,156
Securities purchased under agreements to resell	500,000	7,000.000
Commercial paper	10,000,000	
TOTAL	$137,783,958	$493,427,071
Amounts Due to the State General Fund	(1,948,764)	(19,668,698)
Net Assets	$138,546,742	$483,208,487

Source: Alaska Department of Administration,
Annual Financial Report, State of Alaska for Fiscal Year 1980,
June 30, 1980.

*As of March 31, 1981 the Permanent Fund exceeded $1.7 billion.

the 1971 Alaska Native Land Claims Settlement.[31]   These corporations, with few exceptions, have chosen to pursue the established income maximizing approach and because of heavy pressures to "succeed" have sought investment opportunities that were more defensible as standard corporate activities. Because these large privately owned corporations have chosen to invest outside their regions in an attempt to generate maximum revenue, they overlook the development potential of rural Alaska and encourage a continuation of established patterns of centralization, concentration, and outside control. One very interesting illustration of an alternative development strategy is the Northwest Alaska Native Association (NANA). NANA, one of the twelve profit corporations, and its non-profit counterpart Manueluk, Inc. have taken a leadership role in promoting local human resource development in their home region. According to Gaffney,

> NANA corporate functioning shows a consistently maintained balance between profit-making statewide operations and less solvent regional operations—that is, between profitable de-localization of capital resources and . . . human resource-oriented localization of capital resources.[32]

The state of Alaska should also consider a similar policy that prevents concentration of resources in a single center, and instead, diffuses investments throughout the entire state. It should be evident that the widening disparities between rural and urban areas and growing trends toward urbanization and industrialization will further exacerbate these inequalities. Since a large part of the problem stems from the fact that financial assistance is more easily accessible to large scale projects, a more extensive effort should be made to expand credit and financial assistance to smaller scale projects such as: small businesses, cottage industries, and arts and crafts. Redirecting the state's resources will slow urban growth and may improve the quality of life in rural areas by promoting self-sufficiency, employment, and productivity.

This type of decentralized, grass-roots approach involves three basic policy initiatives. First, in rural areas with a viable population there is a need for the establishment of a basic level of public services such as fire protection, health care, day care, and youth centers. Second, instead of committing large amounts of money to investments in "lumpy" social overhead capital where there is a limited absorptive capacity, a new type of economic infrastructure should be created which would expand job opportunities in rural Alaska without increasing social tensions. Toward this end, the state's telecommunications and university facilities could be utilized and expanded to provide more relevant educational learning programs that better prepare residents for local jobs. Third, employment training programs should be broadened to include cooperative enterprises and internships for rural youth.

Our intention is to, in fairly general terms, encourage a process that could introduce some new possibilities and then through careful, beneficiary directed procedures allow local groups who would be the most affected to determine for themselves what activities they want to pursue. This has not always happened in the past, especially when the metropolitan dominated power structure has determined in advance the beneficiaries of development or failed to allow people to make their own intelligent choices.

The purpose of this article has been to introduce the perspective of economic dependency in analysis of Alaska development. While there are numerous limitations to this theoretical construct, it does provide some useful insights into the dynamic processes inherent in interregional economic relationships.   Patterns of resource exploitation and metropolitan control introduced in an earlier historical period still condition Alaska's economic prospects. These patterns have been recognized, however, and policies are being formulated which will facilitate the possible diversification of Alaska's economic base while at the same time encouraging greater participation by both urban and rural Alaskans.[33]

NOTES

1.   For interesting discussion about this process read, Gordon S. Harrison, ed., Alaska Public Policy: Current Problems and Issues. University of Alaska: Institute of Social, Economic and Government Research, 1973.

2.   The list of standard references in the field is extensive but for an interesting collection of orthodox readings see, Gerald M. Meier, ed., Leading Issues in Economic Development. New York: Oxford University Press, 1976. For a contrasting point of view see, Charles K. Wilber, ed., The Political Economy of Development and Underdevelopment. Second edition. New York: Random House, 1979.

3.   Keith Griffin, Underdevelopment in Spanish America. London: George Allen and Unwin, 1969, pp. 31-48.

4.   Nevin S. Scrinshaw and Lance Taylor, "Food," in Economic Development. San Francisco: W.H. Freeman and Company, 1980, pp. 26-36.

5.   By dualism we mean "the co-existence in one place of two situations or phenomena (one desirable and the other one not) which are mutually exclusive to different groups in society." Michael P. Todaro, Economic Development in the Third World. New York: Longman, 1977, p. 420.

6.   Harold B. Malmgren, "Trade Policies of the Developed Countries for the Next Decade," Jagdish N. Bhagwati, ed., The New International Economic Order: The North-South Debate. Cambridge, Mass.: The M.I.T. Press, 1977, pp. 219-235.

7.   At the present time, the state of Alaska's income tax, a leading source of state's revenue, is being challenged by several major oil companies. For background information see, Christopher P. Wells, "Oil and Gas Taxation in Alaska," UCLA-Alaska Law Review. vol. 6, no. 2, Spring 1977, pp. 301-337; and David M. Reaume, "Government Fiscal Planning in the Face of Declining Resource Revenue: The Alaska Case." mimeographed, September 1978.

8.   For instance, Mahler writes that "many dependency theorists argue, primary product production is not amendable to diversification and is thus often marked by a high concentration of exports in a small number of commodities. This concentration renders trade dependent countries vulnerable to vicissitudes of world commodity markets and offers them little leeway in the event either of a disruption of production because of a bad harvest or other disturbance or, on the other hand, the collapse of commodity prices because of overproduction. In addition a high level of trade dependence is said to make integration both within and among LDCs difficult: dependency theorists often speak of situations in which infrastructural improvements have done little to facilitate internal or regional integration, but instead have been directed towards the port of exit and foreign markets." Dependency Approaches to International Political Economy. New York: Columbia University Press, 1980, pp. 30–31.

9.   For an excellent synthesis see, James A. Caporaso, "Dependence and Dependency in the Global System: A Structural and Behavioral Analysis," International Organization. vol. 32, Winter 1978, pp. 13-44.

10.   Pablo Gonzalez Casanova, "Internal Colonialism and National Development," Studies in Comparative International Development. vol. 1, December 1965, pp. 27-37.

11.   George W. Rogers, The Future of Alaska, Economic Consequences of

200

Statehood. Baltimore: The Johns Hopkins Press, 1962, pp. 268-269.

12.   According to the latest government statistics the per capita income for the state of Alaska in 1980 was $12,406 as compared to a U.S. average of $9,458.

13.   "In 1977 it was conservatively estimated that Japanese corporations had invested over $300 million dollars in Alaska primarily in key industries such as fishing and timber and that figure was certain to increase because Alaska had much of what Japan needed—oil, gas, fish, timber, and hard-rock minerals. Even though Japan and other nations were forbidden by federal law from obtaining any Prudhoe Bay oil, several Japanese corporations had invested in the search for oil, as well as for coal and minerals in other areas of Alaska." John Hanrahan and Peter Gruenstein, Last Frontier: The Marketing of Alaska. New York: W.W. Norton and Co., 1977, p. 310.

14.   Andre Gunder Frank, "The Development of Underdevelopment," Charles K. Wilber, ed., The Political Economy of Development and Underdevelopment. Second edition. New York: Random House, 1979, pp. 3-17.

15.   David T. Kresge, Thomas A. Morehouse, and George W. Rogers, Issues in Alaska Development. Seattle: University of Washington Press, 1977, p. 206.

16.   Much of this discussion originates from the works of Stephen Hymer. See his, "The Multinational Corporation and the Law of Uneven Development," Jagdish Bhagwati, ed., Economics and World Order from the 1970s to the 1990s. New York: Macmillian, 1972, pp. 113-140.

17.   Kresge, Morehouse, and Rogers, Issues in Alaska Development, p. 211.

18.   For further discussion see, Robert M. Solow, "The Economics of Resources or the Resources of Economics," American Economic Review. vol. 2, May 1974, pp. 1-14.

19.   Joseph A. Schumpeter, The Theory of Economic Development. Cambridge, Mass.: Harvard University Press, 1936.

20.   For instance see, K.J. Rea, The Political Economy of Northern Development. Ottawa: Science Council of Canada, 1976, p. 25.

21.   Gary C. Anders and Michael E. Melody, "Dependence and Underdevelopment Among Native Americans," a paper presented to the American Political Science Association Annual Meeting, September 1-4, 1977.

22.   Todaro, Economic Development in the Third World, p. 62.

23.   Rea, The Political Economy of Northern Development, p. 25, 28.

24.   "Since migrants are assumed to respond to differentials in expected incomes, it is vitally important that imbalances between economic opportunities in rural and urban sectors be minimized. Permitting urban wage rates to grow at a greater pace than average rural incomes will stimulate further rural-urban migration in spite of rising levels of urban employment. This heavy influx of people into urban areas gives rise not only to socio-economic problems in the cities, but it may also eventually create problems of labor shortages in rural areas, especially during the busy season." Todaro, Economic Development in the Third World, p. 196.

25.   Given these patterns of migration and the availability it is predicable to expect increased pressures to speed up the exploitation of Alaska's natural resources. For an example of this advocacy see, Commonwealth North, "Solutions to the National Energy Crisis: Why Not Alaska." November 1979.

26.   George W. Rogers, "Alaska's Development and Change: 1950-1980," Inter-Nord, vol. 12, December 1972, pp. 62-70.

27.   Laws of Alaska, Article IX, Section 15.

28.   State of Alaska, Annual Financial Report, June 30, 1980, p. 9.

29.   Fairbanks Daily News-Miner, June 10, 1981, p. 3.

30.   Examples include: the Agriculture Loan Fund, Commercial Fish Loan Fund, the Conservation Loan Fund, Small Business Loan Fund and others.

31.   For an overview and background of the creation of the Alaska Native

Regional Corporations see, Robert D. Arnold, et al., Alaska Native Land Claims. Anchorage: The Alaska Native Foundation, 1978.

32.   Michael J. Gaffney, "The Human Resources Approach to Native Development: A Special Case," in this volume.

33.   The well-known consulting firm, Arthur D. Little, Inc. in a study contracted by the State Department of Revenue in 1977 identified the following areas as those with the greatest economic opportunity: "agriculture, fishing, tourism, oil and gas exploration and refining, coal development, development of hardrock minerals, forest products, hydroelectric power, pulp and paper, chemicals, aluminum, and iron ore mining." Arthur D. Little, Inc., Economic Development in Alaska: A Sectorial Analysis. March 1978.

This article challenges the study's recommendations and instead of endorsing a continuation of Alaska's role as an export economy calls attention to the need for economic diversification, decentralization, and alternative development goals.

Conclusion

Gerald McBeath

The papers collected in this volume describe contradictory processes of statis and change in rural Alaska. The region, comprehending most of American's largest state, is still underdeveloped relative to urban Alaska and the lower 48 states. It is still populated chiefly by indigenous groups with customs, habits, and cultures that differ markedly from those of most Americans. It is the only part of the American population that continues to engage in subsistence pursuits—hunting, fishing, gathering and the rituals that accompany them. In short, rural Alaska in important respects remains a traditional society.

However, pervasive and comprehensive changes have occurred in rural Alaska during the two centuries of contact with western civilization. In some cases, notably that of the Aleuts, these changes have virtually erased the traditional society; but for most of the region and its peoples, the changes have resembled the movement of an undulating tide. Crests of rapid resource exploitation have been followed by troughs of unemployment and lack of opportunities. The changes of the mid- to late-twentieth century have differed in that their effects are irreversible. Rural Alaska is now a part of the cash economy, and it is dependent on "development" in a sense unimaginable previously.

The fifteen authors who have presented their views in this volume have given more than one definition of development in rural Alaska. The various themes they have discussed reflect dissimilar perceptions of the problems of change as well as different disciplinary approaches and values. We can, however, draw some generalizations about Alaska's rural development after reading these papers, even though in a few cases this is little more than a record of areas of disagreement.

The articles in Part One pointed out the uneven distribution of non-renewable and renewable resources in Alaska. Traditional economic growth has occurred in those areas and regions where resources of high market value are located—for example, timber in southeast Alaska and oil and gas on the North Slope. In areas where marketable resources are lacking or where their distance from marketing centers requires an infrastructure that costs more than the economic return, growth has not occurred. These latter areas, comprising the majority of rural regions and including most rural Alaskans, continue to depend on subsistence hunting and gathering, supplemented by transfer payments from the federal or state government. The growth of these areas is thus dependent on a redistribution of resources.

The importance of physical location and infrastructure were shown in two select-ed cases of development—agriculture and mining. Large-scale agricultural development has succeeded only in areas with access to the Alaska road and rail transportation system, and mining is dependent on the same conditions. The regions developed for mining and agriculture are but a small fraction of the areas in which resources are located. Future development is contingent on factors extrinsic to rural regions of the state—for example, federal and state government decisions on lands classification, allocation of state resources to rural areas for construction of roads and energy produc-tion, and the like. There is no consensus about the desirability of establishing a rural infrastructure for traditional capitalistic development. Furthermore, the sparse popula-tion of rural areas of the state (including less than one-third of the state's population) means that these areas will not receive primary consideration except insofar as they use the "special relationship" of their Native population with the federal government, or special political skills in state and federal arenas.

In short, the generalization that can be drawn from these papers is that rural areas are dependent on external factors and conditions—reflected in the boom and bust cycles of rural change and the pattern of colonialism to which several authors have referred; and as they develop economically, their dependence is increased, not lessened. This is a drawback to the classical model of economic development which is mentioned by several authors throughout the volume.

The articles in Part Two illustrated what perhaps has been the greatest and most significant transformation in rural Alaska in the last decade—the proliferation of organ-izations and associations which have as their purpose the improvement of regional and local areas of the state. In the first ten years after statehood in 1959, few locally-controlled organizations addressed the needs of rural Alaskans and buffered rural regions against changes sweeping across the state. One exception was the Native associa-tion which formed in the 1960s to campaign for land Natives claimed by aboriginal rights. A second exception to this was RurAL CAP, an organization that originated in the federal War on Poverty and since that time has initiated social development pro-grams in many villages and trained leaders.

As several authors demonstrate, the Alaska Native Claims Settlement Act of 1971 created change processes which will continue into the future. To the present, the cash settlement has had little direct impact on income, employment opportunities, housing, and other facets of social life in most rural areas of the state. And in the years since ANCSA, only a minority of Native lands have been conveyed to regional and village corporations.

However, ANCSA did create twelve regional for-profit corporations and nearly 200 village corporations, and these are the most likely agents of rural social as well as economic change. Although they are flawed vessels of change—not all possess adequate resources, and not all have skilled, well-trained managers—they are without peers in rural Alaska. They are not simple economic organizations, for in small communities without other agencies and structures they must be multi-functional agencies, even serving as quasi-governments. Much assistance is required in order for village corpora-tions to exercise a directing role in the ordered change of rural Alaska communities. We can be cautiously optimistic, however, in that local organizations are now controlling some resources and can implement strategies and development tactics responsive to community needs and goals.

The Native for-profit corporations have stimulated the revival of regional Native non-profit corporations; and the latter have attempted to address in a comprehensive fashion the social needs of rural Alaskans. The state's oil wealth following the discovery of oil and gas resources at Prudhoe Bay in 1968 and the passage of ANCSA have had two other effects which have improved the basis for rural change. In one region of the state, the North Slope, a regional borough government has been established, and this has led to measureable improvements in employment opportunities and access to education and medical services. In all other regions, educational services have received increased funding, and their control has been partially decentralized through the creation of new school districts following the lines of regional profit-making corporations.

We cannot conclude that regional and local organizations have "solved" the problems of change in rural Alaska. But they have given a voice to villages and regions which they formerly lacked, and they have ensured that rural concerns are presented in state and national centers of power. In the process, however, they have connected rural areas of the state more tightly to these centers, exposing them to broader changes from which rural areas were once isolated.

The articles in Part Three discussed the values of the development process, questioning the traditional and contemporary premises that underlie the changes in rural Alaska since statehood in 1959. One way to recapitulate these views is to mention the issues and conflicts that have figured so prominently in rural social policy considerations.

A focus on economic growth conflicts with an interest in human resources and their development. The traditional, export-based, economic model conflicts with import substitution and decentralized development models. Urban areas differ from rural areas over the rate of exploitation of natural resources, and there are conflicts over subsistence use of fish and game. This issue is interconnected with Native v. Caucasian conflicts regarding not only the preservation of traditional lifestyles but also the question of who should manage rural resources and what arena—local, state, or national—is the appropriate forum for decision.

By expressing these value concerns in dichotomous form, we naturally lose perception of the interconnections among issues in the debate over rural Alaska's present and future. That there is a debate is indicated throughout the pages of this volume. The debating topics, however, have not been consolidated into simple yes/no choices; for, among other factors, the state's wealth has enabled leaders to postpone crucial decisions. For these decisions to be made intelligently and responsively, the issues and values must be defined more clearly and carefully, and basic research must be conducted. The authors of papers in this volume have made a modest beginning in this process.

Contributors

GARY ANDERS is Assistant Professor of Native Studies and Economics at the University of Alaska, Fairbanks, and has authored several studies of Native American economic development.

PETER CORNWALL, Associate Professor of History at the University of Alaska, Fairbanks, is the author of several articles on the modernization of Japan.

MICHAEL DEMAN heads the Economic and Social Development Division, Central Council of the Tlingit and Haida Indian Tribes of Alaska.

RONALD DIXON is a reseach assistant at the University of Alaska, Fairbanks.

MICHAEL GAFFNEY, Associate Professor and Director of the Native Studies Program, University of Alaska, Fairbanks, has written several studies on social change and rural education in Alaska.

CHARLES HAWLEY is an Alaska mining engineer, specialist, and consultant.

LEON HOLLERMAN, Professor of Economics at Claremont College, is the author of Japan's Dependence on the World Economy and several studies of Japan's position in the pattern of international economic development.

LEE HUSKEY, Assistant Professor of Economics, Institute of Social and Economic Research, University of Alaska conducts research and writes in the areas of regional, subregional, and environmental economics.

DAVID MAAS, Assistant Professor of Government, Anchorage Community College, is completing his doctoral dissertation on the Alaska Native Claims Settlement Act.

GERALD MCBEATH, Associate Professor of Political Science at the University of Alaska, Fairbanks, is the author (with Thomas Morehouse) of The Dynamics of Alaska Native Self-Government and other studies of political development in Alaska.

DEAN OLSON, Associate Professor of Business Administration, University of Alaska, Anchorage, is a former executive vice-president of Ahtna, Inc., (a regional Native corporation) and director of the Alaska Renewable Resource Council.

GEORGE ROGERS, Adjunct Professor of Economics and Director Emeritus of the University of Alaska's Institute of Social and Economic Research, has written several books, articles, and reports on regional economics, economics and social history, and the resources and environment of Alaska.

WILLIAM SCHNEIDER was formerly with the National Parks Service, and is now completing a project on oral history in Alaska, through the Rasmuson Library at the University of Alaska, Fairbanks.

PHILIP SMITH is executive director of the Rural Alaska Community Action Program.

TED STEVENS, Alaska's senior senator, is also the assistant majority leader of the U.S. Senate.

WAYNE THOMAS, Associate Professor of Economics, Agricultural Experiment Station of the University of Alaska, Fairbanks, is the author of numerous reports on agricultural marketing and economics.

BRADFORD TUCK, Associate Professor of Economics, University of Alaska, Anchorage, has written several articles on Alaska's regional and natural resource economics.

Index